A BETTER WORLD, INC.

HOW COMPANIES PROFIT BY SOLVING GLOBAL PROBLEMS...WHERE GOVERNMENTS CANNOT

ALICE KORNGOLD

For Poonam,
For all you do
to help build
"a better world!"
With best
wishes
Alice
4/8/14

palgrave
macmillan

A BETTER WORLD, INC.

First published in 2014 by
PALGRAVE MACMILLAN®
in the United States—a division of St. Martin's Press LLC,
175 Fifth Avenue, New York, NY 10010.

Where this book is distributed in the UK, Europe and the rest of the world,
this is by Palgrave Macmillan, a division of Macmillan Publishers Limited,
registered in England, company number 785998, of Houndmills,
Basingstoke, Hampshire RG21 6XS.

Palgrave Macmillan is the global academic imprint of the above companies
and has companies and representatives throughout the world.

Palgrave® and Macmillan® are registered trademarks in the United States,
the United Kingdom, Europe and other countries.

ISBN: 978–1–137–32765–9

Library of Congress Cataloging-in-Publication Data

Korngold, Alice.
    A better world, Inc. : how companies profit by solving global
  problems—where governments cannot / Alice Korngold.
      pages cm
    ISBN 978–1–137–32765–9 (alk. paper)
      1. Social responsibility of business. 2. Industries—Social aspects.
  3. Social problems. 4. Social action. I. Title.

HD60.K66 2014
658.4′08—dc23   2013024608

A catalogue record of the book is available from the British Library.

Design by Newgen Knowledge Works (P) Ltd., Chennai, India.

First edition: January 2014

10 9 8 7 6 5 4 3 2 1

Printed in the United States of America.

For my beloved family
David
Ethan and Ellie
Gabe and Ben
Margaret and Matt
and,
especially, Gerry

CONTENTS

PREFACE

I WAS INSPIRED TO WRITE THIS BOOK BY THE MANY PEOPLE AND ORGANIZATIONS who are dedicated to finding solutions to the world's most challenging social, environmental, and economic issues. Most obvious among them are the ones that lead and work in mission-driven nonprofit organizations (known as "non-governmental organizations" or "NGOs," outside of the United States). So many people who have founded, led, and worked in nonprofits are among my most beloved friends and respected colleagues.

This book puts the spotlight, however, on another, less obvious but critically important player. *A Better World, Inc.* showcases global corporations that are leveraging their formidable resources—often in partnership with NGOs—to help create a better world. Let's be clear: companies are not acting selflessly. Companies are in the business of maximizing profits. Yet many international corporations are learning that solving the world's most pernicious problems is the way to win in the global marketplace—as highly profitable, sustainable businesses.

The book has two purposes. First, to feature companies that are highly innovative in finding solutions to the world's most malignant difficulties as a means to build the corporations' long-term success and value. Second, and most importantly, to show that the most serious issues facing humanity and our planet can only be solved with businesses leading the way. While nonprofits have vital missions and excellent approaches to address social, environmental, and economic matters, NGOs lack the resources to scale for sufficient impact. Governments of some nations represent their people, sometimes effectively, yet they are limited by borders and may be unable to reach agreements among other governments. Only global corporations have the vast resources, international scope, global workforces, and incentives of the marketplace to truly bring about the changes that are necessary in order to achieve global peace and prosperity. Furthermore, as you will see in this book, there are corporate leaders and people who work at companies who are innovative problem solvers and motivated by both mission and markets to build a better world.

The notion that companies are the only organizations that can solve the world's challenges might give pause: corporations are not democratically elected, and their ultimate purpose is profits, not mission. Moreover, many companies caused—and some continue to create—the challenges that the world seeks to remedy. This book is not meant to suggest that we yield the work of global problem solving to businesses. Instead, I am reflecting my observation that some companies are beginning to recognize that energy efficiency, poverty reduction, and access to healthcare, for example, are rich business opportunities, and they are becoming more effective in this role than NGOs and governments ever were or could be.

I also observe that the companies that are the most effective in finding ways to mitigate global warming, provide access to education, and protect human rights, for example, are doing so by collaborating with each other and with NGOs. They also engage with a broad range of stakeholders, including people in the communities where they have operations. These businesses also become transparent about how they conduct themselves, disclose their carbon emissions and labor standards to the broader public through new reporting formats, and engage with consumers via social media.

Companies are not doing these things because they are "nice," but because they are learning that this is the way to be profitable. Corporations understand that customers, employees, and investors expect accountability, transparency, and adherence to labor and environmental norms in order to be brand-worthy. As you will see, studies show that businesses that ignore labor groups, grassroots organizations, consumers, and civil society do so at their peril; costs of such corporate insularity and arrogance can reach billions of dollars annually per company, even affecting their bottom lines into the double digits. Additionally, customers get angry at companies that abuse their workers or spill oil on wildlife and beaches. Furthermore, investors are getting wiser, understanding that companies that do not take social and environmental factors into account are likely to be poor bets.

It has been a great adventure to research and create this book for the past several months. The book is the logical extension of the work that I have been doing for my entire life, and more specifically for the past 20 years. I am by nature practical, mission-oriented, and entrepreneurial. Beginning in childhood, I volunteered after school and during summers, and every job from college and graduate school onward has been mission-focused. In my work, I always had a clear sense of the objective, how it would be accomplished—including generating the revenues and determining how it would be assessed, measured, documented, and reported.

Since 1979, my career has involved creating and building a series of three social enterprises (one was actually the division of a university)—establishing for each a mission, developing a sustainable revenue model, building a great team, developing and implementing an outcome measurement model from day one, instilling the values of transparency and accountability in my team, and engaging businesses as key to the formula for achieving success in the mission. To me, that was just common sense.

Since the early 90s, my work has been focused on three areas: training and placing corporate executives on NGO/nonprofit boards to advance leadership development and effective community engagement, consulting to NGO/nonprofit boards to facilitate the achievement of greater organizational ambitions, and partnering NGOs and corporations for their mutual benefit in accomplishing social, environmental, and economic purposes.

As I've written this book, I've thought a great deal about my grandsons, Gabe and Ben, and the future we are creating for them. My wish is that other readers will consider the children and grandchildren of the world as well.

ACKNOWLEDGMENTS

I AM FORTUNATE TO BE SURROUNDED BY TEACHERS AND MENTORS EVERY DAY. Particularly because of the nature of my work, my life is filled with people of all ages, nationalities, and backgrounds, who work in businesses, NGOs, and universities advancing social, environmental, and economic development. I am endlessly amazed and inspired by their dedication and creativity in finding ways to make this world a better place. It would be impossible to name all of them, but I will do my best to acknowledge many who influenced and informed me in writing this book.

To begin with, thank you to those who generously contributed time and expertise by participating in interviews with me—sometimes multiple and long calls across long distances. Some graciously hosted me in person. Our discussions provided a rich source of learning, research, and delight throughout the past seven months. I am grateful for their bounty as well as their enthusiasm in this book. They include Dunstan Allison-Hope, Sarah Altschuller, Suhas Apte, Andreas Astrup, Brooke Avery, Tanya Barron, Jennifer Beard, Robert Wm Blum, MD, MPH, PhD, Talya Bosch, Richard Brooks, Dan Bross, Antony Bugg-Levine, Laurence Chandy, Ann Charles, Laura Clise, Elaine Cohen, Steve Cohen, Carlos Contreras, Maria Luisa Contursi, Aron Cramer, Deborah Cundy, Luella Chavez D'Angelo, Susan Davis, Paul Dickinson, Paul Ellingstad, Hikmet Ersek, Suzanne Fallender, John Harrington, Nicolas Hazard, Neil Hawkins, Mark Heffernan, Caroline Hempstead, Del Hudson, Fran Hughes, Kara Hurst, Nathan Hurst, Malika Idouaddi, Hannah Jones, Michael Joseph, Julia Taylor Kennedy, Jason Kibbey, Shari King, Gail Klintworth, Jennifer Layke, Chris Librie, Stanley Litow, Thomas Lingard, Naomi Mandelstein, Emmanuel Marchant, Suzanne McCarron, Racheal Meiers, Ahsiya Mencin, Bo Miller, Clara Miller, Tim Mohin, Marilyn Carlson Nelson, Clay Nesler, Jacqueline Novogratz, Allan Pamba, Harry Pastuszek, Deirdre Peterson, Oonagh Puglisi, Robert Rigby-Hall, Linda Rosen, Eric Roston, Paul Scott, Dov Seidman, Sarah Shillito, Robin Smalley, Carol Smolenski, Peter Sweatman, Julie Tanner, Emilio Tenuta, Mark Tercek,

Gina Tesla, Andrea Thomas, Pierre Victoria, Catherine Von Altheer, Jane Wales, Elaine Weidman-Grunewald, Jeannette Weisschuh, Deirdre White, Sir Andrew Witty, Yasmina Zaidman, and Gabi Zedlmayer.

Special appreciation goes to Aron Cramer, president and CEO of BSR. Our discussions about business coalitions, corporate-NGO partnerships, and stakeholder engagement—areas where BSR excels—were invaluable. Aron Cramer also provided background regarding BSR programs that are featured in this book and introductions to members of his team who were outstanding resources.

I want to thank Deirdre White, president and CEO of PYXERA Global for her keen insights and expertise, particularly related to two topic areas: international corporate volunteering and national content development. Deidre White also made important introductions including to corporations that are featured in case studies in *A Better World, Inc.*

Laura Clise, director of Sustainable Development for AREVA Inc., was a valuable resource particularly for the chapter on climate change and energy. Additionally, Laura Clise made introductions to several of the companies that are featured in case studies in *A Better World, Inc.* I am grateful for her expertise, enthusiasm, and generosity.

Thank you also to David and Christopher Mikkelsen, co-founders of Refugees United, for their support for this book and introductions as well.

Thank you especially to friends, colleagues, and loved ones who provided context on issues about which I was writing, either in interviews or in the course of our usual conversations—at seminars, online, over dinners, or just hanging out: David Addams, Debra Beck, Tamara Belinfanti, Donna Callejon, Donna Colonna, Susan Davis, Terril Gagnier, Holly Gregory, Andrew Green, Amos Guiora, Hagit Guiora, Fabiola Girardi, James Hagy, Fran Hauser, Carly Hoffmann, Madeline Kerner, Elena Korngold, Mari Kuraishi, Susan McPherson, Craig Medwick, Margaret Mo, Matthew Mo, Sherry Mueller, Semida Munteanu, Shai Reshef, Carolyn Powell, Teri Steele, Joan Youngman, Brian Walsh, Naomi Waibel, Bonnie Weill, and Douglas Weill.

Thank you also to Paul Besserie and Dana Gluck at the Brooklyn Museum. What could be more inspiring than visits to El Anatsui's exhibit, "Gravity and Grace," during the time I was writing this book.

Thank you to my friends and colleagues at the Clinton Global Initiative (CGI) whom I've had the pleasure to work with for the past six years while blogging on Fast Company about the partnership commitments made by corporations, NGOs, and funders year-round and at the CGI annual meetings.

Special appreciation to Shannon Newberry, who has moved on to Google, to Erika Gudmundson, who made introductions to some of the people who are featured in this book, and to Craig Minassian. Thank you also to Judit

Arenas, James Robinson, and the outstanding team at APCO who provide communications support to CGI at the annual meetings. And to Jove Oliver who is involved in the CGI annual meetings as well. Through these individuals, I've met many of the people who are featured in *A Better World, Inc.*

Thank you to Noah Robischon, executive editor at Fast Company for the opportunity to blog on the topics of corporate social responsibility, leadership, and corporate governance for the past several years. And to Erin Schulte, senior editor—my editor—whose excellence and expertise I greatly appreciate. I'm quite sure that the momentum of blogging for Fast Company about CGI was an inspiration to me in writing this book.

Special gratitude to Melanie Meyer, my right hand person at Korngold Consulting and at my previous social enterprise as well. Melanie is to be credited with the firm's website, social media, board surveys, client service, and much more. An abundance of thank yous to Denise O'Brien—my colleague in shaping three social enterprises for 25 years—who has influenced me in so many ways.

Thank you to my editor, Laurie Harting, executive editor at Palgrave Macmillan. Because of you, there is *A Better World, Inc.* Our first conversation felt more like a third conversation. She got right to the essence of the book. Given her experience as an editor and in the substantive issues I proposed to write about, it was particularly meaningful that she chose this book, and I am forever grateful. Her comments to drafts along the way were encouraging, insightful, and valuable. Lauren LoPinto, Editorial Assistant, thank you for reviews and comments on drafts and guidance along the way.

And finally, my book agent, John Willig, where this all began. He "got me" from our first conversation. He also had the fine instinct to figure out the right match in introducing Palgrave Macmillan and me. Thank you for believing in me and for your wise counsel throughout the process. John made things that seemed complicated quite simple. He is a delight to work with.

Our home, while loving and fun, has always been a round-the-clock seminar since the time our two sons could speak—with us learning more from them and their friends than they from us. The conversations continue via the Internet whether or not we are together in person—sharing and sharply opining about the day's news—including friends who are also involved in the issues. Topics range from human rights to literature, global conflicts to climate change. We also often invoke the wisdom of Homer Simpson, Fletch, and so on.

My husband and I have been each other's mentors for more decades than I care to mention. Gerry read nearly every iteration of these chapters, often asking provocative questions to help me anticipate what people might want to know or understand better. As a professor, author, and former law school dean, his experience is quite relevant, as is his expertise in land rights.

My older son is a physician-scientist. He is a purist, deeply concerned about climate change. In discussing this book, he questioned and prodded, providing thoughtful insights. He also shared authors and thinkers that he most appreciates.

David, a Bain & Company consulting alumnus, now consults to global corporations on sustainability in his position at BSR. David's input was valuable as I shaped the book proposal, in discussions of issues during the writing, and finally in reading the book manuscript a week before I submitted it to my editor. He posed provocative questions that inspired me to return to my laptop with additional thoughts. Primarily, he emboldened me to add more of my own voice to the manuscript.

The two greatest inspirations and motivations for me in writing this book are—without contest—my grandchildren, Gabe (8) and Ben (6). They have also been the most enthusiastic about the book, often asking me: "What page are you on, Oma?" The boys and I have had many discussions about the various topics in *A Better World, Inc.* Ben is animated by concern for people less fortunate than he. One evening at bedtime, Gabe listened thoughtfully as Ben was suggesting how I should organize the chapters. Then Gabe chimed in. "Well, Oma, we've been learning a lot about 'respect' in school. And actually, I think that's really what you're writing about. Respecting the environment and respecting other people." That left the three of us quiet and pensive. That seemed to say it all.

CHAPTER 1

ONLY GLOBAL CORPORATIONS HAVE THE RESOURCES, GLOBAL REACH, AND SELF-INTEREST TO BUILD A BETTER WORLD

> What people can positively achieve is influenced by economic opportunities, political liberties, social powers, and the enabling conditions of good health, basic education, and the encouragement and cultivation of initiatives.[1]
>
> —Amartya Sen

THE WORLD FACES SOCIAL, ENVIRONMENTAL, AND ECONOMIC CHALLENGES that are projected to increase exponentially over the coming decades. Many of these issues, such as environmental degradation, climate change, access to healthcare, poverty, and human rights, are cross-border issues. National governments acting alone lack the authority and resources to provide adequate responses. The international community has too often failed to achieve binding and actionable agreements to deal with these global problems. For example, global climate change conferences have not resulted in implementable accords to address global warming. Conflicting interests between developed and developing nations, rich and poor countries, North and South, East and West, and various political ideologies interfere with agreements on many world issues. The NGO sector has made strides in advancing the human condition but lacks resources and scalability sufficient to make transformational progress.

In the face of these difficult challenges, some creative responses are emerging from the business sector. Unlike governments, businesses in the twenty-first century cross national borders, spanning oceans and continents. Modern corporations respond to customers, employees, and investors across the globe in order to profit and thrive. Moreover, companies are learning that they must be attuned to the needs of the world's population in order to maximize profits. This book tells the story of a number of global corporations that have aligned their profit-making missions with efforts to build a better world. These companies have come to understand that they can enhance their bottom lines while improving global conditions, often through partnerships with NGOs and governments.

Every country on the globe encounters a variety of struggles. Poverty continues to plague over one billion people; the growing disparity between rich and poor is a top concern of global leaders as it threatens peace and prosperity. Climate change is causing extreme weather events that trigger human dislocation and geopolitical destabilization. The degradation of water, forests, and arable land threatens human existence. The failure to adequately educate the world's children, particularly in science, technology, engineering, and math, creates a disconnect between jobs and job-seekers, leaving too many people unemployed and a workforce without the skills to tackle global concerns. Millions of children and adults continue to die from preventable diseases and illnesses due to lack of access to healthcare, medicines, and vaccines. People suffer the loss of human rights across the globe: as victims of human trafficking, or as a result of labor abuses, violence over conflict minerals, and limits to free expression. All of these world problems bring suffering to people and their families. Companies have begun to realize that these global struggles also undermine economic progress and their businesses.

Future trends will magnify the challenges. The world population is on a trajectory to grow from seven billion today to nine billion within the next few decades. The majority of people around the globe will live in cities, particularly in developed countries. Three billion additional new consumers will enter the middle class, primarily from developing markets. These emerging middle-class consumers will seek more affluent lifestyles.[2] With today's global population already consuming resources equivalent to more than 1.5 Earths, we are on an unsustainable path to meet the demands of this growing population.

Furthermore, without any course corrections, we are on track to surpass the safety threshold of two degrees Celsius that scientists predict will unleash the worst effects of climate change. Extreme weather events will exacerbate human hardship, bringing about violence over scarce resources. This is a likely future by the time today's kindergartners become adults. Experts already see such patterns occurring in Syria and elsewhere in the world, as people are forced from their farms in the face of droughts, find no jobs in the cities, and resort to civil war in their frustration. Destabilizing conflicts in sensitive geopolitical areas could threaten peace and prosperity worldwide.

In the past, companies might have seemed an unlikely source for finding solutions to social, environmental, and economic challenges. Businesses and nonprofits sat at either end of a spectrum, often quite mistrustful of one another. Businesses distinctly stayed at one end, creating products and services for profit, while nonprofits clearly stayed at the other end, pursuing missions for the betterment of the world. Too often, elements of the corporate sector were responsible for creating the human rights abuses, environmental degradation, and economic injustices that continue to plague the world today. In the past, if a business wanted to "do good," it would make a financial contribution to a charity or give its employees a pat on the back for volunteering.

By the 1990s, some corporations became more strategic in their philanthropy, focusing their dollars on charities that related to their businesses.

There were a number of drivers for this change. In a weak economy—marked by the stock market crash of 1987, a recession, and high oil prices—and facing increased global competition, companies became more attentive to how they were spending each of their dollars. Businesses began to notice that they had been dispensing charitable funds fairly idiosyncratically. They realized that these monies could be assets to be invested more strategically in strengthening the communities in which the company operated, while also building corporate goodwill. Perhaps most importantly, corporations saw that they could align their contributions with causes that would enhance their direct business interests, thereby boosting revenues, their brands, and their public image. Newspaper companies began giving to literacy organizations, for example; banks invested in small business development, and some phone companies supported crisis hotlines.

Eventually, even more purposeful companies recognized the value of integrating service—including volunteering, skills-based service, and nonprofit board participation—with philanthropy, in order to advance community relations, marketing, leadership development, and other forms of personal and professional development.[3] One example is Clifford Chance, a leading global law firm. As described in *Fast Company*, the firm integrated NGO/nonprofit board participation, pro bono service, volunteerism, and strategic philanthropy to maximize the firm's impact in strengthening communities, while developing leadership and fostering personal and professional development among its attorneys and employees.[4]

Additional examples are provided in *Leveraging Good Will: Strengthening Nonprofits by Engaging Businesses*.[5] As companies recognized the benefits of community engagement, collaboration, and partnerships, as well as opportunities for social and environmental impact, these issues moved up to the C-suite, and took on names like "corporate social responsibility"[6] and "sustainability."[7]

Around the turn of the twenty-first century, some leading businesses advanced to a new stage by embracing the concepts of social, environmental, and economic opportunity as part of their core corporate missions. These companies became motivated by two forces: they understood that they could thrive only if they operated in a healthy and sustainable environment with customers who had the economic capability and longevity to purchase their products. Additionally, these companies saw opportunity in developing and producing goods and services for a market that was increasingly demanding sustainable, socially responsible products. These global corporations, therefore, incorporated these values as a key part of their business philosophy and plans. Social issues were no longer a "feel good" or public relations adjunct to the company's core mission. In this way, these leading companies moved toward embracing the values held by the NGO sector.

Not only have the missions of some businesses and nonprofits become somewhat aligned, their operational approaches have also coalesced. Leading companies have realized that they need a purposeful mission, a sustainable environment and supply chain, a healthy, educated, and economically empowered customer base, and a motivated workforce—values traditionally identified with the NGO sector—in order to thrive. Nonprofits have come to understand that they need to make a compelling case for significant resources, create robust business models, demonstrate replicability, see issues in terms of the "win-win," and build effective infrastructures—ideas historically touted by business—in order to achieve scale to address mighty global challenges.

This book will explore programs developed by a number of global corporations, often in partnership with each other, or with NGOs and governments, that provide visionary and innovative solutions to the challenges facing the world now and in the future. These companies believe that by improving social, environmental, and economic conditions, they will meet the interests of customers, employees, and investors, increase their profits, and become more sustainable. As a result, companies are engaging in economic development initiatives to reduce poverty and create opportunity: cutting carbon emissions in their own operations as well as supply chains, while developing energy efficient products and services for private and governmental customers; internalizing the costs of natural resources that they consume while producing and marketing environmentally responsible goods; investing in technology-based educational programs to prepare the next generation for twenty-first century jobs; offering access to healthcare, medicines, and vaccines—often enabled by mobile technology—to save lives and improve the quality of life for people in underserved regions; and developing programs to prevent human trafficking, labor abuses, violence over conflict minerals, and limits on free expression.

This book features specific approaches that some corporations are taking that appear to be effective or promising in addressing particular social, environmental, and economic challenges. A number of businesses have emerged as global leaders in corporate social responsibility, while others have demonstrated strength in certain programs but lag in other areas. Moreover, one must remember that some corporate actors have created and continue to perpetuate the social, environmental, and economic threats facing the world; only with such an understanding can we move forward together to find solutions. The purpose of this book is to look ahead by highlighting effective and promising corporate initiatives and to rally the business sector and its stakeholders to continue to think creatively and collaboratively about building a better world.

This book is organized into chapters on economic development, climate change and energy, ecosystems, education, healthcare, and human rights. Chapter 2 focuses on economic development. It demonstrates that, although progress has been made in halving the rate of poverty in just over 20 years to 1.2 billion people, progress is at risk due to various factors: droughts, floods, and other extreme weather events that are driving people from farmlands into cities where there are not enough jobs; insufficient access to healthcare and education; negative attitudes toward girls and women; and corrupt governance in some countries.

Global poverty threatens all of society, not only those who are marginalized. Reports from leading institutions, including the International Monetary Fund[8] and Brookings,[9] indicate that poverty threatens global peace and prosperity. Moreover, wealth gaps—defined as severe income disparity—topped the list of the 50 greatest threats to the world according to the *Global Risks Report 2013*,[10] a survey of over one thousand experts from industry, government, academia, and civil society. Chapter 2 argues that while governments alone have been unable to resolve this pernicious issue of poverty, global corporations are finding some innovative solutions through partnerships with NGOs and governments. Furthermore, companies are profiting by strengthening economies in developing countries, providing employment, facilitating the creation and expansion of small and medium businesses, and reversing poverty.

Chapter 3, which addresses climate change and energy, examines a variety of ways that companies are profiting by reducing carbon emissions, investing in greater use of renewable energy resources, and innovating and marketing energy-efficient goods and services. While governments have done a good deal of talking about climate change, the planet's temperature continues to rise. In the meantime, companies are moving forward with concrete action. Intel, for example, is shifting its operations to meet 100 percent of its electricity use in the United States in 2013 through green power. The company is driven to reduce costs, prepare itself for longer-term energy challenges, and burnish its brand among customers, employees, and investors. Other global corporations, such as Walmart, Unilever, and Nike, are creating sustainable products and materials that require less energy and natural resources in their supply chains, and throughout the lifecycles of their products: from raw materials to ultimate creation, production, use, and recycling. These companies are also enjoying cost savings, while decoupling business growth from scarce resources and appealing to stakeholders. Companies like Intel, Ericsson, and Johnson Controls are promoting and constructing "smart cities" and "smart buildings" to cut carbon emissions in entire communities of the world, thereby selling profitable services. These business approaches promise to enrich companies' bottom lines while advancing the global agenda to mitigate climate change.

Chapter 4 explores ecosystems, including clean air, water, timber, and arable land, which are vital for human sustenance. Already hundreds of millions of people lack access to clean drinking water. Droughts and other extreme weather events, combined with population growth, will exacerbate demands for food and water. Governments have been ineffective in protecting forests, land, and water. Yet many businesses are finding that it is their interests to protect the natural resources on which their company's profitability and long-term health depend.

Some companies are transforming their approaches to source alternative materials for manufacturing, and redesigning their products, rather than relying on natural resources that will become more scarce. For example, Kimberly-Clark shifted its sourcing of fibers from endangered areas to certified forests. Unilever committed to source 100 percent of its agricultural raw materials sustainably by 2020 and reports that it is on track to that record. In this way, corporations are making their businesses more sustainable for the future while also increasing their brand value by addressing consumer and investor concerns about the environment.

Chapter 5 demonstrates that education—particularly in science, technology, engineering, and math (STEM)—is vital for people in the United States and worldwide to qualify for jobs in the twenty-first century. Education is the win-win that ensures a qualified workforce for companies while preparing people for employment and opportunities for a good life. Businesses also benefit when people earn incomes that allow them to consume those businesses' goods. Through its Catalyst program, Hewlett-Packard leverages its technology, expertise, and resources to stimulate international collaboration among innovators in science, technology, engineering, and math education to prepare students for twenty-first century problem-solving. Ericsson enables access to world-class information and educational resources for students and teachers in developing countries through low-cost mobile broadband and cloud computing. Companies are seeking to solve the global education crisis because it is in their own interests, and this benefits the world.

Chapter 6 addresses healthcare, another area where humanitarian concerns intersect with business interests. Developing countries suffer from high death rates due to preventable illnesses and diseases. Governments have not been able to provide sufficient access to care, medicines, and vaccines due to the legacy of colonialism, including wars and weak infrastructure, lack of national resources, and sometimes poor governance. In response to this health crisis, a number of companies are providing innovative solutions while also benefiting themselves. These companies are enhancing access to healthcare, medicines, and vaccines—including through mobile technology—by partnering with each other, and with NGOs and governments. Although some projects may begin as proof-of-concept pilot programs, they are designed to be expanded in order to lead to substantial sales, including for vaccines and medicines. For example, GSK and Vodafone are collaborating to increase the vaccination rate of children in Mozambique, using mobile phones to register new mothers and send reminders for appointments; this serves Vodafone's customers and may ultimately increase GSK's sales if the pilot is successfully replicated.

Moreover, many businesses recognize that it is in their interests to help develop robust and thriving communities for the well-being of their employees and consumers. For example, AstraZeneca partnered with Johns Hopkins University and two NGOs to combat noncommunicable diseases (NCDs) in young people through research, high-level advocacy, education, and health skills training.

Chapter 7 explores human rights abuses, including human trafficking, worker safety, and conflict minerals (which are mined in conditions of armed conflict). These human rights violations are reflected in products used and worn in everyday life throughout the world—including cellphones and other electronic equipment made from conflict minerals and clothing made in sweatshops in Asia. This chapter also addresses infringements of freedom of expression and privacy on the Internet—issues which affect people worldwide, including in the United States and other developed countries.

Humanitarian interests alone would seem to be sufficient to motivate companies to protect human rights. Yet the reality is that businesses are sensitive to matters that concern customers, employees, and investors—especially in an era when news of egregious abuses spreads quickly on the Internet. Additionally, companies are realizing that their reputations can rise or fall based on the positions they take on sensitive matters. The Global Coalition Against Human Trafficking, founded by several international corporations such as Coca-Cola, Delta Airlines, ExxonMobil, and Microsoft, mobilizes the power, resources, and thought leadership of the business community to end human trafficking.

Furthermore, a variety of multi-stakeholder groups involving the high technology industry are addressing conflict minerals. Moreover, companies have learned that violating human rights can cost a company billions of dollars in a single year, due to conflicts in labor markets and resistance from communities and other stakeholders that can delay permits, construction, and operations. Companies are learning that doing the right thing benefits their bottom lines by protecting[11] and building their brands, reducing financial risks, elevating employee morale, and attracting responsible investors.

Chapter 8 shows that the success of a company's sustainability strategy rests on its effectiveness in engaging with stakeholders, collaborating with other companies and NGOs, and ensuring effective board oversight of the company's social, environmental, and economic development agenda. Companies can effectively build trust with customers, communities, employees, and investors by involving them in an iterative conversation for global problem-solving. This chapter describes strategies for stakeholder engagement, along with best practices for establishing stakeholder advisory councils (SACs). A global corporation will create an SAC—a small group of highly qualified people with diverse backgrounds and expertise—to meet with the company's executives for candid discussions about corporate strategies and their implications for social and environmental impact. Additionally, forward-looking boards of directors recognize that sustainability drives innovation, growth, and profits, while mitigating risks. Sustainability is a governance matter. The boards of leading sustainability companies have "corporate responsibility committees"—or "sustainability committees"—to oversee the sustainability strategy and its performance and to discuss it with the board.

A number of international companies are seeing that solving global challenges can increase their profits and long-term sustainability. They are developing programs to advance the social, environmental, and economic condition of the world in ways that government cannot. There is much to celebrate and hope for as companies build a better world.

Here are a few definitions that will be helpful to readers. NGOs *refers to "non-governmental organizations," the term used for nonprofits in most parts of the world outside of the United States. In the United States, the term* nonprofit *is most commonly used. In this book, NGO is usually used to refer to international organizations that span multiple countries,* nonprofit *to refer to organizations that serve the United States only, and* NGOs/nonprofits *when referring to both types.*

The words sustainability *and* resilience *are used throughout the book. Sustainability here refers to the long-term viability of a natural resource, community, or business. Resilience refers to the ability of a structure or community to withstand and survive a trauma or attack, usually from an extreme weather event. Both terms are used in the context of threats due to climate change, the demands of a growing population, and scarcity of natural resources, as well as opportunities for businesses to innovate.*

Transparency *and* disclosure *are also terms and concepts that you will read about here.* Transparency *refers to the availability of information about companies, NGOs, and governments, and their activities and operations. There is a trend toward greater transparency, shifting away from previous decades when so much in government, business, and NGOs happened behind closed doors. With the advent of social media, and the democratization and immediacy of information exchange, barriers have been eliminated, so it has become increasingly difficult for institutions to keep secrets. Companies that make information about their social, environmental, and economic impacts easily available and understandable—also known as "disclosing"—look better to the public and their customers than companies that appear to be failing to "disclose." By disclosing, corporations are being more transparent and hence, seem more trustworthy. Legal obligations are also requiring a higher level of disclosure.*

Accountability, oversight, and board governance—or corporate governance—are also important terms. Accountability refers to a company's responsibility to act with integrity with regard to its finances, employees, products, services, customers, and all communities it affects, and to give an honest report to all of its stakeholders accordingly. Oversight refers to legal and regulatory bodies that are responsible for ensuring that companies act with integrity and within the law. Board governance, or corporate governance, refers to the corporation's board of directors' legal and fiduciary responsibility to ensure that the corporation acts with integrity to fulfill its purposes.

The term ESG refers to a company's "environmental, social, and [board] governance" practices. There is a growing understanding that environmental, social, and governance factors affect a company's value as well as the public.

CHAPTER 2

ECONOMIC DEVELOPMENT

If a man doesn't have a job or an income, he has neither life nor liberty nor the possibility for the pursuit of happiness. He merely exists.[1]
—The Rev. Dr. Martin Luther King, Jr.

THERE HAS BEEN STEADY PROGRESS IN REDUCING POVERTY DURING THE PAST three decades. According to the World Bank, 22 percent of the developing world's population—or 1.29 billion people—lived on $1.25 or less a day in 2008.[2] While this is still a staggering number, it represents a steep drop from 43 percent in 1990 and 52 percent in 1981. "The growth rates of the world's emerging and developing economies have surged ... Since 1980, over one billion people around the world have ascended from poverty."[3]

Furthermore, estimates indicate that by 2010, the poverty rate fell to less than half of the 1990 rate.[4] That means the developing world has achieved, five years ahead of the goal, the United Nation's first Millennium Development Goal (MDG): to cut the 1990 extreme-poverty rate in half by 2015.

The eight MDGs were established following the Millennium Summit of the United Nations in 2000. Approved by the UN's member states and global institutions, the MDGs range from halving extreme poverty to halting the spread of HIV/AIDS and providing universal primary education, all by the target date of 2015.[5]

According to a 2013 report by the Center for Strategic and International Studies, a nonprofit chaired by former US Senator Sam Nunn, the private sector, rather than US foreign assistance or philanthropy is the key driver in such global prosperity. "At no other time in history has US foreign aid made up such a small share of global capital flows. In 1960, public capital accounted for 71 percent of financial flows to the developing world. Today, it stands at only 9 percent. Although this aid and US leadership make a tremendous difference in international relations, the private sector, through its flows of capital, technology, and knowledge, has become a vital force in development."[6]

For business, alleviating poverty presents opportunity, while addressing a pernicious global issue. By helping to advance people from extreme poverty to the middle class, businesses anticipate achieving long-term strategic growth through access to new markets, workforce development, product innovation, and product distribution.[7] In Africa, Asia, Latin America, and formerly Communist countries, businesses are teaming up with NGOs and governments to foster employment, business development, and regional capacity-building to strengthen economies. Companies recognize that these locales will provide vast and growing market opportunities as wealth increases and consumers seek to increase their quality of life. According to McKinsey & Company, "Africa's consumer-facing industries are expected to grow by more than $400 billion by 2020."[8] Consumer-facing industries include retail and wholesale, retail banking, telecommunications, and tourism.

In spite of tremendous gains in fighting poverty, progress is fragile. There is still a long way to go, and failure could bring disastrous results throughout the world. Martin Ravallion is director of the Development Research Group, the World Bank's in-house research department. As leader of the team that produces the World Bank's poverty data, he cautions that "even with the current rate of progress, about one billion people would still live in extreme poverty in 2015. And the bunching up we see just above the $1.25-a-day line points to the continuing vulnerability of poor people across the world."[9] The numbers are stark but hardly capture the full degree of human deprivation and suffering.

Achieving success in eliminating poverty is complicated. To begin with, it's difficult to measure progress accurately. According to Laurence Chandy, a fellow at Brookings working on global poverty, aid effectiveness, and fragile states, "the global headcount (based on the $1.25 poverty line) has been dominated by three population groups: sub-Saharan Africa, India and China. These three account for a remarkably constant three-quarters of the world's poor—a share which has never deviated by more than three percentage points on either side. Yet poverty estimates for each of the three suffer from glaring problems: insufficient survey data, flawed surveys, and faulty PPP [purchasing power parity] conversions, respectively. If we cannot believe the poverty estimates for sub-Saharan Africa, India, and China, then we cannot believe the World Bank's global estimates, and we must admit that our knowledge of the state of global poverty is glaringly limited."[10]

Another challenge is defining goals and success. In order to define success, it is important to understand the origins of the baseline. The figure of $1.25 a day was determined based on an average of the 15 poorest countries; the notion of poverty in the United States or Europe would be much higher, of course.[11] According to Chandy, success is actually achieved when the poorest people in developing countries earn $10 a day. "Below the $10 threshold, one is highly vulnerable to slipping back into extreme poverty, susceptible to disease, and losing one's limited assets to theft. At $10 a day, people become global citizens, making demands for democracy and education, and wanting to buy cars. Most importantly, at $10, there is less likelihood of dropping back," explained Chandy. "The President of the World Bank talks about shared prosperity. If we're going to deal with poverty, we need to get people permanently above $1.25, which means above $10."[12]

Susan Davis has another way to describe success in eliminating poverty. Davis is the founder, president, and CEO of BRAC USA, an independent grant-making affiliate of BRAC.[13] BRAC is a development success story, spreading solutions born in Bangladesh to ten other countries around the world – a global leader in creating opportunity for the world's poor.[14] According to Davis, "The question of relative poverty is harder to address because we get into debates on what is 'enough.' We all deserve to have our basic needs for food, water, shelter, healthcare, sanitation, and education met, but at what standard, and who decides? Different groups measure poverty at different levels of purchasing power: $1.25, $2, or $2.50 a day. But even relative poverty is possible to eliminate given the combined impact of economic growth, social protection programs, and access of the poorest to jobs and self-employment. That's where microfinance is essential. When there isn't enough decent work for everyone who needs it, people need to be able to create their own livelihoods. Microfinance is an essential tool in creating freedom and opportunity for the poor, though it's not the only tool. Education, healthcare, legal empowerment, community empowerment, livelihood training—these are important as well."[15]

Advances against poverty are tentative with a volatile global economy, especially for people who live in countries with unstable and corrupt governments. Additionally, climate change will increasingly undermine efforts to combat poverty. According to the United Nations Development Fund, "the impacts of climate change will reverse decades worth of human development gains and threaten achievement of the Millennium Development Goals."[16] As evidenced by natural disasters and droughts in the past decade, these extreme conditions impede people's access to water, sanitation, food, and energy, especially in countries with weak infrastructure and institutions.

Global poverty threatens all of society, not only those who are marginalized. According to an article published by the International Monetary Fund, the result of rising inequality in world income distribution "is a large mass of unemployed and angry young people, mostly males, to whom the new information technologies have given the means to threaten the stability of the societies they live in, and even threaten social stability in countries of the wealthy zone."[17]

Impediments and threats to success include not only climate change and corrupt governance, but also the lack of healthcare and education, and—to a very great extent—negative attitudes toward girls and women. According to the UK's Department for International Development (DFID), "Across the developing world, girls and women continue to bear a disproportionate burden of poverty. Yet we know it is possible to take effective, practical action that enables girls and women to fulfill their potential. And we know that the benefits of investing in girls and women are transformational—for their own lives and for their families, communities, societies, and economies. Empowering girls and women has multiplier effects for economic growth and achieving all of the MDGs. If we reach girls in particular, early enough in their lives, we can transform their life chances. Giving girls greater choice and control over decisions that affect them helps break the cycle of poverty between one generation and the next. It enables us to stop poverty before it starts."[18]

DFID describes four pillars for action: delaying first pregnancy and supporting safe childbirth; channelling economic assets directly to girls and women; getting girls through secondary school; and preventing violence.

Additionally, wealth gaps, defined as severe income disparity, topped the list of the 50 greatest threats to the world, according to the *Global Risks Report 2013*.[19] This top 50 report was presented by the World Economic Forum's Risk Response Network to global leaders in Davos, Switzerland. The results were based on a survey of over a thousand experts from industry, government, academia, and civil society who were polled as to how they expect 50 global risks to play out over the next ten years. Furthermore, leaders indicate that there are limited public resources to address economic or climate issues, both areas requiring investment.

Data from a number of sources indicate that income inequality has grown significantly since the early 1970s, after several decades of stability. While inequality has risen among most developed countries, and especially English-speaking ones, the United States is among those countries with the highest Gini indeces.[20] The Gini index "measures the extent to which the distribution of income or consumption expenditure among individuals or households within an economy deviates from a perfectly equal distribution."[21] An index of 100 represents perfect inequality, with an inedex of 0 representing perfect equality. Causes of growing income inequality include different rates of population growth among rich and poor countries, the fall in non-oil commodities, the debt trap, and technological change.[22] According to a report by the *Global Post*, funded by the Ford Foundation, "income inequality is surging, and there are few countries where it is rising faster than the United States. The distance between rich and poor is greater in America than (in) nearly all other developed countries, making the US a leader in a trend that economists warn has dire consequences."[23]

"In fact," the *Global Post* report continues, "the most recent data compiled by the Organization for Economic Cooperation and Development (OECD) show that Chile, Mexico, and Turkey are the only OECD member countries that rank higher than the US in terms of inequality. And it's only getting worse."[24]

The OECD helps governments tackle the economic, social, and governance challenges of a globalized economy. "The OECD brings around its table 40 countries that account for 80 percent of world trade and investment, giving it a pivotal role in addressing the challenges facing the world economy."[25] According to the *Global Post* report, Branko Milanovic, lead economist in the World Bank research department, said that "rising inequality in the United States means that the American Dream is becoming steadily less achievable."[26]

There are many reasons to care about the world's poorer citizens. Ethics, morality, and justice are motivating forces. Wealth inequality may also pose geo-political threats. "Global poverty is not solely a humanitarian concern. Over the long term, it can also threaten US national security," according to the results of an investigation conducted by Brookings. "In the twenty-first century, poverty is an important driver of transnational threats...With the advent of globalization and the rapid international movement of people, goods, funds, and information, transnational security threats can arise from and spread with dangerous speed to any part of the planet. They can emerge from remote regions and poor, weak states, turning them into potentially high-risk zones that may eventually, often indirectly, pose significant risks to distant peoples."[27] The report gives examples including deadly flu viruses, terrorist cell attacks on US navy vessels, the theft of biological or nuclear materials from poorly secured facilities in any of 40 countries, narcotics traffickers and crime syndicates, and flooding and other effects of climate change that can lead to millions of deaths.

In a recent article about Syria, "Without Water, Revolution," *New York Times* columnist Thomas Friedman asserted that drought drove masses of farmers from their land to the cities, where there were insufficient jobs and infrastructure, and a lack of government response. The ensuing poverty ultimately led to frustration and civil war. "Young people and farmers starved for jobs—and land starved for water—were a prescription for revolution."[28]

As shown in the chapter on climate change and energy, a special report by the Council on Foreign Relations[29] brings attention to the destabilizing affects of storms, droughts, and floods. The threat arises from damage caused domestically from extreme weather, in addition to the disruption of "US interests in strategically important countries."[30]

The Computer Network Assurance Corporation, a think tank funded by the US Navy, released a report on climate change and national security prepared by a panel of retired US generals and admirals. The Council for Foreign Relations Special Report concluded that "declining food production, extreme weather events, and drought from climate change could further inflame tensions in Africa, weaken governance and economic growth, and contribute to massive migration and possibly state failure, leaving 'ungoverned spaces' where terrorists can organize."[31]

It is in our power to create a better world where all people will have food, shelter, healthcare, an education, and the opportunity to work. There are two routes that must be pursued concurrently. First, the economies of regions where there has been extreme poverty must be transformed. Second, girls and women, as well as boys and men, must be empowered and provided access to education, healthcare, and the opportunity to earn a living. This vision of economic development and individual empowerment is possible when businesses, NGOs, and governments work in partnership. What is required is the regional infrastructure to promote and support education, healthcare, financial services, business development, regional capacity-building, open markets and free trade, and equal opportunity.

Corporations are recognizing financial and strategic opportunities by investing human, social, and economic capital in emerging markets. As you will see in this chapter, businesses are a powerful force in economic development and individual empowerment in some of the poorest regions of the world. By building stronger and more vibrant communities in previously impoverished regions, businesses in partnership with NGOs and governments benefit by advancing the vision of all people sharing in global prosperity. The cases in this chapter were selected for their innovation, variety, and impact, as well as for the capacity of the parties to accomplish their goals.

THE DOW CHEMICAL COMPANY AND ACUMEN PARTNER TO SCALE SOCIAL ENTERPRISES IN EAST AND WEST AFRICA

The Dow Chemical Company and Acumen, an NGO global venture fund that uses entrepreneurial approaches to solve the problems of global poverty, announced their partnership at the Clinton Global Initiative (CGI) Annual Meeting in 2012. Dow's commitment included $300,000 in funds as well as technical assistance to scale innovative business enterprises in East and West Africa.

As described in chapter one, the mission of CGI is to turn ideas into action. Established in 2005 by former president Bill Clinton, CGI, an initiative of the Clinton Foundation, convenes global leaders to create and implement innovative solutions to the world's most pressing challenges. CGI Annual Meetings have brought together more than one hundred-fifty heads of state, twenty Nobel Prize laureates, and hundreds of leading CEOs, heads of foundations and NGOs, major philanthropists, and members of the media. To date CGI members have made more than 2,300 commitments, which have improved the lives of over 400 million people in more than 180 countries. When fully funded and implemented, these commitments will be valued at more than $73.1 billion. Each chapter of this book includes at least one partnership that is a CGI commitment.[32]

Dow's expertise was perfect for helping the companies in which Acumen invests. Dow's "portfolio of specialty chemical, advanced materials, agro sciences and plastics businesses delivers a broad range of technology-based products and solutions to customers in approximately 160 countries and in high growth sectors such as electronics, water, energy, coatings, and agriculture."[33] Acumen is an NGO that works to create "a world beyond poverty" by investing in social enterprises, emerging leaders, and breakthrough ideas. Acumen invests in what they call "patient capital" in business models that deliver critical goods and services to the world's poor, improving the lives of millions. Since 2001, Acumen has globally invested more than $75 million in 69 companies.

The Dow and Acumen investment portfolio will advance businesses that provide low-income people with water, sanitation, agriculture, and energy services. Thus, not only does the initiative promote promising companies, it also provides the infrastructure to improve the lives of entire communities.

"This is a multi-stakeholder approach," explained Jacqueline Novogratz, founder, president and CEO of Acumen, with tremendous enthusiasm. "We are developing leaders across sectors and ideology," referring to civil society (NGOs), corporations, and governments.[34] Acumen's portfolio companies, averaging between one and two million dollars in revenues annually, needed help scaling their business models to deliver critical goods and services to low-income people in the areas of energy, water, sanitation, and agriculture. Acumen requested problem-solving expertise and general capacity-building consulting, such as marketing, IT services, finance, product design, product development, business strategy, supply chain, impact measurement, and market expansion in new geographies.[35]

Acumen's interests aligned geographically for Dow. Although Dow has had a presence in Africa for 50 years, it was seeking to expand to East and West Africa, where Acumen is engaged. Dow believed through its work with Acumen and its portfolio companies, it would be able to gain access into markets, develop insights and relationships with people in the regulatory agencies, and send the message to local business and civic leaders that the company was there to engage and bring solutions.

Furthermore, Dow saw this engagement as a way to understand the regional economy—where the opportunities and challenges lay. "When we enter, we'll be building manufacturing plants that will have a life of 50 to

60 to 100 years, investing billions of dollars, making operational decisions," said Bo Miller, global director of Corporate Citizenship of The Dow Chemical Company, and president and executive director of The Dow Chemical Company Foundation. "We need clarity on market opportunities, how the market works. With this Acumen project, we can have an impact, while helping with our own process." Miller also emphasized that this was a new way for Dow to do business.

In addition to making the world a better place, Miller described the partnership with Acumen as one big market research project for Dow. "We will learn by doing. How does Africa think about growing its business in the region?" Additionally, Miller talked about the value of employee engagement. "Employees are demonstrating in real terms their commitment to world challenges and that they have real talents to contribute. These are life-changing experiences for employees. They are proud of the company and derive great personal satisfaction." Miller added that while they are engaged in their Acumen projects, employees are expected to perform on their pro bono assignments as if they are working at Dow, and they are evaluated accordingly.

"We work with companies that value innovation," explained Yasmina Zaidman, director of Communications and Strategic Partnerships at Acumen. "What will Dow look like when it has 30 percent of its revenues from Africa, not 5 percent? The companies that are most successful are the most adaptable. Closest to the ground. And how do you get close to the ground? By adding value. And what will it take to solve big problems? Become a big leader in these emerging markets." Zaidman also talked about the opportunity to "get a glimpse into the future by working on the ground in Africa. Perhaps this is also about helping to create the future—a better future."

Representatives of The Dow Chemical Company and Acumen first met in 2006 when Dow became an investor in WaterHealth International, a business that today processes healthy drinking water for more than five million people in India, Bangladesh, Ghana, and the Philippines. WaterHealth's award-winning water purifying technology, UV Waterworks, is based on a novel approach to the use of ultraviolet light for the inactivation of microbial pathogens. WaterHealth contributes to job growth and economic development as well as improved health in the communities it serves.[36] Acumen had been an investor in WaterHealth since 2004; Dow became an investor in 2006.

"Dow and we got to know each other while we were working together in support of this breakthrough water company," Zaidman said. "Dow was really interested in the application of innovative technologies in emerging markets and helping the poor. It was an "A-ha! moment" for us to think that we might have mutual interests, and that we might be able help each other."

Zaidman explained that Acumen identifies companies in which to invest, like WaterHealth, while Dow was looking for companies like WaterHealth to provide technical assistance. "Through this shared experience, Dow gained an appreciation that Acumen could identify such opportunities early on," according to Zaidman. "Together, we recognized the value of working alongside each other on the ground with social enterprises like WaterHealth to promote innovation. We decided to pursue additional ways to collaborate."[37]

The relationship between Dow and Acumen deepened with the next step. Through the Dow Sustainability Corps (DSC), an employee engagement initiative, a chemical engineer helped a small biotech business in Nairobi to prepare a tech assessment in order to qualify for a new round of financing. The biotech business was part of Acumen's social enterprise portfolio.

Bo Miller notes that legal and regulatory barriers were challenges to scaling social enterprises in Africa. These matters are referenced as well in the Global Entrepreneurship Monitor 2012 Global Report.[38] While the report stresses the imperative of fostering entrepreneurship to develop regional economies, it also cautions readers about legal and regulatory impediments. It states that "with unemployment and a growing youth population a key issue in regions such as sub-Saharan Africa, identifying and successfully implementing policies that both encourage youth to start businesses and support businesses with high employee growth expectations will be critical to creating jobs and ensuring economic growth and societal stability." However, the report also points out that an ineffective legal system will diminish the economic impact of entrepreneurship.

The Organization for Economic Cooperation and Development (OECD) points out that one of the most basic barriers to entry is the number of days required simply to open a business. In 2010 in Brazil that number was 120, compared to an average of 14 days in the OECD area.[39] Additionally, "poor judicial enforcement of property rights and inadequate availability of land with clear titles has forced entrepreneurs to make unproductive investments in fixed assets."[40] Thus, until governments take greater steps to establish legal and regulatory frameworks that promote and support entrepreneurship, business opportunities in emerging markets will not be fully realized.

EXTRACTIVE COMPANIES DEVELOP NATIONAL CONTENT IN EMERGING COUNTRIES

"Local content development," sometimes referred to as "national content development," is an approach used more recently by global corporations—often extractive companies (oil, gas, mining)—to help develop the capacity of a region where the company is locating a major extractive or manufacturing site. Local content development focuses in particular on employment and job training, in addition to fostering the creation of local business enterprises that can provide everything from basic services up to fabrication and construction, logistics, operations support, and professional services. Companies are conducting local content work in emerging and formerly Communist countries, so there are many challenges, including the lack of an educated workforce and poor health conditions.

Through local content development, corporations have a powerful opportunity to improve lives, bringing economic development to some of the world's poorest countries. Furthermore, companies are learning that in order to be effective, they must engage a multitude of stakeholders—from government ministries to NGOs, local trade associations, businesses, and suppliers. "Nowhere are the current and potential activities of large companies more dynamic and influential on development than through their local-content policies, programs, and practices,"[41] according to NGO leaders Michael Levett and Ashley E. Chandler.

There are compelling business reasons for companies to develop local content. Increasingly, such practices are mandated by host countries in return for the company's license to operate. Additionally, cost savings occur with hiring and sourcing locally, while also strengthening communities. Local content is essential for doing business in key parts of the world.

Beginning in 2003, PYXERA Global, a global NGO, worked on a project in Angola to help several oil and gas companies to fulfill the state's mandate for them to source locally. The NGO was needed in order to assist local businesses in growing their technical capacity. PYXERA's mission is to leverage public, private, and volunteer resources to strengthen small and medium enterprises (SMEs) and the institutions, governments, and industries that drive economic growth in emerging markets. By the project's end, "more than 1,500 Angolan-owned businesses had participated in the...program through training and technical assistance, 125 companies were certified as suppliers for the oil industry, and some 300 contracts and contract extensions resulted." The project "generated more than $214 million in oil industry contracts, while supporting the creation of more than 2,700 Angolan jobs."[42]

ExxonMobil, part of the CDS project in Angola, applies a local content approach in Angola, Chad, Equatorial Guinea, Indonesia, Malaysia, Nigeria, and Russia (Sakhalin). In these countries where the company has extractive sites, ExxonMobil seeks to advance human, social, and economic capacity. Its initiatives include workforce development—recruiting and developing nationals for construction and ongoing operations; supplier development—purchasing local goods and services and developing local companies to form a competitive industrial base; and strategic community investments—in health, education, and infrastructure, especially to advance socioeconomic opportunities.

There are numerous benefits to the company. "Most fundamentally is the license to operate," explained John Harrington, ExxonMobil's Public Affairs manager for Africa and Asia Pacific.[43] "As a company, we have to compete to secure a license to operate, Harrington said. "Not only do host governments have expectations that we employ people from within the country, and foster business and economic development, but they will consider how we've performed in other countries. It matters."

Harry Pastuszek, vice president of enterprise and community development at PYXERA Global concurs. As an NGO leader, with experience at the International Finance Corporation and Bechtel Corporation, he observes that "national oil companies and official ministries in the African frontier markets expect all IOC [international oil companies] concession holders to implement plans to enhance local economic development. Such vigilance extends beyond officialdom, down to the community level. Local people, with access to the Internet and other communications channels, are learning from the experiences of communities similar to their own that have already engaged with oil companies. Indeed, support from the people is often the primary prerequisite for social license to operate."[44]

Effective local content strategies are also vital to companies for securing reliable supply chains, shortening delivery time, and reducing the cost of operations, according to Harrington: "Developing local suppliers is a key component of our business model."[45]

Not only is local content good for ExxonMobil's business, it has also led to the development of local economies and businesses. According to Harrington, "As a direct result of the company's efforts to maximize Russian capacity within the Sakhalin-1 project, the value of contracts awarded to Russian companies during implementation has totaled about $7.9 billion, representing nearly two-thirds of the total contracts awarded to date. This ongoing support has allowed many local suppliers to expand their businesses." Harrington gave the example of SFERA Limited Liability Construction Firm that had started out in the Sakhalin construction industry in 1988 as a building cooperative with only 30 employees. "With mentorship and continued business from Exxon Neftegas Limited (ENL), SFERA has grown to more than 1,500 employees and is now one of the largest and most successful construction companies in Sakhalin," Harrington said.

ExxonMobil is also fostering economic development by co-funding a research initiative with the United Nations Foundation to catalyze program and policy action for women's economic empowerment. "Having a shared interest in enhancing the lives of women in developing countries, we are seeking empirical evidence in order to understand exactly what policy and program interventions would most effectively increase women's productivity and earnings in developing countries," explained Suzanne McCarron,[46] president of the ExxonMobil Foundation, the primary philanthropic arm of the Exxon Mobil Corporation in the United States. The foundation's grants totaled $273 million in 2012. "Specifically, we want to know what works in the categories of entrepreneurship, agriculture, wage employment, and youth employment." The final report will provide a roadmap, showing which interventions are most promising in helping young women to find employment. The evidence-based "roadmap" report will include guideposts for investments in program interventions in addition to recommendations for further research.

Furthermore, ExxonMobil leverages its philanthropy through its foundation by investing strategically in education, healthcare, and women's empowerment in regions where the company has a major presence. For example, ExxonMobil's attention to reducing the incidence of malaria is not only good for the community, it also benefits the company by reducing absenteeism at work.

In fact, helping to end deaths from malaria is one of the company's three key focus areas. ExxonMobil's partnerships with the Family Care Association, Roll Back Malaria, and the Federal Ministry of Health in Nigeria achieved a multitude of goals in 2012, including distributing 17,270 insecticide-treated mosquito nets (ITNs), and training thousands in malaria prevention, control, and treatment. In follow-up home visits, it was observed that 82 percent of the households were using the ITNs correctly, a testament to the training and education they had received. Success has also been achieved with bed net use in Cameroon as a result of ExxonMobil's partnership with Malaria No More.

Malaria control is Millennium Development Goal 4 (MDG 4) and MDG 6. MDG 4 is to "reduce by two-thirds the mortality rate among children under 5" by 2015. MDG 6 is to "have halted and begun to reverse the incidence of malaria and other major diseases" by 2015. Consequently, ExxonMobil is serving its own business interests in reducing the incidence of malaria, while also playing a vital role in helping to accelerate the success of critical United Nation's goals.

Deidre White, president and CEO of PYXERA Global, is emphatic about the scope and impact of corporate engagement in developing national economies. "The level of economic development that's required in these regions is not going to happen without global corporations."[47] PYXERA helps to facilitate local content development initiatives for numerous extractive companies, global pro bono programs for corporations in all industries, and

MBAs Without Borders. Prior to heading up PYXERA, White led USAID and World Bank-funded international development programs at Arthur D. Little, a management consulting firm.

White has observed a shift in the attitudes of companies regarding local content development. In comparing her participation at the CWC Group's 14th Gulf of Guinea Oil and Gas Summit in Equatorial Guinea in 2012 to her experience at this same event for the past several years, White noted "a distinct change in tone on the subject of the amount and value of jobs and contracts going to local individuals and businesses, otherwise known as local/national content. In past years, I heard largely industry dissatisfaction with the unrealistic nature (even unfairness) of the local content requirements and expectations. This year I sensed a rapidly shifting ground where this subject is concerned. As leader of the National Content Seminar, I arrived prepared to make the compelling arguments for why the industry should invest in local content: risk management; community engagement; existing or upcoming legislation; and just because it's the right thing to do to ensure that citizens can participate in the benefits of their own country's natural resources. What I found was that industry was prepared to make the arguments for me."[48]

White further noted that she had observed the same change in tone at the International Quality and Productivity Center (IQPC) 8th Annual Global Local Content Summit in the Fall of 2012, which she has also been attending for several years. "Many presentations and off-line conversations proudly declared how a company has exceeded local content requirements or implemented local content programming even where there were no requirements in place. We could also measure the change in that more than 50 people registered for our practical local content planning workshop, where two years ago we had just under 20 participants."[49]

White explained that while compliance is often the starting point to get a company to focus on local content, the hope is that corporations will shift to recognize the business case for local content. And in fact, during the IQPC conference, White said she was "heartened to hear companies state clearly that their business rationale is manifold: sustainable human, social and economic capacity-building reduces the company's political and security risks, demonstrates their responsible corporate citizenship, reduces their costs over time, secures their license to operate, and therefore makes good business sense."

White's vision is for local content to expand to *regional* content development, which she describes as "a strategic approach to the development of certain supplier sectors in neighboring oil producing companies...think about how powerful this idea could be for a region like the Gulf of Guinea where you have the massive, decades-old oil economies of Nigeria and Angola, a brand new producer like Ghana, and countries like Liberia and Sierra Leone which look to become producers in the near term. You also have populations that range from 150 million in Nigeria to 700,000 in Equatorial Guinea, and widely varied levels of education and infrastructure among the countries, factors which significantly affect each nation's capability to deliver local content. Or how about Southeast Asia, which ranges from a century-plus of production in Indonesia to a Cambodia that may see first oil in 2016? Or the countries of East Africa, long ignored by major producers but now courted by majors and independents for their gas reserves?"[50]

Local content development has brought socioeconomic advances for host country businesses and citizens, while promoting the interests of extractive companies worldwide.

BSR FOSTERS CORPORATE-NGO PARTNERSHIPS IN CHINA THROUGH CIYUAN

The strategic partnerships between companies and NGOs that are discussed in these chapters have been taking root in many parts of the world. China has been an exception, however. Following the Sichuan earthquake in May 2008, corporations and foundations seeking to provide philanthropic support to communities were ill-prepared to do so in any meaningful way. Moreover, nonprofits lacked the expertise to conduct fundraising and strategic planning or to engage with businesses and donors. Within a year of the earthquake, and at the request of businesses and NGOs, BSR established CiYuan, the China Philanthropy Incubator, to build cross-sector relationships to enhance the value of social investment in China.[51]

Established more than twenty years ago, BSR is a global NGO with a network of nearly 300 member companies worldwide. BSR's mission is to work with businesses to create a just and sustainable world. From its offices in Asia, Europe, and North and South America, BSR develops sustainable business strategies and solutions through consulting, research, and cross-sector collaboration.[52]

With CiYuan, BSR's goal has been to help move companies along the continuum from philanthropy to sustainable business strategies that benefit businesses and the community.[53] NGOs gain access to valuable resources including volunteers with business skills and funding. Businesses benefit by providing leadership development experiences for their employees, deepening their understanding of the China market, and building relationships, while strengthening the communities in which they live and work.

In one case, for example, BSR worked with several partners from the Shanghai office of SAP—a leading provider of business management software that provides Fortune 500 companies with management solutions—to match them with four nonprofits that required assistance with information technology (IT) matters. SAP's ultimate purpose with the project was not only to assist the four nonprofits but also to develop and provide tools and lessons for the broader NGO sector in Shanghai. The SAP volunteers assisted a nonprofit that provides a hotline and counseling for migrants, an organization that provides grants to grassroots organizations, an education foundation, and a community health foundation. The results of their work included recommendations on how businesses can be useful in assisting NGOs by providing management and technical assistance.

In another case, BSR facilitated a partnership between B&Q, originally known as Block & Quayle, China's largest do-it-yourself retail chain, and Friends of Nature, China's oldest nonprofit environmental organization, to increase consumer awareness of environmentally friendly and energy-saving home improvement solutions. Together, the company and the nonprofit trained 120 customers at five B&Q stores in Beijing, as well as 60 B&Q designers and store managers, in environmentally friendly home improvement solutions; they also strengthened the trainees' ability to explain and promote various aspects of "green" and energy-saving home and residential products to B&Q customers. According to BSR, the lessons learned from this project will advance the organization's work in facilitating additional business-NGO partnerships to further social and environmental benefits that are also good for business.

WESTERN UNION MOVES MONEY TO SUPPORT THE WORK OF NGOS IN ADVANCING ECONOMIC DEVELOPMENT

NGOs face challenges in moving funds to their agencies, staff, and aid recipients worldwide. This is the result of highly complex and tangled global financial systems. Moreover, billions of underserved people live "the last mile" away from financial systems and resources that are essential for them to access basic daily commodities and services as well as education and healthcare. Furthermore, while many people prefer cash, vulnerable people—often women and aid workers in remote and dangerous places—benefit from the security of stored value options such as prepaid cards or electronic/mobile wallets. These new technologies are only effective if they are connected to the global financial system. This is the challenge as described by Luella Chavez D'Angelo,[54] chief communications officer at Western Union, and in the Clinton Global Initiative (CGI) 2012 Commitment to Action.[55]

To better connect NGOs and the people they serve, Western Union committed $10 million dollars to create a financial platform called Western Union NGO GlobalPay. By the end of 2014, Western Union promises to have designed an efficient, transparent, and accessible infrastructure that spans the last mile and improves access to funds and payment/disbursement solutions.

Western Union aims to partner with at least one thousand nonprofits and NGOs to benefit at least one hundred thousand people annually. The countries that will be directly impacted include Haiti, Turkey, Syria, Lebanon, and the Democratic Republic of the Congo.[56] "We're going to solve social problems using our unique geographic reach and our products and services," said Hikmet Ersek,[57] president and CEO of Western Union. Ersek seeks to expand Western Union's products and services to drive additional revenue streams while also solving new problems around the planet. "More than two billion people are financially underserved in this world. This is an opportunity, a necessity, and a privilege to create financial products for the underserved," he said.

ERICSSON ADVANCES MYANMAR SOCIOECONOMIC DEVELOPMENT THROUGH COMMUNICATIONS

In Myanmar today, fewer than five percent of the population has mobile phones, and even fewer have an Internet connection. In the twenty-first century, with more than 6.5 billion mobile phone subscriptions globally, lack of connectivity in Myanmar severely limits access to commerce, education, and healthcare, among other things.

Ericsson, a Swedish company and global leader in mobile broadband infrastructure and services, re-entered Myanmar in 2012 (after having left in 1998 due to human rights concerns). "We felt we could reenter because of progress being made in the country," said Elaine Weidman-Grunewald, vice president of Sustainability and Responsibility at Ericsson. "The European Union and the United States were in the process of suspending sanctions, and progress was being made from social, economic, and human rights perspectives. While there are still many challenges to be worked through, we strongly believe that a well-functioning telecommunications network will greatly benefit the people and the society of Myanmar."[58]

In its commitment to responsible business, Ericsson is part of the Burma (Myanmar) Human Rights and Business Framework. This initiative, led by the Institute for Human Rights and Business and the Danish Human Rights Institute, explores how to apply the UN Guiding Principles for Business and Human Rights in the Myanmar business context.

Ericsson will also evaluate the socioeconomic impact that access to mobile communications can bring to Myanmar in health, commerce, and education, for example. By working in a multi-stakeholder context, Ericsson will bring coordinated, high-performing networks that allow developing countries to advance while adding to Ericsson's bottom line through increased subscriptions.

Ericsson is in 180 countries, with 110,000 employees worldwide. 40 percent of mobile traffic runs through Ericsson networks. As an information and communication technology (ICT) company, Ericsson commits itself to a vision it calls "Technology for Good"—using connectivity to make a positive socioeconomic and environmental impact, and addressing vital issues such as poverty alleviation, human rights, education, healthcare, and climate change.[59]

"Many of the world's major challenges—such as urbanization, climate change, and poverty—could benefit from solutions offered by mobile broadband," said Hans Vestberg, president and CEO of Ericsson.[60]

A study conducted by Ericsson and Deloitte in 2012 forecasts that the potential GDP impact of telecommunications in Myanmar could be around 7.4 percent over the next three years, if subscriber penetration rises to 35 percent, in line with regional trends.[61] Additionally, the introduction of the mobile communication industry to Myanmar will lead to nearly 70,000 jobs within two years. Furthermore, Ericsson studies show that, on average, for every 10 percent increase in broadband penetration, GDP rises by 1 percent.[62]

Mobile commerce and banking is a powerful tool for social and digital inclusion. Financial access via mobile will eliminate barriers to services such as distance, a lack of credit history, and transaction costs. Furthermore, mobile commerce and banking enables the future workforce, customers, and investors. And finally, mobile communications will facilitate agricultural sales by enabling small-scale trading by mobile and Internet, and will also enable access to quality education.[63]

Weidman-Grunewald reported at the Burma (Myanmar) Human Rights and Business Framework on the growth potential for mobile market development in Myanmar: Broadband will contribute to social and economic development; services in education and health will benefit people and businesses; responsible business practices that respect human rights can be exercised; and Swedish companies can share best practices and help to build local capacity.[64]

Ericsson has also engaged in partnerships with NGOs at the Clinton Global Initiative, including the commitment to support Refugees United with mobile communications in 2010.[65] Refugees United is a global NGO that uses secure web and mobile technology to enable refugees to find loved ones throughout the world.[66] "By making commitments at CGI," Vestberg said, "we were able to reach a wider audience and demonstrate the potential impact that broadband technology can have on society as a whole and for one of the most underserved populations—refugees. The CGI platform has also allowed us to reach across borders—to form new partnerships, learn from others, and share experiences."[67]

VODAFONE LAUNCHES M-PESA IN KENYA TO PROVIDE MOBILE BANKING TO THE UNBANKED POOR

M-PESA is an electronic payment system accessible from ordinary mobile phones. It was developed by Vodafone,[68] a British multinational telecommunications company, and launched commercially by the company's Kenyan affiliate, Safaricom.[69] With an M-PESA account, customers can use their phones to transfer funds to M-PESA users and non-users, pay bills, and purchase mobile airtime credit for a small, flat, per-transaction fee. The affordability of the service has provided access to formal financial services for Kenya's poor.[70] Pesa means "cash" in Swahili, so M-PESA means "mobile money."

Data show strong evidence of M-PESA's market penetration among the unbanked poor. "Among the population outside Nairobi, during a period of four years when the prevalence of bank accounts remained relatively flat, the share of the unbanked who used M-PESA rose from about 21 percent in 2008 to 75 percent in 2011," according to *Slate*. [71] "Similarly," the article continued, "the share of non-Nairobi households with very low incomes who use M-PESA has also risen over time. According to our data, in 2008 fewer than 20 percent of the population outside the capital living on less than $1.25 per day used M-PESA, but by 2011, this share had steadily expanded to 72 percent."

Michael Joseph, managing director for Mobile Money for Vodafone, explained the origins of M-PESA.[72] At the time, Joseph was the CEO of Safaricom in Kenya. Joseph recalled the period prior to 2007 when "there was a request for proposals (RFP) from the UK Department for International Development (DFID) to deepen the financial access of the unbanked poor." DFID leads the UK government's fight against world poverty by implementing long-term projects "to help stop the underlying causes of poverty and respond to humanitarian emergencies."[73] Joseph explained that "Nick Hughes, who was at Vodafone, came across this RFP and thought of using cell phones for the disbursement and repayment of microfinance loans. DFID awarded Vodafone £1 million which the company had to match. Hughes then approached a software company in Cambridge to write the original software program and build the hardware platform." By late 2006, Joseph said, Vodafone piloted the project in the town of Thika, just north of Nairobi, through his company Safaricom, in partnership with a microfinance provider, a bank, and other partners.

Joseph explained that they soon observed that the participants used the phone for its ability to send money from one person to another, even though this was not the intention of the project. At Joseph's request, Hughes built a bigger and better platform to accommodate the interests of customers. "You see, many people leave their families to find work," Joseph said. "The challenge had been to find ways to send money home. You'd either have to travel home yourself, give the money to a bus driver, or not send it at all and leave them destitute."[74] In expanding the mobile phone service to provide banking services, Vodafone worked with the telecoms' regulator and the Central Bank of Kenya, the banking regulator. With the blessing of these two regulators to launch the mobile money products in March 2007, "the rest is history."[75]

"We pushed it hard. Added functionalities. Signed up a million subscribers in the first nine months. People could take money out of an ATM with their mobile phones, pay water and electricity bills, and buy air times," explained Joseph. "This was not designed to be profitable, but rather to break even at best. And although this was a tremendous economic and social value for the community, this was not designed as a corporate social responsibility project. The business case was to build customer loyalty."[76]

Joseph elaborated by explaining that there are four mobile phone operators in Kenya; it is a highly competitive market. Furthermore, the investment in software and hardware is very costly, and has been through many iterations. So it took a number of years and many mobile transactions for particular mobile services to become profitable. "This is about customer retention in a highly competitive market, and Safaricom is premium-priced. We want to keep subscribers in our network."[77]

M-PESA is now available in Tanzania,[78] South Africa,[79] and India.[80] Joseph observed that there are many companies seeking to replicate M-PESA, but few are successful. He described M-PESA's unique success factors: "There's a lot of investment in making it successful: in cash, dedication of effort, passion, and determination. It's a financial service that we are selling to poor people at the bottom of the pyramid. Not many companies have made that investment. Secondly, it's truly a social revolutionary product. It changes the lives of people enormously. People in emerging markets have no access to financial services in rural Africa. If you wanted to start a small business, you had to go to the city. What M-PESA has done is to bring financial services to people's phones. And that enables them to participate in the economy and conduct business. People are operating new businesses and feeling more secure."[81]

Joseph also pointed out that there are sixty to seventy thousand M-PESA agents throughout the country, so down the road they will be available for people throughout the country.

The M-PESA venture by Vodafone and Safaricom that originated in Kenya was designed to serve the companies' strategy of maintaining customer loyalty in order to build the bottom line over the long term. These companies have empowered millions of people and entrepreneurs by linking them to financial services for the first time.

BSR's Role in Engaging Corporations in Empowering Women

The World Bank Report on Gender Equality and Development, 2012 identified four priority areas to advance global development: "reducing gender gaps in health and education—particularly among severely disadvantaged populations, promoting access to economic opportunities among women, closing gender gaps in voice and agency, and preventing the intergenerational reproduction of gender inequality."[82] Furthermore, the report states, "gendered differences matter for women's well-being but also for a whole set of outcomes for their families and for society in general. Women's agency influences their ability to build their human capital and take up economic opportunities. In Bangladesh, women with greater control over health care and household purchases have higher nutritional status. Women's agency also matters for the welfare of their children."[83]

While numerous companies sponsor programs aimed at advancing women in developing countries, BSR is working with multiple global corporations to foster women's economic empowerment.[84] Launched in 2007 in China, BSR's HERproject links multinational companies and their factories to local NGOs to create sustainable workplace programs that increase women's health awareness. Working with a global network of partners, BSR is demonstrating the return on investment for factory-based women's health programs. Today, HERproject is active in Bangladesh, China, Egypt, Kenya, India, Indonesia, Pakistan, and Vietnam.[85]

BSR shows that investing in worker health is more than a moral imperative: there's a compelling business case for the investment. "For every $1 invested in women's health, one Bangladeshi factory saw a $3 return through higher productivity, lower turnover and reduced absenteeism,"[86] said Racheal Meiers, director of HERproject at BSR.[87] Meiers also pointed out that in participating factories globally, HERproject women's health education programs have delivered the following benefits for companies and workers: [88]

- Productivity Gains: HERproject factories have seen reductions in absenteeism and turnover, and/or product quality improvements. Workplace improvements have also been observed, both due to worker behavior changes and to factory investments.

- Healthier workers: Workers are healthier as a result of better access to nearby and onsite health services.
- Better worker-manager relations: Workers feel more valued by management and have increased communication skills. Some factories observed improved grievance-handling processes.
- Enhanced recruitment and reputation: Factories benefit from women sharing information about HERproject in their communities.
- Sunk costs better utilized: Existing resources such as factory nurses, clinics, and visiting doctors play an enhanced role when they are integrated into program activities.

Participating companies in HERproject include: Abercrombie & Fitch, ANN INC., Belk, Bestseller, Boden, Children's Place, Clarks, Columbia Sportswear, George at ASDA, H&M, Hewlett Packard, J.Crew, Levi Strauss & Co., Li & Fung, Lindex, Marks & Spencer, Microsoft, Nordstrom, Primark, Sainsbury's, Talbots, and Timberland. BSR receives funding from the Levi Strauss Foundation, the Ministry of Foreign Affairs of the Netherlands, and the Swedish International Development Cooperation Agency for HERproject. International companies provide funding to cover the cost of program activities in their individual supplier factories. Suppliers absorb the costs associated with program implementation, and sometimes also share program costs with international companies.[89]

Through these employers, HERproject has reached more than 200,000 female and more than 25,000 male workers in factories around the world since it began in 2007. The impact is even greater, however, as 80 percent of workers report sharing the health information they've learned outside the factory walls—in their homes, places of worship, and communities.[90]

Company programs to empower women, such as HERproject, improve lives and benefit the bottom line for companies.

THE POVERTY RATE IS DECLINING IN ALL SIX REGIONS OF THE DEVELOPING WORLD: GOOD FOR BUSINESS AND GOOD FOR THE WORLD

Business growth and engagement is a powerful force in alleviating poverty. "Over the past 30 years, the private sector has been a primary driver of economic growth and has contributed significantly to poverty reduction. Businesses provide vital jobs and services and pay taxes, which help fund public services," according to "Exploring the Links Between International Business and Poverty Reduction," a report by Oxfam, The Coca-Cola Company, and SABMiller.[91]

Additionally, the report recommends that companies focus on helping to achieve the MDGs by 2015. The report quotes United Nations Secretary-General Ban-Ki Moon: "Government leadership will be crucial. But more than ever before, we depend on the resources and capacities of the private sector to make things happen. Business is a primary driver of innovation, investment, and job creation. There is no longer any doubt that business plays an integral role in delivering economic and social progress."[92]

Many global corporations are recognizing that developing small and medium enterprises, training and preparing qualified workforces, and creating robust markets in developing countries is good for business.

CHAPTER 3

CLIMATE CHANGE AND ENERGY

There must be the look ahead, there must be a realization of the fact that to waste, to destroy, our natural resources, to skin and exhaust the land instead of using it so as to increase its usefulness, will result in undermining in the days of our children the very prosperity which we ought by right to hand down to them amplified and developed.[1]

—Theodore Roosevelt

WE ARE EMBARKING ON A PERIOD OF CHAOS WHERE GLOBAL CLIMATE change is causing storms, droughts, heat waves, wildfires, and other natural disasters that kill people, disrupt lives, and destroy homes, offices, schools, and cities.[2] Scientific leaders, including the National Aeronautics and Space Administration (NASA), the United States National Academy of Sciences, the American Association for the Advancement of Science, and the American Meteorological Association, affirm that climate change is a real and growing threat to the world.[3] Hurricane Sandy provided a "mild" preview, damaging or destroying 650,000 homes, causing 8.5 million customers to lose power, and precipitating $50 billion of damage in the northeastern United States.[4] The droughts and flooding that will result as climate change worsens will increase hunger and starvation. A number of experts predict that in some regions, climate change will likely provoke violence and threaten global security as people fight for clean water, food, and shelter.[5] Those are the conditions that our children and our grandchildren will face.

In the face of these immense challenges, some global corporations are recognizing the business imperative to address global warming. These companies realize that their existence and profitability are threatened by climate change that results from global warming. Moreover, they see that they can add to their bottom lines by creating and marketing goods and services to put the Earth on a better course. International businesses have the resources, global reach, and self-interest to make progress on the global warming agenda. Governments, in contrast, have had many worldwide meetings, but have been unable to agree on any actionable plans.

Global warming—caused primarily by growing concentrations of greenhouse gases in the atmosphere—refers to the increase in average temperature near Earth's surface. Although global warming brings about changes in climate patterns, it represents only one aspect of climate change. Climate change, on the other hand, refers to a major alteration in the measures of climate over several decades or longer. Examples include significant changes in temperature, precipitation, or wind patterns, among other effects.[6]

"Warming of the climate system is unequivocal,"[7] This was the conclusion of the Fourth Intergovernmental Panel on Climate Change (IPCC) in 2007. The IPCC was established in 1988 by the World Meteorological Organization and the United Nations Environment Programme. In its 2007 "Summary for Policymakers," the IPCC reported that its conclusion was based on "observations of increases in global average air and ocean temperatures, widespread melting of snow and ice, and rising global average sea level."[8] A two degrees Celsius rise in global temperatures from pre-industrial levels is the highest rise we can afford if we want a 50 percent chance of avoiding the worst effects of climate change.[9]

The world must stay at or remain under 450 parts per million concentration of carbon dioxide equivalent in the atmosphere to remain true to the two degrees Celsius goal; the current concentration will surpass 400 parts per million by the time this book is published.

Before the Industrial Revolution, concentrations were fairly stable at 280 parts per million. This has increased 41 percent since then. Leading causes of global warming include excessive and inefficient use of fossil fuels in industrial operations, power generation, commercial and private vehicles, and deforestation. Unfortunately, we cannot turn back. The best we can do is slow down and postpone the rise in temperature and prepare for the worst.

Population growth adds to the exigency of addressing climate change, since more people will further tax the world's resources. The global population will increase from 7 billion today to 8 billion by 2025 and to 9 billion by 2043.[10] Moreover, consumer demands will grow with 3 billion people rising to the middle class by 2030.[11] Experts question whether the Earth will be able to support the increase in living standards for these affluent new consumers.[12] In fact, since the 1970s, humanity has been extracting more natural resources from the planet than it can renew. At this point, it would take 1.5 years for earth to regenerate the natural resources that are being consumed in one year. This is referred to as "ecological overshoot."[13] Knowing the urgency of limiting carbon emissions, one might wonder just how major countries of the world are managing their responsibilities. The PwC Low Carbon Economy Index tracks the annual carbon reductions required by G20 countries to achieve the UN ambition to limit temperature rise to 2°C. The G20 is the "Group of 20" finance ministers and central bank governors from 19 countries (Argentina, Australia, Brazil, Canada, China, France, Germany, India, Indonesia, Italy, Japan, the Republic of Korea, Mexico, Russia, Saudi Arabia, South Africa, Turkey, the United Kingdom, the United States of America)

CLIMATE CHANGE AND ENERGY

plus the European Union. The G20 economies account for 90 percent of the world's gross domestic product (GDP), and 84 percent of fossil fuel emissions are produced by G20 countries.[14] Unfortunately, the 2011 PwC Low Carbon Economy Index "shows that the G20 economies have moved from travelling too slowly in the right direction, to travelling in the wrong direction. The annual percentage reduction now required is 4.8 percent per year, a figure in excess of what has been proven to be historically sustainable. The results call into question the current likelihood of our global decarbonization ever happening rapidly enough to avoid two degrees of global warming."[15] Moreover, the report asserts that "the events of the Arab Spring have shown the social, economic, and political necessity of delivering not just low carbon growth, but growth that delivers on the basic needs, including power, of the billions at the bottom of the pyramid."

Many businesses are realizing market opportunities in advancing solutions to create energy efficiencies that will mitigate and postpone the worst impacts of climate change. A number of information and communications technology (ICT) companies are pioneering solutions to conserve energy which they use in their own operations and sell to other businesses. ICTs also develop and market "smart city" technology (digital and communication technologies that support the community's needs) that adds to their bottom lines while creating efficient and resilient communities.

Other companies are boosting sales by retrofitting old buildings or constructing new ones that reduce carbon emissions and costs. Still other businesses integrate sustainability in their corporate strategy, including designing and manufacturing products with materials and processes that mitigate harm to the environment.

Driving such changes are employees, customers, and investors. With growing demands for reporting and transparency, and daily coverage in the media, companies understand that they are being scrutinized for their environmental and climate impact. The Carbon Disclosure Project (CDP) has taken this to a new level by engaging 722 investors with $87 trillion in assets in monitoring how companies and their suppliers manage and reduce their carbon emissions and their environmental footprint. CDP is an international, not-for-profit organization providing the only global system for companies and cities to measure, disclose, manage, and share vital environmental information.

While this chapter describes the efforts of companies that are leading the way, most companies are not doing their part when it comes to long-term planning to reduce emissions. According to the CDP, "Although 82 percent of companies set absolute or intensity emissions targets, only 20 percent of companies have set targets to 2020 and beyond. The average of the longer-term absolute targets outlined by CDP respondents is only around a 1 percent reduction per year, which is well below the level of ambition needed to limit the temperature rise to 2°C."[16]

"Several factors still hold us back from achieving the large-scale energy transformation necessary to stabilize the climate," remarked United Nations Secretary-General Ban Ki-moon to 800 business leaders at the Bloomberg New Energy Finance Summit on "The Future of Energy," in April 2013.[17] "Globally, clean energy investment is insufficient to prevent the worst impacts of climate change. Proven innovations and solutions—from energy efficiency to emissions reductions—lack adequate incentives, while fossil fuels still enjoy generous subsidies. Too many companies limit their sustainability efforts to pilot programs that never take off. We need to scale up our efforts and our ambition. The climate clock is ticking. The longer we delay, the greater the costs—to communities, to businesses, to economies and to the planet."[18]

It is possible for us to mitigate and postpone the damage to the planet that future generations will inherit—by increasing energy efficiency and the use of renewable energy. According to the businesses that you will read about in this chapter, we have the technology to build "resilient" cities—with structures and infrastructures that are adaptable to adverse circumstances, particularly to extreme weather and natural disasters. The challenge is not about capability as much as it is about our will to change.

Some businesses are leading the way to change. The featured companies understand that climate change is a severe risk to business and society. They also recognize that reducing and limiting carbon emissions, using renewable energy, designing and manufacturing sustainable products, and constructing resilient buildings and communities is a great opportunity to profit, while helping to improve the world.

Intel Applies Its Expertise and Technology To Reduce Its Own Carbon Emissions, Create Products and Services, and Build Coalitions

Intel has taken action to reduce the carbon footprint of its own operations for well over a decade, including investment in energy conservation projects. According to Suzanne Fallender, director of CSR Strategy and Communications at Intel, "We have adopted a portfolio approach to reducing emissions which has included investments in energy conservation, investments in renewable energy credits, and onsite solar installations."[19]

The US Environmental Protection Agency (EPA) has recognized Intel as the largest voluntary purchaser of green power in the United States for five consecutive years, from 2008–2013.[20] Intel's 2013 purchase of approximately 3.1 billion kilowatt hours (kWh) of green power in 2013 will meet 100 percent of the company's US electricity use for the year. This is the equivalent environmental impact of eliminating the CO_2 emissions from the annual electricity use of more than 320,000 US homes. Intel's commitment to purchase a total of approximately 12.4 billion kWh of green power from 2008 through 2013 is equivalent to the greenhouse gas emissions impact of taking 1.8 million cars off the road for one year.[21]

"Intel's renewable energy efforts are intended to provide leadership, help spur the market, make renewables less expensive and more accessible over the long term, and reduce the overall carbon emissions from electricity generation," said Fallender. "We increased our investment levels over the past five years despite the economic downturn, because of the projected long-term benefits. All purchases will be certified by the nonprofit Center for Resource Solutions' Green-e Energy program, which certifies and verifies green power products to meet the requirements of the US EPA's Green Power Purchasing Program."[22]

ENERGY-EFFICIENT PRODUCT STRATEGY

Beyond reducing its own carbon footprint, Intel's goal is to drive energy-efficient performance across all of the major product lines that it sells—from smartphones, tablets, and embedded microprocessors, to those used in laptops, desktops, and servers.[23] The company estimates that its newer technology will enable the billion PCs and servers installed between 2007 and 2014 to consume half the energy and deliver 17 times the compute capacity of the first billion PCs and servers installed between 1980 and 2007.

Furthermore, Intel works to lower the energy costs associated with its business customers' computing and data center needs. For example, said Fallender, "Panasonic Taiwan expanded its server capabilities using the Intel Xeon processor 5600 series running Dell servers, which reduced server rack space by up to 50 percent while lowering server room energy consumption by up to 45 percent. In another example, a new University of Oklahoma High Performance Computing (HPC) cluster built using Intel Xeon processors delivered 3.5 times the sustained performance per server over the previous cluster and reduced energy consumption by approximately 30 percent."

Intel produces energy efficient products and services to meet market demand. These are market opportunities. "Energy conservation is important to our customers," Fallender explained. "Our customers include original equipment manufacturers or other technology companies that are making technology products. They are concerned about making energy efficient products that require less power. This is especially critical with the shift toward more mobile computing in the market."[24]

APPLYING TECHNOLOGY TO SMART CITIES AND TRANSPORTATION

The greater the challenge, the greater the opportunity; clearly that's the case with climate change. Intel is providing smart solutions for cities and transportation, thereby producing a triple bottom line for urban communities—advancing social, economic, and environmental development. A "smart city" has networked, digital, and communications technologies that support the community's information needs, creating streamlined and improved services for traffic and transportation, emergencies, crime prevention, sanitation, pollution mitigation, education, and health care. This is particularly meaningful since urban areas worldwide are expected to absorb the population growth expected over the next four decades.[25]

Put another way, by 2030, "an estimated 59 percent of the world's population will live in urban areas."[26] Smart solutions are critical for energy efficiency since cities are already responsible for 70 percent of greenhouse gas emissions.[27]

By 2050, 70 percent of the world's population will be city-dwellers.[28] According to the United Nations, "the world urban population is expected to increase from 3.6 billion in 2011 to 6.3 billion in 2050. Virtually all of the expected growth in the world population will be concentrated in the urban areas of the less developed regions, whose population is projected to increase from 2.7 billion in 2011 to 5.1 billion in 2050. In the more developed regions, the urban population is projected to increase modestly, from 1 billion in 2011 to 1.1 billion in 2050."[29]

Intel is engaged in designing and providing new technologies to advance sustainability challenges, including developing more energy-efficient production and transportation systems, and applying IT to help measure (sense), model (analyze), and manage (control) energy and natural resources more efficiently. Intel's Energy and Sustainability Lab (ESL) is researching approaches to help the European Union achieve its 2020 sustainability goals for a high-tech, low-carbon economy. Additionally, ESL is researching the use of micro-grids to enable neighborhoods to share energy, and sensors to help buildings conserve energy intelligently, while also monitoring weather or rush-hour traffic.[30] Intel ESL launched the Intel Collaborative Research Institute for Sustainable Connected Cities in 2012 in partnership with researchers from Imperial College London and University College London to drive the application of computing technologies to advance the social, economic, and environmental well-being of cities.[31]

Additionally, Intel has been working with Pecan Street Inc.[32] to help gather and analyze usage patterns based on two years of energy consumption data from sensor systems in Austin, Texas. [33] Pecan Street is a nonprofit consortium of universities, technology companies, and utility providers collaborating on testing, piloting, and commercializing smart grid technologies to advance energy efficiency. Pecan Street seeks to drive new products, services, and economic opportunities in the area of consumer energy management. The overarching vision of Pecan Street Inc. is to reimagine Austin's energy distribution system in a way that can support and accelerate the installation and management of smarter and cleaner electricity services. This includes the integration of clean distributed generation, storage, demand response, energy efficiency, new pricing/rate models, and other technical and economic issues.

PUBLIC POLICY ENGAGEMENT: DIGITAL ENERGY AND SUSTAINABILITY SOLUTIONS CAMPAIGN

Intel founded and co-chairs the Digital Energy and Sustainability Solutions Campaign (DESSC),[34] a coalition of information and communications technology (ICT) companies and associations, NGOs, customers and other stakeholders who recognize the enabling role that ICT plays in improving the environment and driving long-term economic growth.[35] Launched in 2008, DESSC is hosted by the Information Technology Industry Council.[36] DESSC believes that "governments can take many actions to encourage ICT-enabled energy efficiency, clean energy innovation, and sustainable growth." DESSC recommendations include establishing a national strategy to improve energy efficiency and reduce greenhouse gas emissions by using ICT; increasing broadband penetration throughout society to encourage energy efficiency and innovations through intelligent connected devices; and raising funding for research, development, and deployment in energy efficiency and clean energy innovations."[37] The organization also advocates for creating protocols to measure energy efficiency and climate impacts of ICT in a variety of economic sectors, and involving consumers in better managing their electricity use.

According to DESSC, "increasingly, the barriers to applying smart technologies for a sustainable economy stem less from a lack of technical know-how and more from legal, regulatory and cultural questions that inhibit the deployment and use of smart solutions at the scale needed to transform systems like the electricity grid, transportation, and energy use in buildings and homes...The use of smart technologies could reduce US CO_2 emissions by as much as 22 percent by 2020—that's $240 billion in cost savings or a reduction of 36 percent in imported oil. Globally, smart technologies can reduce CO_2 by as much as 15 percent."[38]

Intel is making energy efficiency its business—to generate profits while advancing the global agenda to address climate change.

ERICSSON APPLIES INFORMATION AND COMMUNICATIONS TECHNOLOGY TO ADVANCE SUSTAINABLE CITIES

Ericsson believes that there are opportunities to advance "the triple bottom line"—people, planet, and profit—given that 70 percent of the world's population is expected to live in cities by 2050.[39] Ericsson analyzed 25 urban areas to assess the economic, social, and environmental value of ICT maturity for citizens, cities, and businesses. In its report focusing on the benefits to businesses, Ericsson concluded: "New media services and business concepts such as smart grids, intelligent traffic and e-health, are examples of recent responses to this new landscape. Governments and leaders in society recognize that connectivity along with ICT policy, literacy, and sustainable business models are all crucial in order to create a positive climate for innovation and business."[40]

Ericsson is a leading provider of technology and services to telecom operators, supporting two billion subscribers worldwide. Working in 180 countries, with 110,000 employees, and revenues over 27 billion SEK, the company is headquartered in Stockholm, Sweden.[41] Through its work with cities around the world, as well as in research, advocacy, and new product development, Ericsson is helping to transform the global marketplace—from consumer behavior to new businesses and processes. According to Ericsson, "mobility, cloud computing services, broadband, big data and social media are at the center of the transformation that is occurring in both developed and emerging economies."[42]

Furthermore, Ericsson and Arthur D. Little, a management consultancy that links strategy, innovation, and technology, have demonstrated the economic case for greater connectivity. According to their studies, "for every 1,000 new connections, 80 new jobs are created, and for every 10 percent increase in mobile and broadband penetration, GDP increases by 1 percentage point."[43] Additionally, the report indicates that ICT advances entrepreneurship, while reducing transaction costs between firms.

Ericsson is identifying the key enablers to further advance city progress through its Networked Society City Index in order to engage with forward-looking decision makers in business, civil society, and government. The Index also analyzes the impact of ICT on economic, social, and environmental progress. According to the Index, currently the top ranked cities using ICT to benefit businesses are New York City, Stockholm, and London.[44]

The Stockholm Royal Seaport represents an Ericsson city initiative where Ericsson is heading up the ICT portion of a climate-positive Urban Smart Grid project that is central to the new infrastructure. Ericsson is also providing broadband technologies to businesses throughout Johannesburg, South Africa, making it the first true Digital City in sub-Saharan Africa.

Ericsson is further expanding the dissemination of its expertise and advocacy as a founding member of the New Cities Foundation, a Swiss NGO that fosters innovative urban solutions through public-private partnerships. The company also contributes ICT know-how to SymbioCity, an initiative of the Swedish Trade Council to advance sustainable cities worldwide.

Elaine Weidman-Grunewald, vice president of Sustainability and Corporate Responsibility at Ericsson, explained why the company is committed to developing energy efficient products. "Our customers are mobile operators. Their telecommunications networks cover large geographies— usually entire countries or cities, so energy efficiency is paramount to them. If we can find a way to help them to reduce their monthly electricity bills, that makes Ericsson highly competitive for operators."[45]

Weidman-Grunewald provided some perspective on the past 20 years at the company, which has been producing a corporate social responsibility report for as many years. "I've seen a shift with our customers," she explained. "Their attention to climate change and reducing their carbon emissions has become much more of a priority. So one of the solutions we highlighted in our recent report is called 'Psi.' That product is really a game-changer in building geographic coverage and capacity."[46] Psi brings mobile broadband 3G coverage to three antennas rather than the traditional deployment of a single radio per antenna. This reduces power use by up to forty percent.[47] "Psi is an energy-unique technology," commented Weidman-Grunewald. "Ericsson profits when our products are highly competitive in meeting our customers' interests, and that means lowering their energy costs."

As a board member of the Global e-Sustainability Initiative (GeSI),[48] Weidman-Grunewald is passionate about the power of ICT to reduce carbon emissions. GeSI, an NGO whose members include major ICT companies from around the globe, envisions a sustainable world through responsible, ICT-enabled transformation. Like others in the ICT and the broader business sector, Weidman-Grunewald implores governments to link policies with climate change. She pointed to GeSI's SMARTer2020[49] report that evaluates the potential to reduce carbon emissions through ICT-enabled solutions "ranging across six sectors of the economy: power, transportation, manufacturing, consumer and service, agriculture, and buildings. Emission reductions come from virtualization initiatives such as cloud computing and video conferencing, and also through efficiency gains such as optimization of variable-speed motors in manufacturing, smart livestock management to reduce methane emissions, and 32 other ICT-enabled solutions identified in the study."

The GeSi report also shows how the increased use of ICT "such as video conferencing and smart building management could cut the projected 2020 global greenhouse gas (GHG) emissions by 16.5 percent, amounting to $1.9 trillion in gross energy and fuel savings and a reduction of 9.1 gigatonnes of carbon dioxide equivalent ($GtCO_2e$) of greenhouse gases. This is equivalent to more than seven times the ICT sector's emissions in the same period."[50]

Weidman-Grunewald also calls for government to stimulate changes in the public's behavior. "People talk about carbon capture sequestration to reduce carbon in the atmosphere as if it's 20 years away," she said, "but there are ways to better use existing technology today. The average consumer needs to know the tradeoffs and best way to use technology. For example, services like Spotify or Netflix help dematerialize the economy; we don't need DVDs or videocassettes. Digitization reduces carbon emissions. So does mobile money. Governments can promote awareness among consumers and incentives to encourage smarter behavior, such as working at home, buying electric cars, and taking public transportation."[51]

Ericsson recognizes that climate change coupled with population growth present challenges that require transformative solutions. The company also understands that addressing threats to society and our planet provides business opportunities. Under leadership by CEO Hans Vestberg, Ericsson has positioned the company as a global leader in finding answers. Ericsson is at the table every year with heads of governments, corporations, and NGOs at the Clinton Global Initiative. Ericsson joined other industry partners in promoting ICT solutions at the Conferences of the Parties (COP-18) in Doha, Qatar and at the United Nations Framework Convention on Climate Change.

The company plays a vital role with GeSI, including launching SMARTer2020, which calls for concerted action by global policy makers—in Brazil, Canada, China, Germany, India, the United Kingdom and the United States.[52] For Ericsson, leadership in developing and applying innovative ICT-enabled solutions to climate change is a profitable business that is good for the world.

JOHNSON CONTROLS BUILDS SUSTAINABLE BUILDINGS WITH THE CLINTON CLIMATE INITIATIVE

The building sector consumes up to 40 percent of the world's energy and is responsible for 30 percent of greenhouse gas emissions, according to the

United Nations Environment Programme Sustainable Buildings and Climate Initiative.[53] Furthermore, given the inefficiencies of old structures, and the massive growth of new construction, greenhouse gas emissions from buildings will more than double by 2030 if no action is taken. As noted earlier by Elaine Weidman-Gruneman, solutions are readily available and present opportunities to businesses. As with other energy matters discussed earlier, governments have been slow to create policies that encourage transformation and accelerate market solutions. Johnson Controls, however, has built a vibrant business by reducing energy consumption in buildings.

Building on the legacy of the company's founder, who invented the thermostat in 1883,[54] Johnson Controls is a leading provider of equipment, controls, and services for heating, cooling, and security systems for buildings. The company participates in more than 500 renewable energy projects that use solar, wind, and geothermal technologies. Johnson Controls claims to have reduced carbon dioxide equivalent emissions by 19.2 million metric tons[55] and to have generated savings of $7.0 billion through guaranteed energy savings performance contracts in North America since 2000.[56]

Johnson Controls has established an Institute for Building Efficiency,[57] specifically to focus on existing building retrofits, green buildings, smart grid and smart buildings, renewable and distributed energy, clean energy finance, and energy and climate policy. The Institute conducted a 2012 Energy Efficiency Indicator[58] survey in partnership with the Urban Land Institute[59]—a nonprofit research and education organization with members in 95 countries who represent a wide spectrum of land use and real estate development disciplines—as well as the International Facility Management Association,[60] which supports 19,000 facility managers in 78 countries, and sixteen in-country strategic partners.

The following were key findings from the survey of 3,479 respondents from six regions worldwide—Europe, India, China, United States/Canada, Australia, and Brazil.

1. Interest in energy management increased over previous years. In 2012, 85 percent of respondents said energy management was extremely or very important, compared to 70 percent in 2011 and 60 percent in 2010.
2. Respondents in China (81 percent) and India (74 percent) planned to increase energy efficiency or renewable energy investments in the coming year. Globally, just over half indicated that they planned to do so.
3. The primary driver of energy efficiency decisions in all regions was energy cost savings. In Europe and China, the secondary driver was to increase energy security. Government and utility incentives and rebates

were viewed as a secondary driver in the United States, Canada, and
Australia.

4. "In all regions, tax incentives and rebates for implementing energy
   efficiency measures were the most favored policy, although those in
   developed regions supported such measures more strongly than those
   in emerging regions. Respondents in emerging regions felt that tax
   incentives, stricter building codes and equipment standards, and adoption of green appraisal standards would have a nearly equal likelihood
   on improving energy efficiency in buildings."[61]

5. Respondents cited lack of funding as the top barrier to energy efficiency
   projects, especially in the United States and Canada. "Respondents in
   emerging countries faced more struggles with awareness, technical
   expertise, and certainty of savings."[62]

6. Interest in "green" buildings continues to grow. Globally, 44 percent
   (compared to 35 percent in 2011) planned to seek voluntary green
   building certifications for existing buildings in the next 12 months,
   while 43 percent will seek certification for new construction (compared
   to 39 percent in 2011).

Johnson Controls joined the real estate firm Jones Lang LaSalle and
the Rocky Mountain Institute to complete a highly public retrofit of the
Empire State Building in 2012. The Empire State Building plan involved
refurbishing 6,500 windows, retrofitting the chiller plant, and introducing
an Internet-based tenant management system and new building controls.
It is estimated that energy costs will be cut by 38 percent, saving $4.4 mil-
lion each year and reducing carbon emissions by 105,000 metric tons over
15 years.[63] The savings will pay for the project over the term of the contract.
If not, Johnson Controls will pay the difference between the actual energy
consumption and the guaranteed consumption stated in the contract. In
addition, an online dashboard installed in each office suite gives tenants full
transparency regarding their energy consumption, and helps them analyze
the data to find ways to be more efficient and save on their monthly energy
bills.[64] The project is credited with having won over new tenants including
LinkedIn, Skanska, LF USA, Coty Inc., and the FDIC.[65]

The Empire State Building project was conducted under the auspices of the
Clinton Climate Initiative (CCI),[66] an initiative of the Clinton Foundation.[67]
Clay Nesler, vice president of Global Energy and Sustainability for the
Building Efficiency Business at Johnson Controls, explained the importance
of this project, not only for its impact on the environment but also as a
demonstration of what is possible worldwide.[68] "The first building retrofit
we did with the Clinton Climate Initiative was the Inorbit Mall, the largest

mall in Mumbai,"[69] Nesler explained. "Now we've created a toolkit with templates that governments can use to engage stakeholders. We've trained energy efficiency experts at the World Bank, presented in Singapore to the Building Construction Association, which has trained other building councils throughout Asia, and presented during a thematic debate on the green economy at the United Nations Headquarters in New York City."

As far as generating profits for Johnson Controls, Nesler said his role is to "make the pie bigger" by growing worldwide demand for energy efficient products and services. "We are market-shaping," he said. "We are already in 150 countries, on seven continents. We are trying to make these countries more educated about the opportunities and more committed."[70] By building on its legacy of energy efficient controls, Johnson Controls is advancing its business while playing an important role worldwide in addressing climate change.

UNILEVER PROMOTES SUSTAINABLE LIVING

Unilever, an international Anglo-Dutch company[71] with $160 billion in annual sales and 400 brand products for health, wellbeing, and food, including soaps and detergents, is a global leader in building profits through responsible business practices. Under the leadership of CEO Paul Polman, Unilever has put "sustainable and equitable growth at the heart of its business model"[72] in order to double the size of its business[73] while reducing costs and risks.

By 2020, Unilever has committed to "help more than a billion people to improve their health and well-being; halve the environmental footprint of our products; and source 100 percent of our agricultural raw materials sustainably and enhance the livelihoods of people across our value chain."[74] The company believes that this will allow it to grow by "winning shares and building markets everywhere."[75]

Unilever's strategy to halve the greenhouse gas impact of its products across their life cycles by 2020 includes reducing carbon emissions from its manufacturing, transport, refrigeration, offices, and employee travel. These are areas where the company has direct control, yet Unilever's greatest challenge is lowering the carbon footprint related to consumers' use of the company's products. Importantly, this is where emissions are most significant. "24 percent of the greenhouse gas emissions from our company are around our sourcing, and 4 percent are in our own operations," explained Gail Klintworth, chief sustainability officer of Unilever. "A whopping 68 percent are in the consumers' use of our products—like taking showers. So we are seeking, through our brand, to be innovative in providing consumers with tools to change their behaviors."[76]

The company aims to inspire sustainable living among its customers through the following "five levers of change,"[77] according to Thomas Lingard, global advocacy director at Unilever.

1. Make it understood. Sometimes people don't know about a behaviour and why they should do it. This Lever raises awareness and encourages acceptance.
2. Make it easy. People are likely to take action if it's easy, but not if it requires extra effort. This Lever establishes convenience and confidence.
3. Make it desirable. The new behaviour needs to fit with how people like to think of themselves, and how they like others to think of them. This Lever is about self and society.
4. Make it rewarding. New behaviours need to articulate the tangible benefits that people care about. This Lever demonstrates the proof and payoff.
5. Make it a habit. Once consumers have changed, it is important to create a strategy to help hold the behaviour in place over time. This Lever is about reinforcing and reminding.[78]

Klintworth described the external factors that inform the company's strategy: "Two billion people will become first-time consumers by 2020. Three billion people will join the ranks of the middle class by 2030. If we have problems at the moment living on 1.5 times the planet's resources, extracting out of nature's account so that we are already in the red, just imagine all of these additional people living resource-intensive lives," said Klintworth.[79] She also discussed the hazardous implications of an unsustainable lifestyle. "We're beginning to see that warming the planet leads to extreme weather conditions, and not having enough water to drink, not enough food, and then related migration issues and public health issues." Klintworth concluded, "This is why Unilever's mission is to create a sustainable living plan. Our company's purpose is to make sustainable living commonplace!"

Unilever uses a number of campaigns to promote sustainable living through health and well-being. For example, the company has endeavored to limit the spread of preventable illness, reduce the number of school days missed, and save lives by encouraging hand washing in schools and communities worldwide.[80] Since Global Handwashing Day was co-founded by Unilever's Lifebouy brand in 2008, "the number of children dying from diarrhea each year has halved – that's 1.1 million lives saved." Unfortunately, however, the company notes that "3,000 children under the age of five still die every day from diarrhea alone, making it the second most common cause of child mortality worldwide."

According to Myriam Sidibe, Lifebuoy Global Social Mission Director, clinical research shows that "handwashing with soap at key occasions can reduce the risk of diarrhea by up to approximately 45 percent. That means that handwashing with soap could help over 600,000 children reach their fifth birthday every year."[81]

Another Unilever campaign to advance environmental and economic impacts is its Sustainable Tea Agriculture project in Turkey, benefiting farmers, consumers, the environment, and the company. Turkey is one of Unilever's main centers of tea agriculture, with more than 15,000 farmers and 3 factories based in the country. This Unilever initiative is conducted in partnership with the Rainforest Alliance,[82] a global NGO that works to conserve biodiversity and ensure sustainable livelihoods by transforming land-use practices, business practices, and consumer behavior. By training Turkish tea growers to help them to move to sustainable agricultural practices by 2014 and to become Rainforest Alliance certified, Unilever will help to restore the soil to a rich, fertile state to protect the future of tea agriculture for years to come. This is good for the farmers, good for the environment, and good for Unilever.[83]

For Unilever, finding solutions for people to live sustainably now and into the future is a profitable business enterprise. According to Klintworth, the company even sees this as "making sure the business is 'future-fit'. If people don't have water, our consumer base melts before our very eyes."[84]

Business leaders who understand the gravity of climate change also understand that the challenge cannot be addressed one company at a time, but requires solutions across industries. Polman, for example, is highly engaged in public policy and advocacy, as well as in NGO partnerships. At the World Economic Forum's Annual Meeting 2013 in Davos, Unilever CEO Paul Polman was notably outspoken in his views about sustainability and the role of business. "We have a very bizarre situation in the world right now where 890 million people go to bed hungry, not knowing if they will wake up the next day," Polman said. "And yet we waste about 30–40% of the food as if it doesn't matter. Businesses understand that any system where too many people are excluded or left behind is not a system that is in equilibrium."[85]

To further industry-wide solutions, Polman serves on the board of the Consumer Goods Forum[86] and co-sponsors its Sustainability Program. The Forum is an industry association that brings together more than 400 retailers, manufacturers, service providers and other stakeholders from over 70 countries. The board of the Consumer Goods Forum endorsed two resolutions

proposed by Polman: eliminating deforestation from the supply chains of
all member companies by 2020, and replacing hydrofluorocarbon (HFC)
refrigerants with "natural" refrigerants that have a much lower global warming potential. The Forum seeks to achieve these two goals through individual
company initiatives and partnership with NGOs.[87]

Unilever built a business strategy to profit by providing a sustainable living plan that is designed to meet consumers' needs in the face of a growing
population, climate change, and resource challenges.

NIKE PROMOTES SUSTAINABLE MATERIALS FOR THE
APPAREL AND FOOTWEAR INDUSTRY

Nike is not only altering the design of its footwear and apparel to reduce its
own impact on the environment, but the company also works with NGOs,
companies, and governments in an effort to catalyze transformation of the
entire supply chain for the apparel and footwear industry.

Nike, Inc. has come a long way since Hannah Jones joined the company
in 1998. Under her direction as vice president of Sustainable Business and
Innovation, the company has shifted from a defensive position regarding
toxic chemicals in its materials—hazardous for employees as well as for the
local water supply—to a leadership role in the apparel and footwear industry
by addressing social and environmental issues.

"Like so many others we learned the hard way what it means to ignore our
social and environmental footprint," said Jones.[88] Today, not only is Nike
committed to using environmentally preferred materials throughout its own
supply chain,[89] but Nike also contributed the Materials Sustainability Index
portion of the Higg Index—a tool that is used by companies throughout
the industry to measure the environmental and social performance of their
apparel and footwear products.[90]

Additionally, Nike is collaborating with NASA, the US Agency for
International Development, and the US Department of State to challenge
materials manufacturers to transform the system of producing fabrics to
reduce their environmental impact.[91] According to Jones, "about 60 percent
of the environmental footprint of a pair of Nike shoes is embedded in the
materials used to make them. When you multiply that across our business,
and across the industry, it's clear that innovation in sustainable materials is a
huge opportunity, not just for Nike, but for the world."[92]

While many companies regard sustainability as a defensive approach
to mitigate risk, Jones views sustainability as a strategic opportunity to
increase business. "Sustainability triggers innovation and growth. Designing
new products with materials that are environmentally friendly makes our

company more competitive," explained Jones. She also believes that some investors will likely recognize that companies with effective sustainability strategies will be the ones to bet on. "Socially responsible investment firms (SRIs) were born out of a negative screening approach," she explained. "Now, we will see mainstream investors asking about the extent to which your company has a strong sustainability strategy. As we navigate through the next ten years, there will be scarce resources and greater volatility. Investors will take bets on companies for looking to the future, not in the rear view mirror."[93]

Jason Kibbey is executive director of the Sustainable Apparel Coalition,[94] a nonprofit organization founded in 2008 by a group of sustainability leaders from global apparel and footwear companies who recognized that addressing the industry's current social and environmental challenges is both a business imperative and an opportunity. Its current focus is expanding adoption of the Higg Index for measuring the environmental and social performance of apparel products.

Kibbey observed that, in the past, the few companies that invested in sustainability strategies regarded this as brand-enhancement. "Looking forward, however, companies understand that they will be expected to be transparent with information about their materials and supply chain, so we are helping to prepare for that," he said. "Customers and investors will expect companies to use materials that limit their environmental impact. Companies know that they will be punished in the marketplace if they do not respect that." Kibbey also noted that companies like Nike recognize that the drive for sustainability presents opportunities for innovation.[95]

On stage with President Clinton at the Clinton Global Initiative 2013 Winter Meeting,[96] wearing her Nike footwear in front of hundreds of global leaders, Hannah Jones declared that Nike seeks to "decouple growth from limited resources. This is our corporate strategy." Nike is modeling both a collaborative and competitive approach: The company is collaborative in sharing its measurement tool with its industry colleagues and in encouraging transformation throughout the materials supply chain. And it is competitive in designing the most creative products that will reduce the environmental footprint while meeting the interests of today's and tomorrow's consumers. For Nike, sustainability is a business opportunity for profitability.

INVESTORS WITH THE CARBON DISCLOSURE PROJECT DRIVE CORPORATE REPORTING ON CARBON EMISSIONS

Many investors are banking on their conviction that companies that integrate sustainability into their strategies are more valuable. In 2013, 722 investors with $87 trillion in assets—more than half of the world's invested capital—became signatories to the Carbon Disclosure Project's (CDP) climate change program, up 10 percent from 2012.[97] CDP is an NGO that provides "the only global system for companies and cities to measure, disclose, manage and share vital environmental information. CDP works with market forces to motivate companies to disclose their impacts on the environment and natural resources and take action to reduce them."[98] CDP has seen more than a twentyfold increase in its investor signatories since its inception in 2002.[99]

By identifying themselves as "signatories," institutional investors, such as banks, pension funds, asset managers, insurance companies, and foundations have access to responses from companies that enable them to evaluate the climate, water, and forest-related risks and opportunities that may have an impact on companies' operations and financial performance, and thereby on investor portfolios.[100] While CDP's original intention was to promote disclosure of carbon emissions, the organization is seeing growing interest from investors in additional environmental issues such as water and forests.[101]

CDP data is also relied upon by companies researching suppliers to make environmentally sound purchasing decisions. "65 major purchasing companies, including Walmart, Dell, and L'Oreal, representing purchasing power of more than $1 trillion dollars, ask us for information about suppliers," said Catherine von Altheer, communications manager at CDP. These companies are concerned about risks to their supply chain resulting from climate change. "Thinking about what has driven continued increasing participation in CDP—the investor and purchaser authority is absolutely what got CDP off the ground and remains a strong authority. But more recently, I think that one could also say that companies increasingly understand the business imperative of environmental management," von Altheer continued. "Companies report both substantial risks and opportunities to us. And disclosing through CDP enables companies and investors to identify the risks and best opportunities."

Von Altheer expanded on this point: "Logica (a UK IT company) found efficiency savings worth £10 million by responding to CDP for the first time. Walmart found disclosing through CDP so valuable that they asked us to extend the program to their suppliers; in fact, this was the birth of our supply chain program."[102]

Companies that are effective in addressing climate change generate superior stock performance and benefit in additional ways as well, according to CDP.

- Since 2006, companies that achieved leadership positions on CDP's Climate Disclosure Leadership Index (CDLI) delivered total returns of 67.4 percent, more than double the 31.1 percent return of the Global 500.

- Climate Performance Leadership Index companies generated average total returns of 15.9 percent since 2010, more than double the 6.4 percent return of the Global 500 index. [103]
- Research in 2012 reveals that carbon reduction activities are producing an average ROI of 34.3 percent, with 88 percent of projects exceeding firm-level return on invested capital.[104]
- Samsung Electronics, for example, reported to investors in their 2010 climate change response to CDP that "a 1% decrease in brand value of the company due to unfavorable evaluations from investment organizations and/or NGOs, caused by insufficient climate change response, is equivalent to losing about 200 million USD."[105]

CDP collects and analyzes data from over 4,100 companies each year and produces a number of reports in key markets in addition to an annual survey of the 500 largest public corporations. This research is conducted on behalf of these companies' investors and asks the companies to measure and report what climate change means for their business.[106]

Following are results based on responses from 379 of the Global 500 companies in 2012.[107]

- 81 percent stated that climate change presents a physical risk to their business; 83 percent identify regulatory risk, and 63 percent say that reputation and change in consumer behavior is a climate change-related risk.
- 96 percent have board or senior executive oversight over climate change (compared to 93 percent in 2011).
- 78 percent have integrated climate change into their overall business strategy (compared to 68 percent in 2011).

Paul Dickinson, CDP's executive chairman and founder, talked about the urgency of addressing climate change as well as the opportunity to imagine a new economic landscape. "The urgency of climate change is not complicated," he observed. "If you can read a graph, you can understand that after being fairly stable for millions of years, CO_2 levels jumped since the Industrial Revolution to precipitous levels today. If we continue on this course, there could be one billion avoidable deaths, or even far more, by 2100. That's twenty times (the deaths in) World War II. We have memorials so that we shouldn't forget. But we are forgetting."

Dickinson went on to remark on the simplicity of the challenge, and called for action, saying, "We can do something about this. This is all quite measurable. And we have a responsibility to the future of the species."

Dickinson explained that the challenge is to meet the needs of the present without compromising the future, which he terms "sustainable development." He also noted that the government either will not or cannot fix it. "Government is failing at its number one job of protecting its citizens. Government is failing to restrict the release of greenhouse gases." As a result, he said, "we have to act." Dickinson praised the leaders who have given so much of themselves to lead the effort—people like President Clinton, Vice President Al Gore, and Ban Ki-moon.

Dickinson believes that climate change presents a major opportunity for companies. "Climate change is not going away," he said. "It's like the Internet. It gets bigger every day. You have to learn how to make money by responding to it. Reimagine a whole different economy." He ticked off the many ways to do so, including 722 investors with $87 trillion among them. "Help them vote with their money."

And this presents companies with opportunities to innovate and profit, while being environmentally responsible. "Tablet computers are replacing newspapers; they're making money through dematerialization," Dickinson noted. "So are sponsors of videoconferencing, and producers of insulation, fiber optic cables, broadband, e-books, and local food. This is a bonanza for companies and industries that help us burn less oil, coal, and gas."

Moreover, explained Dickinson, the ultimate democracy is in how people spend their money—how we invest and what we purchase. "National governments are important, but they are constantly eclipsed by the global business system," he said. "You are in charge of how you spend your money. Enlightened citizens are not going to want to put their money into the problem but into the solution."

Finally, Dickinson implored people to be good stewards as shareholders—to take responsibility as an owner: "The corporation is the most extraordinary and marvelous organization for creating wealth, but like other organizations it needs to have appropriate governance. The price of security is eternal vigilance. It's a very good time to pay a lot of attention to climate change."[108]

The Sustainability Consortium Is Measuring and Reporting the Social and Environmental Impacts of Products by Categories

Corporate efforts to reduce energy consumption in their operations are smart from a cost-savings perspective, while also mitigating damage from global warming. The greatest use of energy, however, is not in company operations, but in the supply chain for manufacturing products. Recall that Gail Klintworth of Unilever said that only 4 percent of the company's greenhouse gas emissions are in operations, while "24 percent of the greenhouse gas emissions from our company are around our sourcing."[109]

McKinsey estimates that "companies that take steps to increase resource productivity could unlock significant value, minimizing costs while establishing greater operational stability. Our experience suggests that manufacturers could reduce the amount of energy they use in production by 20 to 30 percent."[110] McKinsey recommends that "to realize the full resource productivity opportunity, companies need to work across the 'full supply circle.'"

The Sustainability Consortium (TSC), an organization launched by a consortium of global corporations in 2009, is addressing this very issue by developing and disseminating a standardized framework to measure and communicate sustainability-related information throughout the product value chain.[111] Its mission is to "design and implement credible, transparent and scalable science-based measurement and reporting systems accessible for all producers, retailers, and users of consumer products." TSC's membership represents more than one hundred businesses that employ over 57 million people and have combined annual revenues totaling over $1.5 trillion.

"There was a lack of data and scientifically-based information about the environmental and social impacts of products throughout the life cycle," said Kara Hurst, CEO of The Sustainability Consortium.[112] "Companies, as well as NGOs and academic organizations were seeking more information about the sustainability impacts of products and commodities." For global corporations, participating in TSC provides them with access to valuable information about reducing operating costs. Additionally, "pre-competitive collaboration leads to innovation of next generation of products and furthers our impact."[113]

In addition to providing measurement data to evaluate suppliers, TSC's analysis and reports go further. "We also provide assessments about improvement opportunities," Hurst said. She described three aspects of TSC's research and reporting that has already been conducted and disseminated for 120 product categories, including items such as milk, beef, laptops, and laundry detergents, rather than specific brands.

TSC is on track to complete the analysis and distribute information to its members regarding 600 product categories by 2015. Each report includes a large compendium of research, called a "dossier," a sustainability profile, highlighting "hot spots"—social and environmental impacts that stand out for the product, especially ones that consumers care about, improvement opportunities, and key performance indicators—questions that retailers might want to ask their suppliers that relate to social and environmental impacts.

"Our member companies are already using these questions in managing their relationships with their suppliers," said Hurst. "It's no longer discretionary for companies to know where their energy costs are embedded. This is a matter of reducing expenses and mitigating risks in the face of the growing scarcity of resources."[114]

Walmart has already rolled out The Sustainability Consortium research questionnaire to 60,000 of its suppliers and has begun using TSC's reports to assess its supply chain.[115] "At Walmart, we have focused much of our supply chain sustainability work through our involvement in The Sustainability Consortium so we can broaden our global impact," said Andrea Thomas, senior vice president of Sustainability at Walmart. "By collaborating with our suppliers, other retailers, NGOs, and universities, we can align as an industry on the biggest issues and the solutions we need to implement to address these issues. By working collectively we can accomplish much more than any one of us could do individually."[116]

Corporations, motivated by profits and long-term sustainability, align with society's interests to reduce carbon emissions and conserve natural resources. Companies are collaborating to drive progress where governments cannot. NGOs, academic and research institutions, and governments are vital partners.

GOVERNMENT NEEDS TO PLAY A ROLE TOO

As shown in this chapter, many businesses are leading the way by developing new approaches to reduce carbon emissions in their own operations and creating new products and services to assist businesses and customers in achieving energy efficiencies. This is a win-win-win for the businesses that profit from sales, for consumers who lower their bills, and for the world. Despite these advances by the private sector, many corporate and NGO leaders believe that government needs to play a far more effective role in creating policies and approaches to reduce carbon emissions.

In April 2013, for example, 30 companies presented the Climate Declaration to Congress. The declaration was titled: "Tackling climate change is one of America's greatest economic opportunities of the 21st century (and it's simply the right thing to do)."[117] The signatories implored Congress to address the issue by promoting clean energy, increasing efficiency, and limiting carbon emissions—strategies that these businesses already have implemented within their own operations. Participating companies, including Unilever, Intel, Starbucks, and IKEA provide approximately 475,000 US jobs and generate combined annual revenues of approximately $450 billion, according to Business for Innovative Climate & Energy Policy (BICEP), the business group that organized the campaign.[118] BICEP is a project of Ceres, an NGO that mobilizes business leadership for a sustainable world. Additionally, at the Bloomberg New Energy Finance Summit 2013, a number of business leaders called on governments to take an increased role by enabling market forces to drive solutions and to promote greater collaboration between businesses, governments, and civil society.[119]

There have been some efforts in the international arena—most recently in 2012 at the Doha conference—to reach an agreement among nations to reduce global warming. This remains a work in progress.[120] United Nations Secretary-General Ban Ki-moon as recently as February 2013 has continued to call for action: "We must limit global temperature rise to 2 degrees Celsius. We are far from there, and even that is enough to cause dire consequences. If we continue along the current path, we are close to a 6 degree increase."[121]

In addition to grand programs to address climate change, business leaders suggest specific regulatory fixes that would enable markets to provide solutions. Peter Sweatman, the chief executive and founder of Climate Strategy & Partners,[122] has identified opportunities for governments to facilitate greater progress on carbon reduction. Climate Strategy & Partners is the Iberian partner for London-based Climate Change Capital Limited (CCC), which is an investment manager and advisory group specializing in the opportunities generated by the global transition to a low carbon economy. CCC has a green building fund—the Climate Capital Green Building fund—that invests in renovating urban buildings for greater energy efficiency.[123]

Sweatman observed that "most businesses that address energy are regulated. So when you sell energy power you do what your regulator tells you. It's a controlled business. Regulators respond to national policy of the moment. We also have a tax system that provides incentives or disincentives to encourage or discourage certain behavior."[124] Sweatman believes that governments should use this influence on the marketplace to encourage and ease the transition to a low carbon economy.

CLIMATE CHANGE IS A MATTER OF SECURITY

According to "Climate Change and National Security,"[125] a special report by the Council on Foreign Relations, climate change threatens national security. The threat arises from damage caused domestically from extreme weather, in addition to disruption of "US interests in strategically important countries."[126] In the report, author Joshua W. Busby argues that in the United States "extreme weather events, made more likely by climate change, could endanger large numbers of people, damage critical infrastructure (including military installations), and require mobilization and diversion of military assets. Internationally, a number of countries of strategic concern are likely to be vulnerable to climate change, which could lead to refugee and humanitarian crises and, by immiserating tens of thousands, contribute to domestic and regional instability."[127]

The Arab Spring of 2011 is a harbinger of the violence that will come with climate change, according to essays published in *The Arab Spring and Climate Change: A Climate and Security Correlations Series*.[128] In the preface, Anne-Marie Slaughter indicates that "this concept of a 'threat multiplier' is a helpful way to think about climate change and security more broadly," and explains that the authors of the various essays in the book show that "the consequences of climate change are stressors that can ignite a volatile mix of underlying causes that erupt into revolution."

The book was published by the Center for American Progress,[129] an independent nonpartisan educational institute dedicated to improving the lives of Americans through progressive ideas and action; Stimson,[130] a nonprofit, nonpartisan institution devoted to enhancing international peace and security through a unique combination of rigorous analysis and outreach; and the Center for Climate and Security,[131] an action-oriented think tank and convener, with an advisory board of former military leaders and security professionals.

Several of the essays argue that social unrest in the Middle East in 2011 can be traced to food scarcity and prices, which resulted from the 2011 drought in China. "We will realize how interconnected the world has become if climate hazards one day disrupt global agriculture, energy, or water systems," says Michael Werz and Max Hoffman. They also maintain that migration resulting from environmental degradation, social conflict, and food scarcity are likely to complicate future crisis scenarios.[132]

The authors assert that addressing climate change and the needs of people worldwide to live sustainable lives forms the basis for global security. They also argue that the violence in Darfur can be traced to conflicts resulting from climate change. In *The Atlantic*, Alex de Waal, program director at the Social Science Research Council, suggests that the dispute was not racially motivated between Africans and Arabs. Rather, he indicates that this was a battle between Africans (farmers) and nomadic herders (Arabs) over lands that were failing due to droughts. Climate change in the region, said a senior scientist at the National Oceanic and Atmospheric Administration, was from environmental degradation in the 1980s and 1990s. Columbia University's Alessandra Giannini, who led an analysis, says that the roots of the drying of Darfur lay in global climate change.[133]

More disruption is already occurring. According to the Norwegian Refugee Council's International Displacement Monitoring Centre (NRC), 32.4 million people were displaced by floods, hurricanes, typhoons, and cyclones in 2012. According to *Fast Company*, "NRC attributes 98 percent of the disasters to 'climate- and weather-related events.' It expects things to only get worse as climate change increases 'the frequency and severity of weather-related hazards.'"[134]

BUSINESSES WITH PARTNERS LEAD ON REDUCING GLOBAL WARMING

The companies featured in this chapter are profiting by reducing costs through energy efficiencies, and by creating and selling products and services to meet the demands of businesses and consumers seeking to reduce their expenses and carbon footprint. These companies are benefiting while improving the world. Although governments have endorsed the principle that global warming must be contained, their actions are often limited or counterproductive. Customers, employees, and investors can continue to play a powerful role in helping to drive the sustainability agenda, by voting with their dollars and feet for companies who share their values.

CHAPTER 4

ECOSYSTEMS

When we try to pick out anything by itself, we find it hitched to every-thing else in the Universe.[1]

—John Muir

UNTIL 2009, ONE OF THE WORLD'S LARGEST PRODUCERS OF TISSUES AND toilet paper sourced fibers from trees that were clear-cut from Canada's boreal forest. Destruction to these forests threatened the region, which is home to nearly a million aboriginal peoples, as well as the woodland caribou, lynx, grizzly bears, wolverine, and one billion migratory birds.[2] The boreal is also the largest storehouse of terrestrial carbon on Earth, so deforestation in this area undermines its impact in reversing up to 20 percent of global greenhouse gas emissions—more than all the cars, trucks, planes, boats, and trains in the world combined.[3]

Clean air, water, timber, and arable land are essential for human suste-nance; without them, we'd all perish. Yet, already 780 million people lack access to clean drinking water, women spend 200 million hours a day collect-ing water, and 3.4 million people die annually from water-related diseases.[4] With flooding, droughts, natural disasters caused by climate change, and increasing demands for food and potable water resulting from population growth from 7 billion today to 9 billion by 2043,[5] the challenges will only worsen.

The growing population, coupled with the increasing consumer demand from developed and developing nations,[6] is accelerating the stress on Earth's ecosystems. The growth in consumer demand is described in a January 2013 report by the World Economic Forum's Sustainable Consumption Initiative, prepared in collaboration with Accenture, a management consulting, technol-ogy services, and outsourcing company.[7] According to the report, "3 billion consumers are expected to enter the middle class by 2050, the vast majority of them from developing markets. These emerging middle class consumers want a lifestyle like today's western lifestyles, one characterized by conspicu-ous consumption and intense resource use. With a global population already consuming resources equivalent to more than 1.5 Earths annually, we cannot continue on this path."

In "Conservation by Design: A Strategic Framework for Mission Success,"[8] The Nature Conservancy (the Conservancy) reveals the threats of continuing to ignore the value of nature. The Conservancy describes the shrinking opportunities for people to support themselves through sustainable environments when there are "fewer fish to catch, less available clean water, more soil erosion and a growing potential for conflict as people compete to have and control these increasingly limited resources."

Planet Earth is on the wrong course. An expanding consumer population has demonstrated a growing appetite for goods and products, using natural resources in increasing amounts. Moreover, too many companies have exploited and managed resources irresponsibly, degrading and depleting the world's water, forests, and soil. Unfortunately, governments, which are entrusted to protect the interests of the people, have not succeeded in addressing the challenges of the world's ecosystems.

Yet, a better future is possible. The Conservancy shows what is possible as well as the path forward. The Conservancy envisions a world where "forests, grasslands, deserts, rivers and oceans are healthy; where the connection between natural systems and the quality of human life is valued; and where the places that sustain all life endure for future generations."[9] The Conservancy collaborates with businesses, other NGOs, and governments to preserve "healthy ecosystems that support people—their health, their livelihoods, their futures—and host the diversity of life on Earth."

Market forces present the most powerful force to save our planet and all living things. In fact, many businesses are reversing their past practices of harming the environment, and some are now taking affirmative steps to achieve compelling results in advancing the Earth toward the Conservancy's vision. Customers, employees, and investors are proving to be the necessary drivers. This chapter will show how twenty-first century companies have the resources, global reach, and self-interest to be the leading force in ameliorating the ecosystem.

THE RAPID DETERIORATION OF THE WORLD'S ECOSYSTEMS UNDER THE WATCH OF GOVERNMENTS

Earth is facing an environmental crisis that threatens lives, jobs, and global security. According to the Millennium Ecosystems Assessment Conditions and Trends Working Group,[10] "over the past 50 years, humans have changed ecosystems more rapidly and extensively than in any comparable period of time in human history, largely to meet rapidly growing demands for food, fresh water, timber, fiber and fuel. This has resulted in a substantial and largely irreversible loss in the diversity of life on Earth. In addition, approximately 60 percent (15 out of 24) of the ecosystem services it examined are being degraded or used unsustainably, including fresh water, capture fisheries, air and water purification, and the regulation of regional and local climate, natural hazards, and pests."

Drought is already driving mass numbers of farmers from their lands to the cities, where there are insufficient jobs and infrastructure and a lack of government response, which—in countries like Syria—can ultimately lead to hunger, frustration, and civil war.[11]

As shown in the chapter on climate change and energy, a special report by the Council on Foreign Relations,[12] brings attention to the destabilizing affects of storms, droughts, and floods. The threat arises from damage caused domestically from extreme weather, in addition to the disruption of "US interests in strategically important countries."[13]

Governments have attempted to respond to these environmental challenges. Most often, these approaches have taken the form of global summits and compacts between nations, reflecting the fact that environmental threats know no borders. In the summer of 2012, the Rio+20 United Nations Conference on Sustainable Development,[14] also known as Earth Summit 2012, provided an opportunity for 193 United Nations member states— including 57 heads of state and 31 heads of government, private sector companies, NGOs, and other groups to plan for a sustainable future. Rio+20 was the successor to the first Earth Summit of 1992 and 2002's Climate Change Convention in Kyoto.

Rio+20 focused on building "a green economy in the context of sustainable development in poverty eradication" and creating a framework for sustainable development. The outcome of Rio+20 was a nonbinding document, "The Future We Want,"[15] that also supports the development of the Sustainable Development Goals (SDGs). The SDGs, which include measurable goals for global sustainable development, are designed to follow up on the Millennium Development Goals (MDGs). The eight Millennium Development Goals (MDGs), adopted by all 193 UN member states, range from halving extreme poverty rates to halting the spread of HIV/AIDS to providing universal primary education by the target date of 2015. The MDGs form a blueprint to galvanize unprecedented efforts to meet the needs of the world's poorest.[16]

While the goals are laudable and some have been achieved or are on track, some policy experts have raised environmental concerns. "Whether in Davos or almost anywhere else that leaders are discussing the world's problems, they are missing by far the biggest issue: the rapidly deteriorating global environment and its ability to support civilization," according to Thomas E. Lovejoy, professor of science and public policy at George Mason University and biodiversity chairman at the H. John Heinz III Center for Science, Economics and the Environment.[17] Describing Rio+20 as "a failure of epic proportions,"

Kumi Naidoo, the executive director of Greenpeace International, referred to the final negotiated statement as "the longest suicide note in history."[18]

In the June 7, 2012 issue of the journal *Nature*,[19] leading scientists—biologists ecologists, complex-systems theoreticians, geologists, and paleontologists from the United States, Canada, South America, and Europe—predicted that population growth, ecosystem destruction, and climate change could continue to move Earth toward an irreversible change in the biosphere, a planet-wide tipping point that would have perilous consequences. "It really will be a new world, biologically, at that point," cautioned Anthony Barnosky, lead author of the *Nature* article, and professor of integrative biology at the University of California, Berkeley. "The data suggests (*sic*) that there will be a reduction in biodiversity and severe impacts on much of what we depend on to sustain our quality of life, including, for example, fisheries, agriculture, forest products and clean water."

Co-author Elizabeth Hadly of Stanford University reported that she "just returned from a trip to the high Himalayas in Nepal, where I witnessed families fighting each other with machetes for wood—wood that they would burn to cook their food in one evening. In places where governments are lacking basic infrastructure, people fend for themselves, and biodiversity suffers. We desperately need global leadership for planet Earth."

To make matters worse, due to economic challenges, government is slashing its key role of sponsoring scientific research necessary to address the environment. Stephanie Kirchgaessner wrote in the *Financial Times* that "while lawmakers have focused on belt tightening as a response to concerns about the nation's long-term fiscal health, government investment in almost all areas of research is under threat."[20]

Governments face a variety of challenges in attempting to restore and protect the world's ecosystems. First, governments represent nation-states with clearly defined borders; officials are accountable to their constituents who often focus on immediate and parochial interests. Second, governments have an array of stakeholders to manage and many issues to balance. When people are out of jobs, concerns about protecting ecosystems can seem to the voting public as conflicting with what appear to be more immediate needs. Third, government leaders are usually not in office long enough to establish and implement long-term visions and strategies, while ecosystem planning requires longer-term thinking and investments. Finally, many governments are composed of coalitions of parties with a variety of interests and constituents.

If governments have a mandate that is too short-term and parochial to protect ecosystems in a meaningful way, then perhaps corporations spanning borders, driven by market interests, can achieve the promised land.

COMPANIES ARE PIONEERING ADVANCES IN CONSERVATION

A number of companies are paving the way forward by creating solutions to conserve water, forests, and arable land. They are stepping in front of the crowd as innovators and global problem-solvers to distinguish themselves in the marketplace among customers, employees, and investors. These companies are on a trajectory to build a better world, while burnishing their brands and increasing shareholder value.

Four corporations have been chosen for discussion in this chapter because of their leadership and innovation in developing environmentally friendly solutions for the manufacture of their products and their services to customers. As these case studies demonstrate, company efforts are enabled and leveraged by powerful collaborations with NGOs/nonprofits and by healthy interaction with governmental actors.

Ecolab, with a 90-year history of helping hospitals, hotels, and food services to find new solutions that address cleanliness, health, and safety, recently merged with Nalco, a company known for helping its heavy industry clients to be more sustainable. The merged company is creating a new model and brand, integrating sustainable solutions among all of its services.

Kimberly-Clark (K-C), the company noted in the opening of this chapter for its use of wood derived from the boreal forest, is an excellent example because of their bold shift in 2009. After tussling with Greenpeace for four years over the sourcing of their fibers, K-C transformed from a position of resistance and opacity to become a leader in sustainability, transparency, and accountability through a partnership with Greenpeace and other NGOs. Additionally, K-C enhanced its advisory board to involve stakeholder expertise that is a model for its high level of engagement.

The Dow Chemical Company's collaboration with The Nature Conservancy is proving effective in reducing risks and costs, enhancing the brand, and fueling growth. Not only is the work piloted through a business-NGO relationship that is transformative to Dow in valuing nature with metrics for their own corporate decision-making, but the methodologies they developed will soon be adopted by 24 additional companies.

Finally, as discussed in the chapter on climate change and energy, Unilever is at the forefront in tying sustainability and responsibility with human welfare and the environment. At Davos 2013, Unilever chairman and CEO Paul Polman declared, "We have a very bizarre situation in the world right now where 890 million people go to bed hungry, not knowing if they will wake up the next day. And yet we waste about 30 to 40 percent of the food as if it doesn't matter. Businesses understand that any system where too many people are excluded or left behind is not a system that is in equilibrium."[21]

ECOLAB'S WORK IN CONSERVATION IS GROUNDED IN
THE COMPANY'S ORIGINS

With the purpose of making the world cleaner, safer, and healthier, Ecolab has four lines of business: clean water, safe food, abundant energy, and healthy environments. Following the merger of Ecolab with Nalco in December 2011, the company has 40,000 employees in 171 countries, 5,300 patents, and $11 billion in annual sales.[22] Their customers include many of the world's largest companies, such as Pepsico and Marriott, whose products and services range from food service, retail, hospitality, health care, commercial laundries, and food and beverage processing, to heavier industries such as oil, gas, and chemicals, pulp and paper, metals, mining, and mineral processing.[23]

Ecolab is particularly suited to advance the vision of healthy ecosystems that support people for three reasons. First, the company's "Total Impact" approach to products and services is "designed to increase efficiency, minimize the use of natural resources, and improve safety from sourcing to manufacturing to use and through disposal."[24] Second, the company's values derive from its founding in 1923, when a traveling salesman imagined and established a company that would create and sell a better soap for hotel guest rooms and kitchens. Third, the company's science-based approach involves 1,300 scientists around the world who study germs that can make people sick, learn about water, and develop innovations that leverage chemistry, equipment, packaging, and dispensing. Ecolab's 22,500 field experts work with customers on-site.

So while most companies can, at best, only improve their own footprint, Ecolab has an exponential impact by leveraging its expertise to help its customers reduce their use of natural resources. For example, Ecolab reports that in 2010, the company made it possible for its customers to save more than 368 billion liters of water worldwide with Ecolab's patented systems, up to 40 percent of a typical customer's water consumption through the use of another of their innovations, and up to 50 percent of water use by restaurant customers with their patented dish machine.[25]

Ecolab also reports making it possible for companies to save energy, sharing these examples from 2011: helping Marriott to save 17.6 million kWh of energy in 2011, helping one NV Energy station reduce coal consumption by 87,000 tons, and helping one NV Energy station to save $3.5 million in fuel.[26]

Ecolab's NGO partners include Water for People and the World Wildlife Fund (WWF), as described by Emilio Tenuta, vice president of Corporate Sustainability.[27] In the summer of 2012, Ecolab announced a two-year commitment to WWF to support the organization's Alliance for Water Stewardship (AWS) in establishing a global water standard and third-party verification system. Ecolab provides the WWF with financial and technical support to field test the draft AWS standard. Additionally, Ecolab helps to build market awareness of the need for an international water standard to address water challenges.

AWS was formed in 2009 with a belief in collective action to "promote responsible use of freshwater that is socially and economically beneficial as well as environmentally sustainable…Socially beneficial water use recognizes basic human needs and ensures long-term benefits (including economic benefits) for local people and society at large."[28]

AWS includes representation by the following organizations: The Nature Conservancy, Pacific Institute, Water Stewardship Australia, World Wildlife Fund, Water Witness International, Water Environment Federation, European Water Partnership, International Water Management Institute, UN Global Compact's CEO Water Mandate, and Carbon Disclosure Project.[29]

Investors are a key driver for Ecolab's forward progress. Bill Gates is one of the company's largest shareholders.[30] Ecolab considers itself well-positioned in the marketplace in the face of megatrends, such as the increasing world population, an aging demographic that is also living longer, and mutating and more resistant strains of infections.[31]

Ecolab has made sustainability its business by creating solutions that address the scarcity of natural resources that confront their commercial and industrial customers. In doing so, Ecolab adds to their own bottom line and their customers' bottom lines, while helping to preserve the world's ecosystems.

KIMBERLY-CLARK TO GREENPEACE: "YOU MADE US A BETTER COMPANY"

From 2003 until 2009, Kimberly-Clark was an "evil empire" to Greenpeace—an independent organization that uses protest and creative communication to expose global environmental problems and to promote solutions that advance a sustainable future.[32] Beginning in 2004, Greenpeace launched Kleercut, a now legendary campaign against K-C's use of fibers derived from Canada's boreal forest. Earlier rounds of talks between K-C and Greenpeace were unsuccessful until a breakthrough in 2009.[33]

K-C is a publicly traded company listed on the New York Stock Exchange with sales of $21.1 billion in 2012. The company is headquartered in Irving, Texas and has 58,340 full-time employees with sales in more than 175 countries.[34] Its products are marketed under brands such as Kleenex, Huggies, Kotex, and Depend.

This story has a good result, for K-C and for the world. Today, only a few short years after the standoff with Greenpeace, K-C's chairman and CEO,

Tom Falk, stated that "our business success entails providing people with the essentials for a better life while conserving the natural resources on which we all depend." Falk's letter in the company's 2011 Sustainability Report proudly announces that K-C "became the first US branded consumer tissue maker to offer tissue products certified by the Forest Stewardship Council (FSC) to North American consumers, while Kimberly-Clark Professional expanded its FSC certification to more than 95 percent of its tissue and towel lines in North America."[35] The company expanded FSC certification on tissue products in additional countries as well as attaining other achievements and creating initiatives in water conservation and replenishment.

Richard Brooks, who planned and launched Greenpeace Canada's Boreal Forest Campaign beginning in 2003, and who has coordinated and directed Greenpeace Canada's forest campaign since 2006, attests to K-C's transformation to a sustainability leader. "Kimberly Clark has gone from sourcing very little sustainable pulp to majority. That's revolutionary for a company of this size to make such a major change," said Brooks.[36] "They're producing millions of tons of tissue. This is unique."

Scott Paul was director of the US Greenpeace campaign in 2005, when the group decided to combine forces with the Canada campaign against K-C. Paul explained how a company is targeted.[37] Greenpeace works their way backwards, starting with a forest whose valuable ecosystem is under threat by forestry companies that are logging. It then researches the chain of custody to the branded companies that are buying from the destructive operators. Upon discovering that K-C was sourcing fibers from trees that were clear-cut from Canada's boreal forest, Greenpeace appealed to K-C to stop buying pulp from the logging company in Canada.

Paul elaborated that every negotiation is based on three central tenets: "First, (there is) an examination of fiber that is purchased. Greenpeace supports the Forest Stewardship Council (FSC) and encourages companies to purchase FSC-certified fibers. Second, companies must examine their supply chain and establish policies for which areas they will not source from. These are the so-called "threatened" or "endangered" forest regions or areas with particularly important biodiversity, habitat, or carbon value, or regions with important spiritual or cultural value. Here, we talk about mapping, land use planning, and stakeholder relations. Third, the company is expected to examine how it can reduce its fiber needs overall through greater efficiencies, recycling, or the use of alternative fibers like bamboo. Every corporate negotiation regarding forests is different, but they all come down to those three issues."[38]

The first phase of Greenpeace's campaign against K-C lasted from 2004–2007. This period was followed by a highly structured series of two-day meetings spanning several weeks with attorneys and policy experts from both sides. The third such meeting broke down and ended so badly that Paul said that Greenpeace "doubled-down" on the campaign for the next two years.[39]

In 2009, K-C chairman and CEO Tom Falk designated Drew Barfoot, a highly experienced and trusted executive, to negotiate one-on-one with Scott Paul as the exclusive point-of-contact for all intensive discussions. After Barfoot's retirement mid-year, the negotiations with Scott Paul were completed by Suhas Apte, another highly experienced and trusted executive of the company. The negotiations resulted in a notable press conference in Washington, D.C. announcing K-C's new commitments to sustainable forestry. From the time of that agreement forward, K-C embarked on the commitment to using 100 percent credibly certified fiber with strong preference to FSC certified fiber.

"That transformation was pretty significant from who that company was to who they became," said Paul. "Now Greenpeace and K-C get together every four to five months to review the goals to see where they are. One thing I admired about K-C: If K-C writes it down, they are really, really serious."

Paul recalled K-C executive Robert Abernathy slapping him on the back at one meeting and saying to him, "Greenpeace made K-C a better company...you can quote me on that."[40]

Paul also recalled giving a speech to employees several months after the agreement was finalized. He received a standing ovation. "I've heard that this is good for recruitment, retention, and morale," he added.

Suhas Apte followed Barfoot in leading the company's sustainability effort. He served as vice president of Global Sustainability from September 2009 until he retired in August 2012. Apte continues to serve today on the company's Sustainability Advisory Board which advises the company's global strategic leadership team and sustainability staff.[41]

Brooks, with Greenpeace Canada, elaborated on the very significant employee aspect of the campaign. "Throughout the five years, we were communicating with staff in factories via email, keeping them apprised of the campaign. People want to work at a company that they feel proud about," Brooks explained.[42] As a result, many employees were making individual financial contributions to Greenpeace, which depends almost entirely on private donations. Additionally, between 2004–2009 when there were no official conversations between K-C and Greenpeace, employees would encourage Greenpeace, revealing that they were seeing movement in the company's position internally.

Furthermore, by engaging employees in the conversation, Brooks reported that there were two positive outcomes in 2009 when the company finally agreed to change its policy to source sustainable pulp. First, he said, morale jumped. Employees saw their employer as a leader. Second, employees ran with the change. They felt empowered by the company's decision, and this helped K-C to make the transformation.

The legacy of the new directions of 2009 remains strong at K-C today. Sustainability has a central role in the company's strategic, financial, and operational plans.[43] In his letter at the opening of K-C's 2011 Sustainability Report, Apte described the company's Sustainability 2015 strategy and five-year goals under three pillars: People, Planet, Products. "In addition to our Sustainability 2015 goals, we have identified four focus areas in which we believe we can take an industry-leading role," Apte wrote. "These areas include forest conservation, access to water and sanitation in communities, responsible solutions for postconsumer waste, and providing access to essentials for a better life through our global social giving programs developed in partnership with our brands' health and hygiene products."[44]

Moreover, K-C has not just shifted its sustainability goals; the company is now transparent and accountable in reporting those goals, indicating exactly where they succeed and fall short. Additionally, K-C further enhanced its Sustainability Advisory Board (SAB) in order to take full advantage of its access to expertise on trends and best practices on sustainability. The SAB is composed of thought leaders and experts with a variety of perspectives worldwide, including finance, design, governance, and sustainability.[45]

The Greenpeace campaign demonstrates the importance of brand and reputation as drivers of K-C's sustainability strategy. Additionally, as the company expanded its sustainability strategy, it recognized greater values to the sustainability elements of risk-mitigation, energy efficiency savings, and business opportunities through innovation, particularly in emerging markets. When asked about the competitive advantages from the company's sustainability efforts, chairman and CEO Tom Falk cited "tens of millions of dollars in savings."[46] He also noted customer advantages "where we're selling products to our B2B customers as well as our consumer customers." Falk also spoke of gaining a recruiting advantage.

On the investor side, Falk commented in "We Learned How to Listen Better," published in the *MIT Sloan Management Review*, that "I'm starting to get questions from investors. On a recent investor relations trip, I spoke with one of our large longtime shareholders, and for whatever reason that day, all we talked about was sustainability."[47]

The K-C story illustrates many lessons: it's never too late for companies to adopt sustainability strategies, regardless of past opposition and even conflict; sustainability adds to the bottom line, in spite of previously held assumptions; and NGOs/nonprofits can become mutually beneficial partners, which will ultimately improve the world.

DOW AND THE NATURE CONSERVANCY BREAK
NEW GROUND IN VALUING NATURE

Andrew Liveris began to transform The Dow Chemical Company when he became the CEO in 2004. With the acquisition of Rohm and Haas, a specialty chemical company in 2009, Dow was positioned to provide a more comprehensive mix of products to its customers in value-added chemicals, plastics, and materials. With chemistry enabling more than 96 percent of manufactured products, Dow sought to create new technologies and solutions for world challenges, focusing in particular on "alternative energy, water purification, crop productivity, building efficiency, and many more solutions that improved lives while protecting the planet."[48]

Under Liveris' leadership, Dow shifted to become a more transparent and accountable company with a strategy oriented around sustainability. Aligned with these interests, Dow partnered with The Nature Conservancy (the Conservancy), a global NGO, to develop a tool to enable their own company as well as others to measure the impact of their actions on nature and surrounding communities. The tool was designed to provide the data for companies to make decisions to better mitigate risk, improve their bottom lines, benefit communities, and help preserve the ecosystem.[49]

In early 2011, Dow and the Conservancy began their collaboration to create a methodology to measure the value of nature to a company and a community in order to inform business decision-making and purposeful conservation outcomes. The first pilot project at Dow's Texas operations focused on valuing ecosystems services such as air quality, water supply, and coastal hazard protection. The approach included defining business decisions, projecting future scenarios, running biophysical models, assessing economic values, and evaluating options and trade-offs.[50]

"When our conservationists and Dow's engineers had their first conversations, we were speaking in different languages," recalled Mark Tercek, president and CEO of The Nature Conservancy. "But today, we are all on the same page, talking about incorporating the value of nature into business goals, decisions, and strategies."[51]

By the time the 2012 Progress Report was issued by Dow and the Conservancy, the first pilot project had been completed in Dow's Texas operations in Freeport, and the second project had been initiated in Santa Vitoria, Brazil. Moreover, Dow and the Conservancy had begun creating the Biodiversity and Ecosystem Services Trends and Conditions Assessment Tool (BESTCAT) for use by additional companies.[52] In fact, by June 2012, 24 major companies representing $500 million in combined revenue announced commitments to incorporate ecosystems and biodiversity into business strategy.[53] The companies included Alcoa, the Clorox Company, Coca-Cola, Dell, Dow Chemical, Duke Energy, Ecolab, Enterprise Rent-A-Car, FEMSA, General Motors, Hanesbrands, Kimberly-Clark, Lockheed Martin, Marriott International, Nike, Patagonia, TD Bank, Unilever, The Walt Disney Company, Xerox, Weyerhaeuser, and others. With regard to businesses collaborating with NGOs, Tercek commented that "environmentalists should take full advantage of the opportunity that partnerships with forward-thinking companies provide."[54]

The 24 companies also launched a report called "The New Business Imperative: Valuing Natural Capital,"[55] published by the Corporate EcoForum,[56] a membership organization for large companies that demonstrate a serious commitment to environment as a business strategy issue. The Corporate EcoForum report describes the business imperative to safeguard the natural goods and services on which the global economy depends: "Clean water and air, affordable raw materials and commodities, fertile soil to grow crops, abundant fish stocks, buffers to floods, droughts, fires and extreme weather, barriers to the spread of disease, and biological information to propel scientific and medical breakthroughs." The report notes that "each year nature provides $72 trillion of 'free' goods and services essential to a well-functioning global economy."

"The New Business Imperative: Valuing Natural Capital"[57] also explains the four benefits of "prioritizing ecosystems within business strategy: (1) cutting costs, (2) reducing risks, (3) enhancing brand and reputation, and (4) growing revenues."

The article continues with recommendations as to how companies can capture these opportunities: "(1) Assess your company's impacts and dependencies on ecosystems, (2) put a price on nature's value, (3) optimize resource use to minimize environmental degradation, (4) invest strategically in conservation and restoration, (5) engage your value chain to bring solutions to scale, (6) innovate in materials, processes and products, (7) build natural instead of man-made infrastructure, (8) leverage new natural capital markets and investment tools, and (9) join forces."[58]

"For its part, Dow has embedded sustainability and transparency within the company's culture," explained Neil Hawkins, vice president of Global Environment, Health & Safety (EHS) and Sustainability at Dow. The sustainability team for which he is responsible convenes to ensure that environmental, health, and safety standards and expectations of management are being implemented in every business unit. Additionally, Hawkins has product sustainability leaders in every business unit, supporting them in life-cycle analysis work in value chain and EHS implementation. "If you're a chemicals and materials company, you want risks managed well," Hawkins said.[59]

Hawkins is responsible to the Environmental, Health, Safety and Technology Committee of the Board of Directors. Additionally, he works with the Sustainability External Advisory Committee (SEAC), first launched in 1992. The SEAC is composed of leaders from around the world who have expertise in corporate social responsibility and the environment. The role of the SEAC is to provide advice, not oversight, and not to endorse; SEAC offers guidance to Dow executives about where they are not doing as well as they can, and lets them know where the opportunities are.

Dow's collaboration with the Conservancy is not only a value for the company but for many others who are also valuing nature for the benefit of their businesses and a better world.

UNILEVER: LIVING THE GOOD LIFE

No chapter on ecosystems is complete without a discussion of Unilever and its innovation and leadership in sustainability. Chapter two, which addresses climate change and energy, provides a more comprehensive description of Unilever and their sustainability strategy. The company's Sustainable Living Plan, launched in November 2010, commits to three outcomes by 2020: "To help more than one billion people take action to improve their health and well-being; to halve the environmental footprint of the making and use of our products; and, to source 100 percent of our agricultural raw materials sustainably."[60]

Unilever makes the business case for integrating sustainability into its brands by recognizing that sustainability appeals to consumers and retailers, fuels innovation, helps develop new markets in developing countries, saves money for the company and its customers, and inspires employees and prospective employees.[61]

Unilever's strategy for protecting ecosystems includes goals for reducing the use of water in manufacturing and agriculture, as well as in the habits of consumers of the company's personal care products. The company claims significant progress in reducing the use of water in manufacturing and agriculture, yet consumers' use of water appears to be a more elusive goal. The company seeks to cut consumers' water use in half by 2020.[62] To this end, they work on "The Five Levers for Change" to inspire sustainable living: Make it understood, make it easy, make it desirable, make it rewarding, make it a habit. Unilever uses this approach to encourage customers to change their behavior and reduce their use of water.[63]

Half of Unilever's raw materials derive from forests and farms, so sustainable sourcing is important to the company. Unilever commits to source 100 percent of its agricultural raw materials sustainably by 2020 and records being on track to that goal. Similarly, Unilever, in partnership with governments, industry, and NGOs, has set a goal to increase recycling and recovery rates by 5 percent by 2015 and by 15 percent by 2020 in its largest market countries. To do so, Unilever will make it easier for customers to recycle packaging by using materials best aligned with treatment facilities in the various countries.[64]

According to Chief Sustainability Officer Gail Klintworth of Unilever, the company's business case for protecting ecosystems is multi-faceted. It includes risk mitigation with the scarcity of resources; a consumer base that is endangered due to flooding, droughts, hunger, and disease; cost management; and the opportunity for growth by finding sustainable solutions to global challenges. Unilever's sustainability mission and strategy is driven by consumers, employees, and investors.[65]

Unilever explains that "there is a clear business case for Unilever to source its raw materials sustainably. By taking a long-term view we can ensure security of supply, reduce costs and protect scarce resources."[66]

Protecting and restoring ecosystems is at the core of Unilever's business strategy. Its products are designed and manufactured with sustainability in mind. Unilever's success is dependent on their effectiveness in building a better world.

SPURRING GOVERNMENT INTEREST IN PRESERVING GLOBAL ECOSYSTEMS

Protecting the most exceptional ecosystems and habitats is vital to preserving most of life on Earth.[67] Consider the Amazon rainforest in Brazil, the forests and carbon-rich peatlands in Indonesia,[68] and the boreal forest in Canada. These are just a few of the natural resources owned by national governments. Yet, these governments have neglected their responsibilities.

According to Brooks at Greenpeace Canada, involving businesses in demanding changes from governments has been a highly effective approach. "Businesses care about their brands and their employees. And once they're engaged, you have partners worth billions, and you have employees. Then you can go with companies to ask governments to protect forests."

Brooks explained that "governments have to be forced to embrace the responsibility that they inherently have as owners of the forest." As to the motivation for companies to advocate for government regulation of ecosystems: "Companies want an even playing field," he said. "They also want their supply chain operating under the same rules, and as much choice as possible among legitimate fiber suppliers."

BSR (Business for Social Responsibility) is a global NGO that works with businesses to create a just and sustainable world. BSR's study of "Global

Public Sector Trends in Ecosystem Services, 2009–2012,"[69] reveals five trends showing governments' growing interest in ecosystem services. Ecosystem services are defined as benefits that derive from the ecosystem and contribute to personal health, jobs, and safety. Ecosystem services include provisioning services—goods and products such as freshwater, wood, and fiber; regulating services—natural processes regulated by ecosystems, such as filtering water and control of the climate and disease; cultural services—nonmaterial services such as spiritual, cultural, and recreational programs; and supporting services—maintainence of the other services, such as nutrient cycles and crop pollination.[70]

These are the five trends as described by Sissel Waage at BSR:[71]

1. National governments around the world are exploring expansion of GDP measures to include natural capital, which would include ecosystem services measurements.
2. Public-sector exploration of ecosystem services valuation is on the rise.
3. Governments around the world are showing interest in attracting investment in ecosystem services, such as through payments for ecosystem services (PES) and eco-compensation mechanisms.
4. Public sector-funded research on ecosystem services is proliferating.
5. Engagement between the private and public sectors on ecosystem services is limited but has grown each year.

Governments that are increasingly interested in measuring and managing environmental and social impacts of ecosystem services will need to learn about the advances made by the most innovative companies. Businesses will need to understand governments' interests. Collaboration will be required in order for the sectors to move forward together in the best interests of communities and the world. NGOs like BSR play a vital role in helping to facilitate and advance the discussion and progress.

CUSTOMERS, EMPLOYEES, AND INVESTORS DRIVING COMPANIES TO BUILD A BETTER WORLD

Biodiversity—the existence of a wide variety of ecosystems, animals, and plants—is essential to the planet's health. Biodiversity safeguards vital resources such as clean air and water, as well as providing the raw materials for food, medicines, and industries that support life. Yet overexploitation and habitat destruction imperil our Earth and damage is often irreversible.[72] Already 85 percent of ocean fisheries are overexploited or depleted, threatening sources of food and jobs. Nearly one billion people lack access to clean, safe drinking water, leading to poverty, disease, hunger, inequality, and instability.

"Environmental change is happening rapidly and exponentially. We are out of time... Ecosystem destruction is massive and accelerating. Institutional responsiveness seems lethargic to a reptilian degree," according to Lovejoy at George Mason University.[73]

There are a number of impediments to reversing this treacherous course. During these times of economic uncertainty, people too often mistake efforts to protect ecosystems as a threat to jobs. Moreover, while our better instincts are to safeguard the planet, the desire to consume abundantly and even to "have it all" appears to be human nature. Additionally, the vast emerging middle class in the developing world is also looking for its share of creature comforts after centuries of deprivation, if not oppression. Finally, the global nature of ecosystem challenges requires unprecedented cooperation between nation-states that often have diverging interests.

As shown in other chapters, there are cases where a leading NGO makes an example of a major brand that is causing harm. As with Greenpeace and Kimberly-Clark, the NGO can publicly challenge the company until it finally reverses course, embracing best environmental and social standards. Once the NGO sets an example within an industry, other companies will often follow the reformed company in adopting the new environmental and social practices.

With today's digital media, it takes even less effort to raise consumer awareness of a company's practices that harm the environment.[74] As a result, there is greater demand from companies for NGOs to collaborate to help businesses to adopt more environmentally positive approaches. This is leading some NGOs to shift from the role of activist protester to collaborator— and for new NGOs to emerge as consultants and advisors—in order to help achieve the mission of a better world.

Many top company executives understand that success in addressing global challenges will only come through partnerships with NGOs. "Instead of schmoozing clients or doing deals, he [Paul Polman, chairman and CEO, Unilever] will be brainstorming with Greenpeace and Oxfam on food security, persuading other business leaders to commit to sustainability programs, and hanging out with social entrepreneurs, according to a savvy observer at Davos 2013."[75]

Consumers expect companies to be serious about sustainability, and they want action and evidence, not just words. 80 percent of Americans don't believe companies are addressing all of their environmental impacts, and only 44 percent trust companies' green claims. Consumer skepticism can go straight to the company's bottom line, since the 2012 Cone Green Gap Trend

Tracker says that "as many as 77 percent would be willing to boycott if misled."[76] When you read Cone's conclusion that "American consumers expect companies to address the full environmental impact of a product's lifecycle, from the impacts associated with manufacturing the product (90 percent), to using it (88 percent), to disposing of it (89 percent)," it is clear that Ecolab, Kimberly-Clark, Dow, and Unilever are on the right track in understanding the consumer market.

Globally, consumer trust in corporations has dropped as well. According to the Brand Asset Valuator, conducted by BAV Consulting, trust has declined by 50 percent since the financial crisis in Fall 2008.[77] Furthermore, BAV recommends that companies can distinguish themselves in the marketplace through socially responsible practices. Their results show that 63 percent of respondents, who are consumers in 18 countries, make it a point to buy from "companies whose values are similar to their own," and 69 percent feel that "they and their friends can change corporate behavior by supporting companies who do the right thing." BAV concludes that "brands from companies with a strong record of social responsibility have greater usage (+33 percent) and preference (+39 percent), as well as greater loyalty (+27 percent), among consumers worldwide representing 78 percent of global GDP."[78]

Investors, consumers, and employees are key players in a company's increased focus on sustainability. Corporate leaders who seek to maximize long-term shareholder value recognize and promote the importance of the environment. "There's...a strong correlation between financial performance and performance on environmental and social issues—we've found there's an 11 percent higher return from companies that demonstrate high environmental and social standards," says William Bulmer, director for the Environment, Social, and Governance Department at the International Finance Corporation (IFC), the private sector arm of the World Bank.[79] Smart investors see this connection as well.[80]

Companies at the environmental forefront also have better workforces. Studies show that such companies attract and retain the best employees, while enhancing their motivation to deliver higher productivity by as much as 16 percent. "Adopting green practices is...good for your employees and it's good for your bottom line. Employees in such green firms are more motivated, receive more training, and benefit from better interpersonal relationships. The employees at green companies are therefore more productive than employees in more conventional firms," according to Professor Magali Delmas of UCLA and Sanja Pekovic from France's University Paris-Dauphine, who published "Environmental Standards and Labor Productivity: Understanding the Mechanisms That Sustain Sustainability" in the *Journal of Organizational Behavior*.[81] In fact, BAV reports that "70 percent of workers in our survey (and 91 percent of millennials) said they 'would work for less money at a company whose culture they believed in.'"[82]

It will continue to be important to discern which companies are "green washing" as opposed to becoming more sustainable. Let's apply the definition of sustainability from the first chapter—a sustainable company finds solutions to protect the environment and serve society while pursuing their profit motive, measures their impact, and provides the public with an annual sustainability report along with the company's financial report. In order to assess a company's sustainability, consider the NGOs with which the company consults to derive expertise, the level in the company where the NGOs have the relationship and the depth and quality of the engagements, the degree to which the CEO and board of directors seem engaged and aware of significant environmental and social impacts, the nature of stakeholder engagement on material issues, and the company's transparency in reporting on its environmental and social impacts. For each of the companies described in this chapter—Ecolab, Kimberly-Clark, Dow, and Unilever, the standard of being a sustainable company seems to be met.

ACHIEVING THE VISION

The Nature Conservancy describes a better world where "forests, grasslands, deserts, rivers and oceans are healthy; where the connection between natural systems and the quality of human life is valued; and where the places that sustain all life endure for future generations."[83] Some global corporations are recognizing the imperative to achieve this mission and vision in order to build thriving businesses. They are transcending barriers to ecosystem protection by working with their customers, suppliers, and across national boundaries. Only companies have the resources, global reach, and self-interest to achieve what governments cannot.

CHAPTER 5

EDUCATION

> Knowledge emerges only through invention and reinvention, through the
> restless, impatient, continuing, hopeful inquiry human beings pursue in
> the world, with the world, and with each other.[1]
>
> —Paulo Freire

SEVENTY-EIGHT PERCENT OF EIGHTH GRADERS IN MICHIGAN MET THE STATE'S
standard for proficiency in science in 2009. The real story, though, is that
the state's standard is far below the National Assessment of Educational
Process (NAEP) cutoff for merely "Basic" performance in science. In fact,
only 26 percent of the state's eighth graders meet the benchmark for college
readiness when they ultimately graduate high school.[2]

The national picture is even bleaker. Change the Equation indicates that
"two-thirds of states we studied reported that most of their eighth grade
students were proficient in science in 2009. By contrast, ACT reported that
in 2009, only 13 percent of US eighth graders were on track to do well in
introductory college science courses."[3]

A well-educated workforce is essential for businesses to be competitive
in the global marketplace. Skilled talent is necessary to develop advances in
technology, products, and services to meet the needs and demands of existing and emerging populations. New generations who are educated in science,
technology, engineering, and math (STEM) will be valuable to businesses in
advancing solutions to vital global issues such as climate change and energy,
food supply and agriculture, health care, ecosystems, and more.

Through its coalition of business CEOs, Change the Equation pledges to
foster widespread literacy in STEM that sparks an innovative spirit in students and prepares them for postsecondary options.[4] A report by Change the
Equation states that "students who gain a strong STEM foundation today
will face brighter prospects in years to come: Their skills will be resilient even
as markets and technologies change. States that focus on the STEM learning of their youth are investing in a prosperous future where they can attract
innovative new industries."[5]

Success in educating young people in STEM translates into opportunities
for employment and self-sufficiency for families and improved economies
everywhere. During the sluggish economic years between 2009 and 2012,
for example, there were nearly six unemployed people for every job opening
in Michigan. In STEM, by contrast, there was more than one job for every

unemployed person who had STEM skills. Nationally, there were nearly two STEM jobs listed for every unemployed person with a STEM background.[6]

Young people growing up without adequate STEM skills will be on the losing side of the increasing gap between rich and poor in the United States.[7] In the United States, STEM employment grew three times faster than non-STEM employment over the last 12 years, and is expected to grow twice as fast by 2018.[8]

"Not only are STEM educated students advantaged in the obvious fields of computers and technology, but also in careers that one might not associate with them such as fashion, waste management and recycling, and construction. A car, for example, is just a finely tuned computer," explained Linda Rosen, Ph.D., who is the CEO of Change the Equation.[9]

Society's role is to provide all of its children with the education to lead fulfilling lives and to become productive citizens for a sustainable universe. In more basic terms, the education system is intended to prepare students to become employed and contributing members of their communities. Although such aspirations have been fundamental to our way of life in the United States for well over a century, the evidence shows that our education system is failing in this mission.

The imperative to educate children and young adults is not only a matter for the United States but also throughout the world. Governments alone have not been able to achieve society's interests, nor meet the needs of employers, in preparing people for the workforce of today and tomorrow.

Some businesses are emerging as a new and vital force by partnering with governments and NGOs/nonprofits to find new solutions to improve education. Together, they are finding ways to provide the education that students require to be successful, fulfilled, and effective contributors in the world.

THE EDUCATION CRISIS AFFECTS INDIVIDUALS AND SOCIETY

Education is essential for individuals, economic growth and development, and peace and stability. When education is in crisis, so are our communities and our world.

In the United States, people with a high school diploma are nearly twice as likely to be unemployed as those with a college or advanced degree, according to a report by the US Department of the Treasury and the Department of Education.[10] African-American and Latino students are at the greatest disadvantage since they complete college (associates degree and higher) at much lower rates (28 percent and 20 percent, respectively) than whites (46 percent) and Asians (62 percent).[11]

A college degree is critical for employment. It's estimated that three million jobs go unfilled every month in the United States because there are an insufficient number of people who have the necessary educational skills and preparation.[12]

There are even concerns that the quality of high school education in the United States is inadequate to prepare students for college. For example, only 45 percent of high school graduates are ready for college level math, and 30 percent are ready for college level science.[13] In fact, according to Change the Equation, high school students in 17 industrialized nations performed better than US students in math.[14]

Society benefits as well from the higher employment rates and salaries of college graduates. Greater incomes generate more tax revenues for federal, state, and local governments. Furthermore, government expenses for social programs are far lower for college graduates than for others.

But education has an even more profound societal effect. Education facilitates socioeconomic mobility, often referred to as "the American Dream," popularized by James Truslow Adams in his 1931 book *The Epic of America*.[15]

The American dream, that dream of a land in which life should be better and richer and fuller for every man, with opportunity for each according to his ability or achievement. It is a difficult dream for the European upper classes to interpret adequately, and too many of us ourselves have grown weary and mistrustful of it. It is not a dream of motor cars and high wages merely, but a dream of social order in which each man and each woman shall be able to attain to the fullest stature of which they are innately capable, and be recognized by others for what they are, regardless of the fortuitous circumstances of birth or position.

Also referred to as "intergenerational mobility," this cherished principle maintains that education furthers children beyond the limitations of their parents' economic status. A college degree can be powerful in fostering economic advancement. On the one hand, without a college degree, "children born in the lowest income quintile have a 45 percent chance of remaining in the bottom quintile as adults, and a nearly 70 percent chance of ending up in the bottom two quintiles."

On the other hand, according to the Departments of the Treasury and Education report: "with a college degree, children born in the bottom quintile have less than a 20 percent chance of staying in the bottom quintile of the income distribution and about an equal chance of ending up in any of the higher income quintiles."[16] These results are echoed in data provided by Brookings.[17]

Given the power of higher education to influence one's likelihood of employment, compensation level, and socioeconomic status, the trend away from public funding for higher education is concerning. According to the Departments of Treasury and Education report, "previous generations of students attended colleges supported by state funds, which were funded by broad-based taxes on older generations. Now, students and their families increasingly pay their own way, given the increasingly common view that education is a private investment, rather than a public good...Individuals may not be able to finance this high-return investment in higher education on their own, and the economy-wide benefits of higher education suggest that a purely private financing market will lead to under-investment in education."[18]

Moreover, the failure to educate America's students threatens both national security and economic prosperity, according to a Council on Foreign Relations (CFR)—sponsored Independent Task Force report on US Education Reform and National Security:[19] "The lack of preparedness poses threats on five national security fronts: economic growth and competitiveness, physical safety, intellectual property, US global awareness, and US unity and cohesion...Too many young people are not employable in an increasingly high-skilled and global economy, and too many are not qualified to join the military because they are physically unfit, have criminal records, or have an inadequate level of education."[20]

The report shows that more than 25 percent of students do not graduate from high school in four years, and that the figure approaches 40 percent for African American and Hispanic students. Only 22 percent of US high school students are college-ready in all of their core subjects. "Human capital will determine power in the current century, and the failure to produce that capital will undermine America's security," according to the report. "Large, undereducated swaths of the population damage the ability of the United States to physically defend itself, protect its secure information, conduct diplomacy, and grow its economy."[21]

The education crisis is not only an American one. It's global. Worldwide, young people are three times more likely to be unemployed than their adult counterparts, and twice as likely to be underemployed, according to both McKinsey[22] and Gallup World.[23] A 2012 report by the Organization for Economic Cooperation and Development (OECD) also shows concerning results regarding education attainment among its member countries.[24] The OECD's mission is to promote policies that will improve the economic and social well-being of people around the world.

The OECD's 2012 report estimates that an average of only 39 percent of today's young adults in OECD countries are expected to complete tertiary education over their lifetimes—from a high of 50 percent or more in Australia, Denmark, Iceland, Poland and the United Kingdom to less than

25 percent in Mexico, Saudi Arabia and Turkey.[25] The report also indicates that only one-third of young adults are expected to complete tertiary education before the age of 30, from a high of more than 40 percent in Australia, Denmark, Ireland, Poland and the United Kingdom to a low of only 18 percent in Mexico.[26]

Growing unemployment and the accompanying inequality are fueling greater unrest in the world. "More than half of 106 countries surveyed by the International Labour Organization face a growing risk of social unrest and discontent," said the new World of Work Report published by the International Institute for Labour Studies (IILS). According to IILS Director Raymond Torres, "Unemployment rates remain high in the majority of [advanced] countries and income inequality has increased in more than half of the cases."[27]

The plight of education is front and center on the global intergovernmental agenda. The United Nations has been so committed to the primacy of education that "achieving universal primary education" was established as the second out of eight Millennium Development Goals (MDGs) in 2000.[28] The purpose of the MDGs is to support global development by improving social and economic conditions in the world's poorest countries. All 193 United Nations member states and at least 23 international organizations agreed to achieve the eight goals by the year 2015. The education MDG goal is to "ensure that, by 2015, children everywhere, boys and girls alike, will be able to complete a full course of primary schooling."

YOUNG PEOPLE ARE NOT EDUCATED FOR JOBS THAT ARE AVAILABLE

The tragedy of today's unemployment figures, and the corresponding opportunity for redesigning education, is that there *are* jobs for those who are properly prepared. Among the nine countries that were studied by the McKinsey Center for Government, "only 43 percent of employers surveyed agreed that they could find enough skilled entry-level workers." It's anticipated that this challenge for companies will grow. In fact, the McKinsey Global Institute predicts that there will be a shortfall of 85 million high- and middle-skilled workers worldwide by the year 2020.[29]

Furthermore, OECD's report of growing income inequalities in OECD countries shows that trends in globalization (trade integration) and technology, policies (e.g., trade integration, declining union coverage, tax policies, less strict employment protection) and education ("upskilling") were the key drivers of changes in wage inequality and employment.[30]

Changes in the world have the potential to continue to be adverse to all but the very rich. In order to ensure a more equitable and hence a more peaceful world, we must find new ways to educate, include, and connect people throughout the world with gainful employment, while also addressing other factors that widen the breach between the very rich and the very poor.

BUSINESSES PARTNER WITH NGOS/NONPROFITS AND GOVERNMENTS TO ADVANCE EDUCATION

The inadequacy of STEM education and barriers to higher education world-wide will perpetuate the gross mismatch between young adults and tens of millions of jobs. Economic tensions and social unrest will grow. This is bad for business and bad for the world.

Governments alone have not been able to address this education crisis. Businesses recognize the imperative and the value of their intervention as partners with governments and NGOs/nonprofits in finding solutions. Every one of these entities and all of us are mutually interdependent, so that collaboration is essential to this planet's success.

Not only do corporations have a deep and fundamental interest in our developing a highly qualified workforce, but they also bring powerful resources to the table. Financial resources are just part of the equation. Most significantly, businesses bring people with experience and expertise, along with their passion, commitment, and technological assets to create and drive change. Furthermore, unlike governments, companies have a broader global mandate; corporations cross borders, languages, and cultures to accomplish their purposes. When it comes to educating the world's workforce, businesses aren't limited by geographic boundaries. Consider the lack of true national educational standards simply across state borders in the United States alone.

Education is so central to business that it would be difficult to find a major company that does not contribute in some way to addressing this particular crisis, either through philanthropy, employee volunteering, executive involvement on nonprofit boards, or a combination. Companies do so, not only for the reasons discussed in this chapter, but also for education's appeal to employees and consumers.

Fortunately, there is a plethora of outstanding global and national nonprofits that excel at engaging companies to improve education and help students. One compelling approach is by involving business people in classrooms, mentoring, volunteering, and philanthropy. Junior Achievement, City Year, and Teach for America are outstanding examples of such organizations that have a global presence, as well as the College Summit, National Mentoring Partnership, and America's Promise that focus on the United States. These nonprofits and many more galvanize hundreds of the world's major corporations in service and funding to improve schools, keep students engaged and in school, make education more affordable, and help young people to gain access to higher education and jobs.

Successful partnerships have to manage tricky issues. First, some from the corporate sector might demand top-down instant results, while educators might seek more research-oriented, consensus-driven, longer-term approaches. To further complicate matters, leaders with limited terms— including politicians—require short-term solutions in order to show results to their constituents, whereas improving the education system requires longer-term problem solving. Additionally, there is the difficult and sensitive issue of outcome determination and measurement: Are these initiatives truly addressing systemic problems? Can achievement be documented? Can successful initiatives be replicated and scaled?

HP's Unique Approach To Address the Education Challenge

While there are a vast number of corporate initiatives to improve education, Hewlett-Packard's approach stands out as one of the most unique and promising. Hewlett-Packard (HP), headquartered in Palo Alto, California, is a multinational information technology corporation with over $120 billion in annual revenues. With operations in more than 170 countries, HP provides products, technologies, software, solutions, and services to consumers, small- and medium-sized businesses and large enterprises, including customers in the government, health, and education sectors.[31]

One of HP's global education initiatives, HP Catalyst,[32] was launched in 2010 not just to tweak the system or merely to be generous with money and equipment. Instead, HP set out to be a catalyst for NGOs/nonprofits, educational institutions, and schools to entirely reimagine teaching and learning, and to further encourage those who were demonstrating evidence of success. Most fundamentally, HP Catalyst's vision is that education will in fact prepare the next generation to solve the large and seemingly intractable social and environmental global challenges through "STEMx"– not simply Science, Technology, Engineering, and Math, but also important disciplines such as Computer Science, and essential skills such as creativity, collaboration, problem solving, entrepreneurial spirit, and other vital twenty-first century skills. HP committed to leverage the expertise of the company's engineers and scientists, tools and technology, and monetary grants in order to stimulate international collaboration among the most enterprising innovators in STEMx education.

Within less than three years, under the organizational direction of Gabi Zedlmayer, vice president of Sustainability and Social Innovation (SSI) at

HP, and led by Jeannette Weisschuh, director of Education Initiatives, SSI, Catalyst has galvanized and funded 56 NGO/nonprofits and academic institutions in 15 countries. HP's collaborations extend to another 180 organizations, and it has partnered with governments worldwide. Catalyst is creating new ways of raising STEMx literacy and engaging young people in solving vital social and environmental challenges. Further scaling HP Catalyst innovations could represent a major breakthrough in global education and lead the way to a better future.

"What does a powerful learning experience look like? How does technology enable it, and how could it be scaled for the benefit of many more students?" are the questions that HP sought to address, according to Jim Vanides, global program manager for HP Catalyst and member of the HP Sustainability and Social Innovation education team.[33] HP established "an international network of innovation sandboxes" to answer the question, as Vanides described it. Importantly, he explained that "breaking down all barriers is fundamental to success. Barriers between countries, secondary and college education, universities, and NGOs. At work, we solve problems through collaboration with people throughout the world. If young people learn to engage in learning and problem-solving without any silos, they will be prepared to have an enormous impact."

"We wanted to figure out how to create immersion learning experiences," said Zedlmayer.[34] "We know that technology alone is not the solution. So we decided to build a network of schools and people across boundaries and frontiers to find a different way of learning."

HP's Catalytic Approach Yields New Learning Experiences Worldwide

Exciting learning is occurring in the innovation sandboxes that have been catalyzed and funded by HP. For example, students in underfunded schools in Chicago have been conducting lab experiments remotely by using laboratories at MIT and the University of Queensland in Australia. For one project, they measure radiation emissions as a function of how far they hold their cell phones from their ears. They design the experiments themselves and watch the Geiger counter in Australia via live media. They run the experiments at home in the evenings at their own pace, produce lab reports, and then compare their results and experiences in the classroom with their teachers and fellow students.

These are classrooms with 35 students that never before had funds for lab equipment until HP established the remote labs. The results are already in: Students who use the virtual instruments show significant increases in test scores.

Dr. Kemi Jona (director, Office of STEM Education Projects, Northwestern University and HP Catalyst partner) explained. "Here's the vision: remote labs can be transformative at a district, state, or national level because you can create a server function or cloud solution that can provide a centralized shared facility of science experiments. A district no longer needs to buy lab equipment for each school as we do now in the current funding model…a model that is financially prohibitive for most communities."[35]

Far away from the streets of Chicago, students in the remotest villages in India are helping to find solutions to waste management issues by participating in science projects via mobile science labs, science fairs, and young instructor leader programs. This is happening through the Agastya International Foundation, another HP-funded Catalyst partner.

"This experience has transformed me," said Ajith Basu (chief program executive, Agastya International Foundation, and head, HP Catalyst "New Learner" consortium). "My greatest learning has been that children have no problems anywhere. The problem is the system and the lack of resources."[36] Even in the poorest, most remote neighborhoods of India, Basu says, "the children are much smarter than we were. Much faster. We must create systems around that. We can create powerful learning communities."

Catalyst is also bringing young people together from far-reaching parts of the world to collaborate. At a magnet middle school in Stamford, Connecticut, where 50 percent of the students are from educationally disadvantaged families, students are helping to solve local well water contamination problems through a partnership with middle school students in Shandong University Middle School in China. Throughout the process, the students from Stamford are learning Mandarin, and the students from China are learning English.

"This began with our seeing water contamination in our local water wells as a teachable moment," said Bryan Olkowski (former assistant principal, Scofield Magnet Middle School). "Then, by engaging in Catalyst, the world has opened up to us."[37] Since 2010, Scofield students have worked in partnership with students at their sister school in China, remotely and through exchange visits. They are collaborating using geospatial information studies (GIS), technology, and systems with university faculty and resources provided by HP.

Scofield teachers traveled to New Dehli in 2011 to present at the international Catalyst Summit, attended by all of the Catalyst members. A second group of Scofield teachers participated in the follow-up Summit in the spring of 2012 in Beijing. And HP has introduced new funders to Scofield, including the International Society for Technology in Education (ISTE).

According to Olkowski, 1,000 students in Connecticut had already benefited from Catalyst in 2011, as well as 640 in China. He believes that the project is a contributing factor to increasing math and reading scores on state tests for kids in his school. "This is what's possible for public school education," said Olkowski. And that key message from this project is spreading: United States Congressman Jim Himes visited Scofield, and Olkowski was asked to brief Congress on the project.

Furthermore, HP learned an important lesson from their most successful projects. "Projects that combine great teaching *plus* the right technology are able to create new and more powerful learning experiences for their students. This combination is what moves the needle on student achievement," Vanides said.[38]

HP: SCALING SOLUTIONS TO MAKE STEMx LEARNING ACCESSIBLE TO ALL STUDENTS

You might wonder how the vision of a universal STEMx education is possible, given that one billion children live in poverty, many in remote rural villages, others in densely populated urban slums. When so many children in developed countries aren't even getting decent educations, much less children in the developing world, how can education be truly transformed?

In fact, in just three years, the educational success of STEMx is already evident. Middle school and high school students from some of the world's most deprived communities are already working together on solutions for sustainable energy sources and to purify water. 130,000 students are already benefiting from the STEMx projects through 60 schools, universities, and NGOs around the world. These are the "innovation sandboxes" that Vanides referred to. Furthermore, plans are well under way to scale such educational opportunities to reach millions.[39]

Essential to Catalyst's success has been its network of partnerships. Catalyst has two lead partners:

- The International Society for Technology in Education (ISTE) describes itself as the premier membership association for educators and education leaders engaged in advancing learning and teaching through innovative and effective uses of technology in PK-12 and teacher education. Founded in 1979, ISTE has become the trusted source for professional development, knowledge generation, advocacy, and leadership for innovation.[40]
- The NMC (New Media Consortium) characterizes itself as an international community of experts in educational technology—from the practitioners who work with new technologies on campuses every day; to the visionaries who are shaping the future of learning at think

tanks, labs, and research centers; to its staff and board of directors; to the advisory boards and others helping the NMC conduct cutting-edge research.[41]

To deepen and broaden partner engagement, Catalyst is organized into six international consortia, each of which is led by a key partner organization. These partners include Carnegie Mellon University (United States), FutureLabs (United Kingdom), Meraka Institute (South Africa), Agastya International Foundation (India), Sloan Consortium (United States), and Tsinghua University (China). Each of these consortia includes international collaborators representing non-profits, schools, and universities.[42]

To further advance sharing and collaboration, Catalyst and its partner, ISTE, convened over 120 educators, education experts, and policy leaders from 21 countries for the 2012 Catalyst Summit in Beijing to exchange best practices and plan next steps. Furthermore, the 2012 Summit provided opportunities for a number of Catalyst grantees to secure eleven million dollars in additional funding from Catalyst's foundation networks.[43]

Beyond the exchanges that occur among the Catalyst consortium partners, further collaboration takes place between HP and corporate, foundation, and government leaders. Jeannette Weisschuh participates in the Education World Forum (EWF), the largest global gathering of education ministers. "The focus here is on innovative concepts to jointly increase student performance around the globe, especially in STEMx education and entrepreneurship, using technology to increase student outcomes and enhance learning experiences and achievement in all disciplines, for the purpose of building a better world."[44]

Scaling solutions is a priority for HP and its partners. HP works closely with ministries of education throughout the world, the Organization for Economic Cooperation and Development (OECD), European SchoolNET, UNESCO, the White House, USAID, the Department of State, and the US Department of Education. Two particularly important HP partners are the World Economic Forum's Global Education Initiative and the Global Business Coalition for Education. Additionally, the Catalyst initiative is being assessed by the Center for Education Research and Innovation at the OECD. OECD's report, issued in May 2013, will be disseminated to governments, education ministries, and policy leaders worldwide.[45]

Zedlmayer and her team recognize the challenges of pursuing such an ambitious vision. "International collaboration is difficult. It takes time to develop trust and a common understanding of the value of working together," Zedlmayer said.[46] This is why Catalyst is designed with a hybrid approach that integrates in-person meetings with online interactions.

Catalyst is effective because it's not prescriptive, explained Gavin Dykes,[47] the program director of the Education World Forum, the largest global gathering of education ministers and the internationally recognized ministerial forum for debating future practice in education. Dykes commented that Catalyst works well because it sets the circumstances where innovation can be leveraged, and then convenes people in hubs through technology, face-to-face interaction, and a combination of both.

In its new report on *Education to Employment*, McKinsey points out that there are two key features that distinguish successful education to employment initiatives. One is that "education providers and employers actively step into one another's worlds." The second is that "employers and education providers work with their students early and intensely."[48] HP's Catalyst initiative meets both of these criteria.

Catalyst is distinctive for its highly strategic approach. Catalyst proves that the amount of money thrown at a problem is not the best predictor of an initiative's effectiveness, and that the value companies bring to bear is not in the money alone. HP's total financial participation in Catalyst from 2010 through 2012 was $12 million in cash grants and technology—a relatively small investment compared to other signature education grants and initiatives. Perhaps the greatest value that HP has contributed is its leadership, imagination, expertise, and leveraging the quality of the education, NGO/nonprofit, and government partnerships that it has galvanized.

With Catalyst, HP is envisioning and achieving the greater potential for both the company and the world by affirming the interdependence of corporate success with the health and prosperity of the planet and its people. What's distinctive about Catalyst is that "all the learning creates far-reaching results in problems facing humanity," explained Ajith Basu, chief program executive for the Agastya International Foundation, and head of one of the six Catalyst consortia.[49]

HP: STEMx EDUCATION FOR YOUNG PEOPLE WORLDWIDE IS GOOD FOR BUSINESS

There are many benefits to HP for investing in STEMx education. To begin with, a 70 percent majority of HP's workforce is composed of engineers and scientists with STEMx educational backgrounds. The company depends on people being well prepared for its innovation agenda and technology. Additionally, HP relies on a global customer base that is STEMx-educated. HP also benefits when new generations grow up with positive familiarity with the company's products and services.

Moreover, through its education initiatives, HP becomes a valuable resource and partner to the world's leading education and policy institutions that are customers and prospective customers. According to Zedlmayer, "through our education initiatives, we have the opportunity to showcase the skills, capabilities, and strength of services that our more than 300,000 employees can bring to the table. Many ministries of education say 'I didn't know the breadth of your solutions.' We are also showcasing to universities, NGOs, and other customers and partners."[50]

Zedlmayer further explained the importance of HP's education initiatives with respect to the company's reputation. "When we started in education, we did research on our reputation around the world and what's important to our customers. First, they look to product, solutions, and services. Next, they look to how we perform with regard to the environment, and then, socially—specifically how we address the digital divide in terms of training and education."

Even more directly, HP has brought products and services to market after establishing their value through SSI. For example, SSI partnered with HP Labs India, a social enterprise, as well as local governments in Bangalore and Gujarat, to pilot a new personalized learning concept with local schools. For the pilot, HP provided students with containers equipped with the latest HP classroom technologies, and a solution developed by HP Labs called VideoBook. VideoBook automatically searches the Internet for relevant videos based on a student's textbook, allowing students to personalize the knowledge they are seeking, and receive it in a format that is engaging. Once VideoBook demonstrated a positive impact on student performance, HP's business division in India capitalized on the opportunity to market VideoBook as a product to education institutions in India. This resulted in a multi-million dollar business initiative. VideoBook went on to win the Education Technology category in *Wall Street Journal*'s 2012 Technology Innovation Awards.

Zedlmayer is particularly emphatic about the value of Catalyst in providing opportunities for HP employees to engage in meaningful service. She indicates that this is a means of recruiting and retaining the most valuable employees and fostering an *esprit de corps*. The positive feelings among the employees who participate in Catalyst, as well as HP's partners, were evident throughout the interviews.

Zedlmayer is devoted to weaving volunteer service throughout every opportunity. For example, when Shai Reshef (founder and CEO, University of the People, a free online university for people worldwide) asked Zedlmayer for funding, her response was consistent with her pro-volunteer philosophy. Zedlmayer agreed to a grant of $200,000, while adding her own recommendation and commitment: that 100 women employees from HP would serve as mentors to women students from University of the People. Zedlmayer understood that by engaging volunteers from her company, she would help transform 200 lives, not 100.

OVERSIGHT AND ACCOUNTABILITY ARE PROVIDED BY HP LEADERSHIP BODIES

Oversight for HP SSI, led by Gabi Zedlmayer, is provided by the Pan-HP Global Citizenship Council. Zedlmayer reports to the executive vice president and chief communications officer who reports to HP's president and CEO.

While HP's Executive Council has overall responsibility for global citizenship as part of the company's business strategy, the Global Citizenship Council, co-chaired by Zedlmayer and Ashley Watson, the vice president of Ethics and Compliance, helps to ensure the company's commitment and alignment to HP's global citizenship objectives company wide. The group meets at least quarterly to strategically promote and advance global citizenship, through integrated risk and opportunity assessment, governance, and policy oversight. Agendas focus on environmental issues, human rights, and supply chain, to name a few.

HP Catalyst has its own advisory council composed of leaders from ISTE, New Media Consortium, the Exploratorium, Hewlett Foundation, World Bank, UNESCO, OECD, the Consortium for School Networking (CoSN), and the six consortia members. The advisory council meets for two hours, three or four times annually, usually coinciding with their Annual Summit, the ISTE conference in the United States, and the Education World Forum, which most of the Advisory Council members attend. The group discusses Catalyst's progress and plans going forward.

Its most recent agenda was the Catalyst Academy, a new initiative to scale Catalyst innovations through global teacher training and sharing of best practices that emerge from the innovation sandboxes. The Academy offers a wide variety of STEMx topics offered as online workshops, mini-courses, or "massively open online courses" (MOOCs).[51]

ERICSSON'S CONNECT TO LEARN: A PARTNERSHIP PROVIDING ACCESS TO EDUCATION FOR STUDENTS IN EMERGING COUNTRIES

Another noteworthy corporate initiative is Connect to Learn, a partnership between Ericsson, the Earth Institute at Columbia University, and Millennium Promise. Its purpose is to end poverty by enabling access for students and teachers to world-class information and educational resources, while fostering collaborative learning, cross-cultural understanding, and global awareness.

According to the UN, 61 million children lack primary school education, and 71 million adolescents, ages 12 to 15, are not in school.[52] Furthermore, the Broadband Commission, together with UNESCO, shows that 774 million adults cannot read or write—primarily people in developing countries—of which 64 percent are women.[53] The second of the eight Millennium Development Goals (MDGs) is to achieve universal primary education by the year 2015. ICTs and broadband can improve the delivery of education, thereby enhancing educational outcomes.[54]

Connect to Learn's partners include the following.

- Ericsson, a leading provider of technology and services to telecom operators, supporting two billion subscribers worldwide. Working in 180 countries, with 110,000 employees, and revenues over 27 billion SEK the company is headquartered in Stockholm, Sweden.[55]
- The Earth Institute, based at Columbia University and led by Jeffrey Sachs, Ph.D. The institute brings together people and tools needed to address some of the world's most difficult problems, from climate change and environmental degradation, to poverty, disease and the sustainable use of resources. For Connect to Learn, the Earth Institute advises on educational monitoring and evaluation.[56]
- Millennium Promise, an international NGO whose mission is to support the achievement of the MDGs. It raises funds to support the initiative.[57]

Key components of the initiative include connecting students and teachers to low-cost, mobile broadband and cloud computing, computer connections to classrooms in the United States, and scholarships for girls. With its power coming from the collaboration of these three partners, Connect to Learn has been implemented in secondary schools in Ghana, Tanzania, Senegal, Rwanda, Kenya, Chile, India, Malawi, Uganda, Brazil, Djibouti, Nigeria, and South Sudan. Within its first year, five thousand students were connected via mobile broadband and cloud computing. By the end of 2012, the number of students being served by Connect to Learn is up to sixteen thousand.

Ericsson leveraged the combination of three major assets to make online content accessible to students—mobility, broadband, and cloud. First, Ericsson made available its unique cloud computing system solution, which includes virus protection and content for all students via Ericsson's central server. Second, Ericsson launched Connect to Learn as a joint, shared value initiative to engage its customers—mobile broadband providers—to offer airtime to schools at a highly discounted rate. As an example, Ericsson was able to develop a public-private partnership with Djibouti Telecom and the ministry of education in Djibouti to deploy educational services and Internet access in half of all secondary schools.

Ericsson also has a project in Ghana. There, they are working with schools in the Millenium Village rural communities, such as Bonsasso—as well as in urban neighborhoods surrounding Accra—together with the local municipality and school systems. "Sharing value among the players in the value chain and in public-private partnership provides real opportunities to get scale," said Elaine Weidman-Grunewald (vice president, Sustainability and Corporate Responsibility, Ericsson).[58]

Connect to Learn focuses in particular on providing quality education for girls because they are most at risk of dropping out due to financial strains on their families. Furthermore, according to the Council on Foreign Relations, when 10 percent more of its girls go to school, a country's GDP increases an average of 3 percent.[59] There are a multitude of gains when girls stay in school, including better health outcomes, fertility patterns, employment opportunities, and women's empowerment.

Here are a few more benefits to girls and society when they have access to education:

- Girls who receive an education marry later, have fewer children, and are more likely to seek healthcare for themselves and their children.
- Girls with secondary schooling are up to six times less likely to be married than those who have little or no schooling.
- The positive impact of girls' education has been shown to transcend generations, resulting in better health outcomes among women, their children, and eventually, their grandchildren.[60]

The business case for Ericsson to invest in Connect to Learn is three-fold, according to Weidman-Grunewald: First, Ericsson is driving mobile broadband use in remote areas among schools and governments, together with its customers. "Bringing the Internet to schools will require adequate bandwidth, which will drive traffic in our network. Second, Ericsson is investing in sustainable development of communities, which is good for business and for helping to build the brand. Third, Ericsson sees a positive business potential in educating girls. "The tech field has traditionally been very male dominated. While none of the girls have completed their educations yet, we do hope that in the future they can be a potential workforce."[61]

Weidman-Grunewald reports directly to Hans Vestberg, Ericsson's CEO. Weidman-Grunewald meets bi-monthly with the internal board that governs the sustainability and corporate relations area, including several members of the company's executive team, and at least annually with the Ericsson board of directors.

Connect to Learn illustrates the power of business collaborations with NGOs and government to transform global education. This partnership leverages Ericsson's technology, expertise, and resources to surmount educational barriers and lack of infrastructure in the developing world.

INTEL STRENGTHENS EDUCATION WORLDWIDE

Intel and the Intel Foundation have invested significant resources in establishing and supporting more than 200 education programs in over 70 countries, and have provided more than one billion dollars in the last ten years to enhance teaching and learning environments. In collaboration with governments, policy makers, NGOs, and local businesses, Intel helps to implement elearning solutions to facilitate professional development for teachers; foster student achievement and development of twenty-first century skills; and enable access to relevant, localized digital content.

Intel's model of education transformation combines advocacy for policy reform, curriculum standards and assessment, sustained professional development, information and communications technology (ICT), and support for research and evaluation. Through scalable programs, technology solutions, and ecosystem support, Intel helps countries improve the quality of their education systems and compete in the global marketplace.[62]

In Argentina, for example, Intel established a program called Conectar Igualdad to distribute three million netbooks over the course of three years to improve educational equality and reduce the web literacy gap. "In addition to delivering Intel-powered classmate PCs and other netbooks to secondary and vocational schools, teacher training institutes, and special education institutions across the country, the program provides much-needed infrastructure improvements, professional development for teachers, and new opportunities for economic growth."[63]

Based on Intel's experience with Conectar Igualdad, the company makes three recommendations for technology integration to transform education:

1. Strong leadership supported by long term funding: Conectar Igualdad was established as a federal initiative, implemented by federal agencies, with support from the President, as well as local governments and school districts. Funded by revenues from the national retirement and pension fund, Conectar Igualdad is ensured of long-term sustainability.
2. Independent oversight: The Organization of Ibero-American States ensured transparency and oversight for the purchase of the netbooks, and an executive committee provides ongoing oversight.
3. Early consideration of all components to transform education: Planning was conducted from the outset for professional training and

development for 19,000 teachers to integrate the use of the new technology into their teaching, and systems were underway for research and evaluation.[64]

It is also clear from the case study that stakeholder engagement was integral to every aspect of the process as well as to the creation of long-term oversight.

Intel is deeply engaged in strengthening education in the United States as well. Craig Barrett (former chairperson and CEO, Intel Corporation) chairs the board of Achieve,[65] a nonprofit that states as its purpose that "all students should graduate from high school ready for college, careers and citizenship."

One of Achieve's main initiatives is helping to attain the Common Core.[66] "The Common Core State Standards provide a consistent, clear understanding of what students are expected to learn, so teachers and parents know what they need to do to help them. The standards are designed to be robust and relevant to the real world, reflecting the knowledge and skills that our young people need for success in college and careers. With American students fully prepared for the future, our communities will be best-positioned to compete successfully in the global economy."

In June 2010, the Common Core State Standards for English Language Arts/Literacy and Mathematics were released by the National Governors Association Center for Best Practices and the Council of Chief State School Officers.[67] Since then, over 45 states have adopted the Common Core State Standards and are now working to implement them.[68] The nonprofit organization Achieve, heavily funded by corporations, is providing advocacy as well as implementation planning tools for teachers and other vital support to advance the Common Core.

Intel describes the business case for investing in education in its corporate responsibility report. The company "views education is the foundation of innovation." Furthermore, as a technology company, Intel's profitability depends on its access to highly skilled employees, "a healthy technology ecosystem, and knowledgeable customers." Additionally, Intel states, "our education programs support our long-term corporate diversity objectives by encouraging girls, women, and students in underserved communities to pursue careers in science, technology, engineering, and math."[69]

BUSINESSES—IN PARTNERSHIP WITH NGOS AND GOVERNMENTS—CAN MAKE THE EDUCATION VISION POSSIBLE

International corporations seek to develop girls and boys, women and men to be educated, contributing members of the global workforce. First, companies need access to highly capable and motivated individuals to be effective problem solvers in communities throughout the world. Second, people who earn become consumers for company goods and services.

Governments have the authority and responsibility to educate young people. Academic institutions and NGOs are crucial partners. And businesses have the resources, global reach, and self-interest to make success possible. It is a win-win for companies, civil society, and governments to collaborate in advancing young people to lead fulfilling lives and become productive citizens for a sustainable universe.

CHAPTER 6

HEALTHCARE

Our greatest obstacle to building a healthier world is not that we don't care about our health...Our greatest obstacle is our imagination.
—Tom Farley and Deborah A. Cohen[1]

LET'S START BY COUNTING THE DEAD. FIRST, BY AGE GROUPINGS: IN LOW-INCOME countries, 40 percent of the dead are ages 14 and under, as compared to 1 percent in high-income countries.[2] Infant mortality, typically defined as death before five years, is the primary contributor to these rates.[3] Next, looking at people in the age group of 15–69, 43 percent are dead in low-income countries compared to 28 percent in high-income countries. That leaves only 17 percent of people in low-income countries who live to age 70 and older, compared to 71 percent in high-income countries. These data, issued by the World Health Organization, make it apparent that health in a country correlates with the country's economic status.

The World Health Organization shows that *how* people die also correlates to a country's economic status. If you live in a low-income country, you are most likely to die from a lower respiratory infection, a diarrheal disease, or HIV/AIDS. If you live in a middle-income country, you are most likely to die from ischaemic heart disease, stroke and other cerebro-vascular disease, or chronic obstructive pulmonary disease. If you live in a high-income country, you are far more likely to die from ischaemic heart disease, or from stroke and other cerebro-vascular disease, or lung, trachea, and bronchus cancers.[4]

Healthcare is a vital concern for companies seeking to expand market opportunities to engage billions of new consumers. Corporations require healthy employees to perform their jobs productively and also to reduce the company's healthcare expenditures. Healthy families at home allow employees to focus on their work. Moreover, healthy consumers have the purchasing power and interest in acquiring goods and services necessary for robust markets. A healthy population and an efficient healthcare system provide a sound economy in which companies can operate and thrive. For pharmaceutical companies in particular, solving healthcare challenges provides a special commercial opportunity to demonstrate their prowess for innovation and to partner with governments and NGOs who are key stakeholders.

Healthcare services, vaccinations, and medicines can reduce the death rate and improve the world's health. Access to these services by all people is key for moral, practical, and economic reasons. "Promoting and protecting health is essential to human welfare and sustained economic and social development. This was recognized more than 30 years ago by the Alma-Alta Declaration signatories, who noted that Health for All would contribute both to a better quality of life and also to global peace and security," according to the most recent World Health Organization (WHO) report, published in 2010.[5] The Alma-Alta Declaration to which the WHO report refers is the International Conference on Primary Healthcare held in 1978. The Declaration expressed the need for urgent action by all governments, all health and development workers, and the world community to protect and promote the health of all the people of the world.[6]

The centrality of global health to peace and prosperity is reflected in the United Nations Millennium Goals (MDGs). Three out of eight of the MDGs focus on improving global health outcomes. Established in 2010, the MDGs seek to reverse poverty, hunger, and disease affecting billions of people worldwide by 2015.[7] Governments, foundations, corporations, and NGOs have pledged over $40 billion to achieve the MDGs. MDG Number Four aims to reduce the under-five child mortality rate by two-thirds.[8] Goal Number Five seeks to improve maternal health by cutting the maternal mortality ratio by three-quarters, and achieving universal access to reproductive health.[9] MDG Number Six undertakes to combat HIV/AIDs, malaria, and other diseases.[10]

Looking beyond the MDGs, the NCD Alliance seeks to put non-communicable diseases (NCDs) on the global agenda and to generate solutions to this deadly threat to world health. "The NCD Alliance was founded by four international NGO federations representing the four main NCDs— cardiovascular disease, diabetes, cancer, and chronic respiratory disease. Together with other major international NGO partners, the NCD Alliance unites a network of over two thousand civil society organizations in more than 170 countries...The NCD Alliance uses targeted advocacy and outreach to ensure that NCDs are recognized as a major cause of poverty, a barrier to economic development, and a global emergency."[11] NCDs include cardiovascular disease, and stroke and cerebro-vascular diseases, the leading causes of death in middle- and high-income countries, which can be ameliorated with healthier lifestyles. Additionally, over one-third of all child deaths are linked to malnutrition, an NCD.[12]

The NCD Alliance proposed a post-2015 development agenda that recognizes NCDs "as an emerging issue in LMICs [low- or middle-income countries] given their epidemiological trends, and attributes the rise and causes of NCDs to complex global patterns of urbanisation, globalisation, and economic development which increase exposure to the leading NCD risk factors: tobacco and alcohol consumption, unhealthy diets and physical inactivity." There is a growing concern that as people in developing countries gain wealth, they are on the wrong path in developing some of the bad habits of people in the West, including obesity, smoking, and alcohol abuse. The report also recommends that "a greater emphasis should be placed on public health, health promotion, behaviour change, and disease prevention, with resources directed to addressing risk factors and creating the conditions for good health.[13]

Unfortunately, governments in the developing world, where the need is the greatest, too often appear to lack the capacity to fully address the healthcare needs of their citizens. A variety of complex factors present impediments: lack of national resources, the legacy of colonialism (including war and local conflicts), high levels of poverty, indigenous diseases, and limited education and infrastructure, among others.

Maureen Lewis, formerly chief economist in Human Development for the World Bank, and currently a visiting professor at Georgetown University, suggested that weak and corrupt governments have also contributed to the healthcare crisis. "Achieving the dramatic and permanent declines in mortality envisioned by the Millennium Development Goals is doubtful unless governments shift their attention to the institutional factors that affect performance in the health sector. A dysfunctional environment limits the chances that more funding can have an impact."

Lewis asserted that "funding without the necessary institutional strengthening could lead to perverse results," and that "priorities cannot be met if institutions don't function and scarce resources are wasted. Bribes, corrupt officials, and mis-procurement undermine healthcare delivery."[14]

The cases in this chapter will show a variety of approaches that companies are taking in partnership with NGOs, academic institutions, and governments to address global healthcare challenges. In each case, companies are benefiting communities while also improving their own financial and strategic opportunities in emerging markets.

ASTRAZENECA SEEKS TO EXTEND LIVES BY PROMOTING HEALTHIER LIFESTYLES AMONG ADOLESCENTS

NCDs such as cardiovascular disease, diabetes, and cancer caused 36 million deaths out of 57 million deaths (63 percent) in the world in 2008, according to the most recent figures provided by the World Health Organization.[15] "NCDs are caused, to a large extent, by four behavioral risk factors that are pervasive aspects of economic transition, rapid urbanization and twenty-first-century lifestyles: tobacco use, unhealthy diet, insufficient physical activity and the harmful use of alcohol," according to the World Health Organization.[16]

Furthermore, "the rapidly growing burden of NCDs in low- and middle-income countries is accelerated by the negative effects of globalization, rapid unplanned urbanization and increasingly sedentary lives. People in developing countries are increasingly eating foods with higher levels of total energy and are being targeted by marketing for tobacco, alcohol and junk food, while availability of these products increases. Overwhelmed by the speed of growth, many governments are not keeping pace with ever-expanding needs for policies, legislation, services and infrastructure that could help protect their citizens from NCDs."[17]

Furthermore, research shows that "NCD behaviors are on the rise among young people, and that they establish patterns of behavior that persist throughout life and are often hard to change,"[18] according to a report by Johns Hopkins University. The report indicates that adolescence is a critical period for intervention. In spite of such evidence, adolescents are rarely on the agenda when issues of NCDs are being discussed.

Young Health Programme

At the Clinton Global Initiative Annual Meeting in 2011, AstraZeneca announced its partnership with Plan International and the Johns Hopkins Bloomberg School of Public Health, to combat NCDs in young people through research, high-level advocacy, education, and health-skills training. AstraZeneca committed nine million dollars to this initiative that would extend over three years. The project is called the Young Health Programme (YHP). Its partners agreed to (1) improve scientific research on the health needs of the most disadvantaged youth to address behaviors that have a direct impact on the later development of NCDs; (2) advocate for policies and programs that address the connection between youth and NCDs over the next decade; and (3) develop "on the ground" community programs that address locally pertinent health issues and risk factors for NCDs.

Plan International is a children's charity that works with the world's poorest children so they can move themselves from a life of poverty to a future with opportunity.[19]

AstraZeneca is a global biopharmaceutical company headquartered in London, with annual sales of $28 billion. Its primary focus is the discovery, development, and commercialization of prescription medicines for six areas of healthcare: cardiovascular, gastrointestinal, infection, neuroscience, oncology and respiratory and inflammation. AstraZeneca views the YHP partnership as valuable in several respects: helping to improve outcomes for young people now and for future generations, engaging with opinion leaders and policy makers at a global level on addressing key barriers to healthcare, and motivating and inspiring employees about the impact of the program on the lives of young people.

"The potential impact of this work is huge," exclaimed Robert Wm. Blum, MD, MPH, PhD (William H. Gates, Sr. Professor and Chair of the Department of Population, Family and Reproductive Health, and Director of Johns Hopkins Urban Health Institute at the Johns Hopkins Bloomberg School of Public Health). "I've been in the field of research and adolescent health for over thirty years. Never before has a major company said that they would focus their work on adolescents. Our focus and mission is built around the most disadvantaged young people. For a company to shine its corporate spotlight on this population: This is major! This has the potential to be a big opportunity to inform public policy and decision making."[20]

Research. For the past three years, Blum has been leading the research for the AstraZeneca initiative. The objective is to develop an understanding of the health needs of the most disadvantaged youth across the world and to identify the barriers to their accessing health. The research program, the Wellbeing of Adolescents in Vulnerable Environments (WAVE study), has focused on very disadvantaged youth in the poorest areas of six cities: Baltimore; Ibadan, Nigeria—a site funded by the Bill and Melinda Gates Institute for Family Planning; Johannesburg; New Delhi; Rio de Janeiro; and Shanghai.

This WAVE study will provide a unique understanding of the health needs of disadvantaged adolescents and explore innovative solutions such as the use of mobile technologies to deliver health information and health services. Research outcomes will be used to update the community programs, inform health providers and health workers in the field of adolescent health about the needs of disadvantaged young people, and direct the improvements in health provision and health monitoring for young people, including addressing those behaviors that have a direct impact on the later development of NCDs.

Advocacy. The program aims to broaden global understanding, inspire support, and develop resources for adolescent health in order to increase access and uptake of services by disadvantaged young people. In conjunction with the NCD Child Alliance, the International Pediatrics Association, and the American Academy of Pediatrics, Blum's research group prepared an advocacy document to present the case for increased attention to adolescent behaviors that contribute to the onset of NCDs in adulthood. This document was presented at the time of the high-level meeting of the UN General Assembly in September 2011. Scientists, policy makers, and program planners came together in an "Emerging Issues Consultation" to review the most current research on a range of youth-related issues in order to guide research, policy, and program agendas related to impacting youth NCDs over the next decade.

A key driver for the consultation is that over the past decade, there has been an explosion of research on adolescent neurodevelopment, the biology of addictions, and the epigenetic influences on health and disease. However, much of this research was yet to be incorporated into youth health programming and policy, especially in low- and middle- income countries.

Programs. The third component of YHP is on-the-ground programs for young people. YHP programs are developed to address the most relevant and urgent local needs. For example, the YHP programs run by Plan focus on hygiene (India) and sexual reproductive health (Brazil, India, Zambia). In the United Kingdom, YHP addresses mental health among young homeless people. In Romania, YHP works to prevent cardiovascular disease. In South Korea, YHP works in suicide prevention and in the United States, YHP works to increase healthy behaviors that help young people achieve academic success, mental health, emotional well-being, and precursors to NCDs.[21]

The international children's charity Plan is YHP's global delivery partner working in Brazil, India, and Zambia. Plan works with the world's poorest children so that they can move themselves from a life of poverty to a future with opportunity. "If the young population is protected from HIV/AIDS and growing problems of health issues that are allied to economic growth—obesity, lifestyle choices, smoking, drinking—then the future is promising. Our hope is that they not succumb to the issues of the Western world," according to Tanya Barron, chief executive at Plan UK.[22]

The opportunity to make a valuable contribution is even greater in countries where the population comprises predominantly young people, noted Barron. "We're from aging countries," she explained, referring to the United States and the United Kingdom. "I've just returned from Uganda, where 80 percent of the population is under the age of 25. It's similar in many parts of Sub-Saharan Africa."[23]

mindyourmind

A key to the success of YHP is exemplified by the activities of another partner, mindyourmind. A Canada-based NGO, they are engaging young people in planning, designing, creating, and shaping programs and messaging for youth services. The organization also serves as a resource center for youth and emerging adults seeking information and resources "during tough times...a place to get unstuck."[24]

Maria Luisa Contursi launched mindyourmind in 2001 as the outreach component of a crisis service for youth and young adults.[25] At the time, the program had barely any resources. Today, the organization provides expertise and assistance to service providers—physicians, social workers, nurses, educators, and others—who wish to engage with youth, by employing young people as advisers on projects. mindyourmind is playing a valuable role within YHP to develop approaches to reach the world's most vulnerable communities, including the development of curricula for educators about mental health prevention, and the expansion of online resources. Based on input from its young advisors, this includes mobile apps for use in appointments or sessions with social workers and mental health providers as well as family physicians to refer young patients.

"We need to be where young people are," said Contursi. "At school, doctors' offices, in their communities, and online."[26]

The Young Health Programme will expand its reach this summer at the International Association of Adolescent Health World Congress in Istanbul. There, all three partners—Johns Hopkins, Plan, and mindyourmind—will serve on a panel that is being shaped and led by young people from YHP to advocate that young people should be involved in determining their own health states.

The partnership with mindyourmind increases the impact of the YHP by engaging young people in the project. It also expands mindyourmind's sphere of influence in connecting the organization to additional global partners like Johns Hopkins University. "Involvement in YHP is an extraordinary opportunity for mindyourmind," said Contursi, when describing the 2013 symposium for adolescent health in which they'll be participating. "Along with our global partners—Plan International and Johns Hopkins University—we'll be speaking to a global audience about the importance of youth engagement in program planning and evaluation. The audience will include the world's most influential, expert organizations in global health: organizations such as the World Health Organization and the United Nations Population Fund. If you had asked me ten years ago if this would be possible, I'd have said it was unimaginable."

The Win-Win Situation

There are numerous benefits to AstraZeneca when it engages in community investment projects such as the YHP, according to Caroline Hempstead, vice president of Group Corporate Affairs at AstraZeneca.[27] "The mission of our company is to bring innovative medicines to market to improve people's lives. Most employees would say that what motivates them to work here is the opportunity to improve the health of patients and their quality of life. YHP is a great example of how we can work in partnership with others to achieve this.

"The vast majority of our medicines are for older people or adults. But you can reduce the burden of disease for the world if you change the habits of people when they're young. At around ages eleven to fourteen or fifteen, young people make their own decisions, look for their own sources of information; that determines how they live their lives. Through research and grass roots programs in many countries in the world, we can make a difference in young people's lives, and influence policy through research.

"As a company, we are learning from our expert partners and the wider stakeholders we work with about the health needs that inform our business and the strategic priorities we have as a company. YHP also gives us a broader platform for developing relationships with opinion formers and others, including governments and NGOs, to tackle the NCD challenge. Additionally, and importantly, our employees are very engaged by our YHP activities and indeed, many of them get involved through local volunteer schemes."[28]

The additional benefits to the company, according to Hempstead, are in developing good will with ministries of health in developing countries. Beyond such obvious relationships, however, she says, there is the opportunity to engage in a conversation and relationship with the company's customers around an issue that is not directly related to its commercial products.

"Our company tagline is that 'health connects us all.' The real value, whether grassroots or advocacy, is to provide a platform to build relationships with people who have relationships with our company in a commercial sense – payers, patients, NGOs, patient organizations, healthcare professionals, therapists, and pharmacists. They are also parents, aunts, and uncles who make healthcare decisions. Having a community investing program allows us to have a completely different dialogue with them which is lifestyle oriented. That gives us the ability to have broader relationships with key stakeholders."

Finally, Hempstead explained that YHP provides an opportunity for AstraZeneca to have an exponential impact with its philanthropy. "In other areas, our contribution would just be a drop in the bucket. But by helping to support and promote the research with Johns Hopkins, through journals, or with public policy makers, we can help the lives of so many. It's a matter of scale. We want to help influence policy makers—like getting NCDs on the agenda of the post-2015 MDGs."

With AstraZeneca's $9 million, the company's thoughtful and strategic selection of NGO and academic partners, and its engagement with the Clinton Global Initiative, the company is reinforcing positive motivation among its employees, engendering good will among ministries of health in countries where its commercial relationships are important, creating an important conversation with its customers and consumers, and playing a vital role in public policy to extend lives and improve the quality of life for all people worldwide.

PHARMACEUTICAL COMPANIES DEPLOY HUMAN CAPITAL IN GLOBAL PRO BONO SERVICE

Two global pharmaceutical companies have advanced their corporate missions while improving world health through innovative employee engagement programs. This section tells the stories of Pfizer and GlaxoSmithKline (GSK) and their NGO partners.

According to PYXERA Global's (formerly known as CDC Development Solutions) Corporate Volunteerism Benchmarking Study 2013, leadership potential is the number one criteria for a company's selection of candidates for international corporate volunteerism programs.[29] Additionally, 95 percent of companies expect the volunteers to share their experiences with others in the company.[30]

From 2006–2013, volunteers have worked in 64 countries, primarily in Africa, Asia, and Latin America.[31] The total number of volunteers has increased steadily each year, from 375 in 2008 for six programs surveyed; to 624 in 2009 for seven programs surveyed; to 884 in 2010 for eleven programs surveyed; to 1,391 in 2011 for 13 programs surveyed; to 1,723 in 2012 for 26 programs surveyed; to 1,061 as of April 2013 for 22 programs surveyed.[32] The majority of programs are team-based with 10 to 20 volunteers per project.[33]

Increasingly, companies are sending volunteers from multiple counties.[34] Key success factors were selecting the right employees to participate, selecting the right projects and having clear project objectives, and selecting experienced third party implementers and partners.[35] Developing the volunteers' professional skills was seen as the greatest potential benefit—leadership development, team building, and entrepreneurship.[36]

PFIZER ASSISTS MOTHERS2MOTHERS WITH ORGANIZATIONAL INFRASTRUCTURE

The global NGO mothers2mothers (m2m) is based in South Africa. It helps to prevent mother-to-child transmission of HIV, keeps mothers healthy, and empowers women.[37] Without any intervention, about 40 percent of children born to an HIV-infected mother will contract the infection: during pregnancy or labor, or through breastfeeding. This translates to over 400,000 new HIV infections passed from mother to child worldwide each year. With appropriate medical intervention, that figure can be reduced to less than 5 percent.

m2m opened its first actual office in South Africa in 2004, according to Robin Smalley, its international co-founder and director.[38] Today, m2m employs 1,060 HIV-positive mentor mothers, serving 242,000 HIV-positive mothers and mothers-to-be, working in nine sub-Saharan

African countries.[39] m2m's budget is $20 million annually, and the United Nations has identified 22 countries where it wants to see m2m programs embedded.

Clearly, m2m is effective in addressing MDGs 4, 5, and 6, which seek to reduce the child mortality rate for children under five years of age, improve maternal health, and combat HIV/AIDs. According to Smalley, "This is about putting women front and center as the solution in keeping mothers alive. And children. Both. You can't separate the two. If the child is born healthy and the mother dies, the child won't reach its fifth birthday. It's not only humane, it's good sense, and it's good business."[40]

While Smalley and Dr. Mitch Besser, founder and medical director, were building programs and support and delivering services, Smalley reports that they had no acumen for establishing the business and financial infrastructure for their rapidly growing enterprise. "Pfizer was a lifesaver," Smalley explained. "As soon as I got in touch, they deployed a Pfizer Global Health Fellow who worked with us for three months, full-time, to establish a financial records system. From then on, we had a series of Fellows, sometimes two at a time, for six months at a time, up until 2011.

"The Pfizer Fellows established a variety of systems to support our growing business, including human resources, payroll, communications, monitoring and evaluation, and so on. We didn't even need a chief financial officer until 2009. Each of the Fellows was outstanding, and each person rolled up their sleeves and jumped right in with great enthusiasm. I don't know how we would have done this."[41]

Pfizer is a US-based, global corporation whose mission is "to be the premier innovative biopharmaceutical company" and whose purpose is to "innovate to bring therapies to patients that significantly improve their lives."[42] At Pfizer, the Global Health Fellows Program (GHF) involves individuals in short term assignments to transfer their professional medical and business expertise in ways that promote access, quality, and efficiency of health services for people in greatest need. Since 2003, Pfizer has engaged over 300 employees, from offices throughout the world, in pro bono engagements with approximately 40 international development organizations in 45 countries. Assignments are focused on optimizing supply chains and business functions, and scaling up promising health prevention approaches.[43]

For the past several years, a number of global corporations have been encouraging and supporting the involvement of their people in short-term pro bono assignments, often in emerging markets. These programs, often referred to as international corporate volunteering (ICV), or global pro bono, are highly competitive for employees to participate in. They are usually designed for people who are being groomed for leadership in the company. International pharmaceutical companies offer ICV programs to healthcare professionals, such as physicians, nurses, and pharmacists, as well as to business professionals, such as people with expertise in strategic planning, information technology, business development, sales and marketing, and other fields.

Businesses invest in global pro bono for a variety of reasons. Most of all, companies believe in the leadership development value. Employees attest to the tremendous personal and professional development, including a more acute sensitivity and awareness of more diverse backgrounds, and improved communications skills. Companies also seek to deepen their knowledge and understanding of needs and cultures in emerging markets where opportunities abound. Finally, companies recognize that having international corporate volunteering programs is a powerful recruitment and retention tool. PYXERA Global, a Washington, DC-based NGO, facilitates ICV programs for many global corporations and conducts an annual conference for sharing of best practices.[44]

PYXERA Global defines ICV programs as "any program in which employees cross international borders to provide services to local clients based primarily on the skills they utilize in their daily jobs. Though not always the traditional volunteerism, as participants may or may not continue to receive their salaries, the employees are engaged in an activity outside of their normal assignments and responsibilities. Some companies also refer to these as 'pro bono' activities. The projects they work on are non-revenue generating for the company, and are intended to provide economic/social benefits to the local organization and community."[45]

Pfizer believes that the Fellows' work benefits the company and the world at the same time. "Business and social purpose are one and the same when your company's mission is to innovate to bring therapies to patients that significantly improve their lives," explained Caroline Roan, vice president of Corporate Responsibility at Pfizer Inc., and president of the Pfizer Foundation. Roan described the value of the GHF program to the communities where they serve and to the company. "Not every country in Africa has healthcare providers," she said. "Pfizer has doctors, nurses, and pharmacists. We can help. That was the original idea. What we learned is about NGOs' needs for core business skills, such as information technology, media planning, social media, finance, and business planning. We want to leverage all of our assets to help, including our people, products, and funding, particularly in areas where we have expertise. This includes non-communicable diseases, neglected tropical diseases, and infectious diseases."[46]

Roan shared the ways in which the Fellows' experience benefits the company as well. "Pfizer colleagues come back from their assignments with a deepened, richer sense of our company's purpose, more committed than ever, and with greater cultural flexibility. As we enter new countries, the broader experiences our Global Health Fellows are gaining are very valuable. It deepens their and our understanding of markets in India, China, and Africa. We learn what patients need and how governments work, as well as how to best structure our talents for success." Roan added, "when we enter the market, we want to ensure that we have a core set of skills and a set of solutions."[47]

Based on surveys conducted by the GHF's third party evaluator, Boston University Center for Global Health and Development of Pfizer Global Health Fellows, GHF experiences provided opportunities for professional development:

- 96 percent of 2012 Fellows strongly agree that they would recommend GHF program to peers.
- 91 percent of 2012 Fellows feel they "somewhat" or "substantially" had the opportunity to apply or expand their professional, technical, or leadership skills while on fellowship – as compared to their regular position at Pfizer.
- 87 percent of 2012 Fellows saw the business value in the projects they worked on.
- 79 percent of 2012 Fellows strongly agreed that the GHF program offered an opportunity to increase understanding of patient populations and health delivery systems.
- 75 percent of 2012 Fellows agree or strongly agree that they are more motivated to perform in their Pfizer job after the GHF experience.
- 55 percent of 2012 Fellows agree or strongly agree that participation in the GHF program sparked new ideas for products, services, and improvements that they can apply at their Pfizer work.[48]

According to surveys conducted by the Boston University Center for Global Health and Development, Pfizer's 2012 NGO Partners reported "extremely significant" and "significant" capacity gains in the areas of

- Human resource training and development (90 percent of partners)
- Leadership and governance (75 percent of partners)
- Health management information systems (72 percent of partners)[49]

Pfizer's NGO partners include Accordia Global Health Foundation, Care, Center for Disease Control and Prevention, GBCHealth, Project HOPE, Save the Children, and USAID, among others. The Pfizer Global Fellowship Program provides value to the company and the world.

GlaxoSmithKline Assists Clinton Health Access Initiative with Vaccination Supply Chain

GlaxoSmithKline (GSK) describes itself as a science-led global healthcare company that is "dedicated to improving the quality of human life by enabling people to do more, feel better, and live longer."[50] GSK, a UK-based company, has three primary areas of business which include pharmaceuticals, vaccines, and consumer healthcare. GSK researches and develops medicines and vaccines for the World Health Organization's three priority diseases—HIV/AIDS, tuberculosis, and malaria.[51]

GSK's global pro bono program is called the PULSE Volunteer Partnership. Since 2009, GSK has deployed nearly 400 volunteers from 45 countries to work full-time for up to six months with 85 different NGOs in 57 countries. In June 2013 alone, GSK deployed approximately one hundred PULSE volunteers on three- or six-month PULSE assignments worldwide.[52]

GSK's global volunteers work on project management, business development, and change management, human resources, information technology, data management, logistics and supply chain, research and clinical development, and communications and marketing. The majority of volunteers work internationally, primarily in emerging markets, although some work domestically in underserved communities.

GSK believes there are a number of reasons to engage in global pro bono, including the win-win-win for the company, the employee, and the NGOs and communities they serve. Ahsiya Mencin, Director of the PULSE Volunteer Partnership at GSK, described being inspired by CEO Sir Andrew Witty's original vision to expand the company's volunteering opportunities. "We built the program around Andrew Witty's vision in the power of partnerships to solve complex global health challenges, and our strong belief in the value of bringing outside perspectives and realities into our company's culture and thinking," Mencin recalled. "PULSE aims to affect a three-fold change: change communities, change oneself, and change GSK."

Mencin also noted that the PULSE program is open to everyone, not just "key talent," as long as the employee has been with the company for a minimum of three years, has a strong track record of performance, has their line manager's endorsement, and has a skill-set that is needed by an NGO partner. Employee volunteers must also demonstrate that they have "the PULSE gene," which is defined as humility, flexibility, adaptability, and cultural sensitivity. Mencin and her team screen for the best candidates who can accomplish the program's mission of improving the well being of people around the world.

This mission is accomplished through projects focused on improving access to medicines and healthcare, and improving the health and education of children, including STEM (science, technology, engineering, and math) education. PULSE volunteers include doctors, nurses, and pharmacists, project managers, and specialists in information technology, finance, and communications, as well as experts in logistics and supply chain who can help NGOs to get medicines in and out of countries.

In order to amplify the benefit to the company, volunteers blog to their colleagues and others while they are deployed, and make presentations about their PULSE experiences upon their return.[53] The employees' appreciation of the program is evidenced by the fact that there is a 33 percent higher retention rate among GSK employees who have participated. Additionally, the leadership development value is seen in a 47 percent higher rate of promotion among returning volunteers.[54]

Malika Idouaddi, a supply chain optimisation project specialist who works for GSK in the UK, applied and was selected to serve as a PULSE volunteer with the Clinton Health Access Initiative (CHAI) in Yaoundé, Cameroon. (CHAI began as the Clinton HIV/AIDS initiative; it has improved markets for medicines and diagnostics, lowered the costs of treatments, and expanded access to life-saving technologies—creating a sustainable model that can be owned and maintained by governments.)[55]

For six months, Idouaddi was based in the Central Medical Stores (CMS) that belong to the Ministry of Health in Cameroon. The CMS received donations of anti-retroviral drugs for pediatrics that came via the Clinton Foundation. Since the CMS was experiencing many stock-outs—too many occasions when it was running out of drugs when they were needed— Idouaddi's job was to apply her expertise in supply chain logistics to improve distribution and supply chain. She conducted a diagnostic, developed an action plan, and then implemented it within six months. "You can't expect to change the entire the organization in six months, so you keep it focused, simple, and efficient," she explained.[56]

Idouaddi had an additional role, which was to help the team develop a system to track and monitor inventory positions. The team included a pharmacist, the director of the national health program in charge of the supply for drugs to treat HIV, tuberculosis, and malaria, the warehouse administrator, and two additional administrators in charge of distribution. Until then, there were no systems to track supplies in the warehouse, and notes were kept on paper. Idouaddi showed them how to set up spreadsheets to monitor inventory position and monthly demand, and to predict how much volume they would need in order to cover demand six to nine months out. Since not everyone was familiar with Excel spreadsheets or data analysis, Idouaddi ran training programs.

As this was complicated for the team, Idouaddi needed to build rapport and help them realize the benefits that the reports would bring. "It took time," said Idouaddi. "It was real business change management. They finally accepted it and were very pleased. In the end, it was very rewarding."

Idouaddi talked about the value of learning to adjust her management style to a new culture. "You can't expect to have the same approach you would have in the United Kingdom, or in France where I come from. You have to consider the local culture. In Cameroon, I liked how warm and friendly people were. What came with that is that if you want to achieve something, you have to get to know and acknowledge each person. That was key to getting their buy-in."

Idouaddi said that the experience prepared her well for a current assignment she has in Turkey. Working in Cameroon has helped her to adjust and be more effective in a variety of new and different cultures and work environments.

While on assignment in Cameroon, Idouaddi also met with representatives of Philippe Douste-Blazy, chair of the executive board of UNITAID, together with her manager from CHAI. UNITAID is a global NGO that is funded by air ticket levies implemented by Cameroon, Chile, Congo, France, Madagascar, Mali, Mauritius, Niger, and the Republic of Korea, in addition to a portion of Norway's tax on CO_2 emissions. The funds are used to buy drugs to treat HIV/AIDS, malaria, and tuberculosis. Idouaddi had the opportunity to take part in the audit of the Central Medical Store that is located in Mali. Based on the audit, UNITAID would buy and contribute drugs to the Central Medical Stores in Mali.

As to whether she would recommend this experience to others, Idouaddi gave an enthusiastic yes: "Did my PULSE experience change anything for me? Yes! It changed a lot!" she said, referring to her appreciation of GSK, her views on life, her sense of self, and her plans for her education and career.

Idouaddi exemplifies Sir Andrew Witty's vision for GSK's PULSE program. Sir Andrew is the chairman and CEO of GSK who inspired the creation of the global pro bono initiative. "We envisioned this as an experience to change the diversity of the way people think inside the company, and how they perceive the way that the world works," he said. "We wanted people from GSK to experience how civil society works as compared to corporations, and to learn how to get things done through partnerships."

When he learned about Idouaddi's PULSE experience, Sir Andrew responded that the feedback is that the program has been transformative— not only for the participants but also for the host NGOs. As to the value to the company's bottom line, Sir Andrew said, "We want to develop more competent decision makers who have a global view. We want to have a company that's part of society, with a cadre of personnel who will behave differently because of what they've experienced."[57]

GSK is advancing its own business interests. At the same time, the company is contributing to the achievement of MDGs 4, 5, and 6.[58]

MOBILE SOLUTIONS AND TECHNOLOGY IMPROVE
ACCESS TO HEALTHCARE

Various companies, from pharmaceuticals to ICT, in partnership with NGOs and governments, are combining their expertise with mobile technology and cloud solutions in order to provide greater access to healthcare services, medicines, and vaccinations. These programs improve access, quality, and efficiencies in healthcare delivery, particularly to underserved and remote regions of the world. GlaxoSmithKline and HP are two examples.

GLAXOSMITHKLINE AND VODAFONE

One out of five infants worldwide does not receive the three required, life-saving doses of diphtheria, tetanus, and pertussis (DPT) vaccine. Children who are not vaccinated are vulnerable to these deadly diseases.[59]

"The role of the private sector in delivering health is growing larger, as traditional sources of funding are drying up. NGOs are seeing that corporate partnerships are valuable. GSK is getting more requests,"[60] according to Dr. Allan Pamba,[61] director of Public Engagement and Access Initiatives for GSK. Pamba is responsible for the sustainable delivery of GSK medicines and vaccines across 50 countries, including the United Nations' 48 Least Developed Countries.[62]

"We've always wanted to play in this space," Pamba said. "Suspicions are beginning to break down. We'll see more partnerships, public-private and private-private. With ministers of health in Africa, where the continent has 24 percent of the global health burden of disease, but only 1 percent of health budget and only 3 percent of global health workforce. That's the situation on the ground. This is a challenge, as well as an opportunity."

Pamba[63] trained as a physician in Kenya and worked in clinical care in the country for government services, mission hospitals, and research hospitals. He is optimistic about improving health in Africa through a partnership between GSK and Vodafone. The collaboration will use the mobile technology platform to register mothers and children to provide them with vaccines to reverse deadly diseases, including diarrhea, pneumonia, and malaria. "Given that a population of just under a billion people are using 700,000 mobile phones, we can leverage that platform to reach people for vaccinations," said Pamba.

The GSK-Vodafone initiative is a pilot project to increase the uptake of DPT vaccinations in Mozambique. On the demand side, explained Pamba, pregnant women are registered on a Mozambique health ministry database when they deliver their babies,and are alerted by text message about the availability and importance of vaccinations. They are able to book vaccination appointments by text and receive reminders about follow-ups so their children can become fully immunized.

Additionally, healthcare workers are provided with smart phones to register a new mother, check the vaccination status of a child, and send text reminders to mothers and caregivers for their children's vaccinations. The pilot will run across all mobile phones, not just those connected with Vodafone.[64] On the supply side, mobile phones are used to provide storehouses with the necessary information in order to avoid stock-outs.

A series of three injections are required in order for the DPT vaccination to be fully effective. "It's been observed that without this intervention, there is a 91 percent coverage rate for the first dose, and only 76 percent coverage by the third dose. With this intervention, we are aiming to increase the uptake for the third dose to 86 percent. A ten percent rise in coverage would be significant. A level that no country could ignore. It would be life-saving. More countries would want this," Pamba stated.

The business case for GSK's and Vodafone's pilot project is business development. "If the solution works in Mozambique, then we will have the opportunity to supply millions of doses of vaccine throughout Africa," explained Pamba. "That's business for us, while we are also impacting the disease."

The vaccinations would be purchased by GAVI, an NGO whose mission is to save children's lives and to protect people's health by increasing access to immunization in poor countries through public-private partnerships.[65] "For Vodafone, once the pilot is completed, if any additional countries choose to use the model, then the mobile company generates revenues through text message traffic," Pamba said.

"When I left Kenya to join GSK in London in 2005, I wanted to drive change from within. Having worked with patients on the front lines, I understood the limitations of patients who are not at the table with big pharma companies. What I do now is drive solutions that are win-win for everyone. We are increasing access to medicines that are life-saving," said Pamba. "We are not a charity. We are a business. But we measure our success by the volume of medicines and vaccines that we get through into the 50 least-developed countries, rather than the profit that we make. Our target—set in 2010—is to grow the volume five-fold by 2015. In the short time that we've existed at the company, we've become the fastest growing unit at GSK," Pamba said.[66]

Pamba showed the link between GSK's profits and good health outcomes for young children. "7 million children die every year before their fifth birthday, many of these from vaccinable diseases such as pneumonia, diarrhea and measles. A 10 percent increase in vaccine uptake could result in hundreds of thousands of lives saved every year."[67]

Pamba expanded further on what he had learned as a physician in Africa, where he conducted clinical trials on the management of severe malaria in children at the Wellcome Trust Research Programme in Kilifi, Kenya and also established one of the country's first HIV Comprehensive Care Clinics. "As a child, I grew up in an environment where all I saw was donated aid. I fell into a trap of 'give me, give me.' As a young physician, I recognized that that doesn't work with HIV. I woke up to the fact that for solutions to be sustainable, you need to earn and buy. That's why I support this approach. It gives people their dignity."

Pamba observed that "the West is waking up to the opportunity that is Africa. The private sector in the United States and Europe is trying to make inroads to build an Africa strategy. But Western governments are one step behind in supporting the private sector."[68]

Through its mobile-enabled vaccination program, GSK and Vodafone are providing a sustainable business solution that involves community healthcare workers on the frontlines. It also engages mothers in taking responsibility for saving the lives of their children.

HP COMBINES EXPERTISE AND TECHNOLOGY TO IMPROVE GLOBAL HEALTH

Under the leadership of Gabi Zedlmayer, vice president of Sustainability and Social Innovation (SSI), and Chris Librie, director of Environmental and Health Initiatives, HP Sustainability and Social Innovation, HP engages its people in finding solutions to global healthcare challenges, while also contributing its technologies to advance progress.

HP Created a Mobile Technology and Cloud Solution for m2m. HP supports m2m by helping the organization to exponentially expand its HIV-prevention work in the Republic of South Africa. "HP is transforming m2m's operations from paper-based records to a digital system that will help the organization," according to Librie.[69]

Mark Heffernan, chief financial officer at m2m,[70] explained the intake process for m2m patients in order to illustrate HP's contribution in saving lives. "We work in clinics alongside state- or privately-employed health workers. The expectant mothers wait outside in long lines for their neonatal visits. When a mother finds out for the first time that she is HIV-positive, the health worker often has insufficient ability and limited time to provide a very complicated explanation about the medications and infant-feeding practices necessary to prevent transmission to the baby."[71]

At that point, the health workers refer the women to m2m down the hall. The women usually arrive in shock and despair, said Heffernan. They are received by m2m's "mentor mothers" who have themselves been through this experience. M2m's mentor mothers are trained to talk with the expectant mothers and prepare them for what lies ahead. The mentor mothers admit the new patients into a program and regime to help them stay on their medications, and follow the right feeding habits, so that they and their children can live healthy lives. "The key to success is in the follow up by the mentors. Our studies have shown that if the women return for three visits, transmission of HIV can be virtually eliminated. The key is follow up," Heffernan explained.

HP provided three important values to m2m, Heffernan said. "First, for the mentor mothers. Until HP helped us shift to an electronic data system, the mentors kept notes on paper when they met with their new patients. Now, the mentors use mobile phones and text messaging, which makes it easier and more efficient for mentors to collect and automatically upload this data to help ensure that mothers return for their follow ups."

The second benefit, according to Heffernan, is that HP helped m2m to establish a database system that "provides much richer analysis of the data in order for us to make decisions about the program and how to make it more effective. This is an immense value to look at outputs and impact."

HP's final contribution was to strengthen the organization's entire information technology infrastructure. "We had various databases, including financial, that weren't talking to one another. HP came up with architecture and design, so we could make more efficient use of data and share information across various applications and platforms."

In total, summarized Heffernan, "at program and site levels, as well as from an IT infrastructure perspective, this has been a fantastic relationship with HP."[72]

From Librie's point of view, "the mentor mothers were limited by the need to document and keep paper records. We were able to create a cloud-based solution by using cell phones, which are ubiquitous. Texting enabled the mentor mothers to maintain records of their mentees and do their follow ups more efficiently. This also allowed the mentors to spend more time with the mothers."[73]

As to the challenges, Librie indicated that HP wanted to ensure that the infrastructure was manageable and sustainable. "We wanted to know that it would be easy for the mentors to use, and that it could be maintained without difficulty: That it would truly be better from a user point of view."

According to Heffernan, "we are fortunate to have worked with very talented and dedicated folks. They gave up their free time and spent countless hours far beyond the call of duty."

As noted earlier, m2m is effective in addressing Millennium Development Goals 4, 5, and 6, which seek to reduce the mortality rate for children under five years of age, improve maternal health, and combat HIV/AIDs. For HP, said Librie, projects like the one with m2m provide the company with an opportunity to demonstrate the value of HP's technology and expertise in providing solutions for social impact. Additionally, "working with various projects in emerging markets facilitates HP's working relationships with ministries of health in emerging markets which often lead to commercial opportunities."[74]

HP PARTNERS WITH PARTNERS IN HEALTH TO ESTABLISH THE HÔPITAL UNIVERSITAIRE DE MIREBALAIS

Another example of how HP is contributing its unique value and assets is through its support for the establishment of the Hôpital Universitaire de Mirebalais (HUM), rural Haiti's first teaching hospital. The hospital will provide primary care services to 185,000 people in Mirebalais and two nearby communities—people who have only had limited access to quality healthcare. The HP project was conducted in partnership with Partners in Health (PIH), the NGO founded and led by the renowned Paul Farmer, who began his global work in Haiti 25 years ago.

As described by HP, the company provided "the information technology infrastructure to support all of the applications needed to run a modern hospital of this scale as well as critical communications systems. HUM was outfitted with a high-capacity server rack that provides connectivity across the campus...HP workstations are situated throughout the hospital, equipped with 27-inch monitors to enable teaching opportunities in the operating rooms and optimum radiology image viewing...In addition to providing technology and funding, HP employees around the world contributed their time and expertise to the design, build-out, and installation of the IT systems at HUM."[75]

Librie commented on the unique challenges of this project. It was essential for the grid to be resilient in the most challenging of environments, providing easy-to-use, fail-proof technology that can be operated with minimal training.[76]

The HUM itself presented a difficult situation. One of the biggest issues was connectivity in a remote part of the country that had been severely damaged by the earthquake in 2010.

"Haiti was already one of the poorest countries in the world, when the devastating earthquake of 2010 damaged its infrastructure even further," explained Librie. "When Paul Farmer said that Partners in Health (PIH) wanted to build a teaching hospital two hours north of Port-au-Prince, that would be a tremendous challenge."

Librie described the vision: "We wanted to bring together the best people from HP and PIH to install the best technology to create an integrated system for the hospital. The backbone is HP technology, computing, networking, switches, and internet. This is a great demonstration project of a fully integrated solution in the most challenging conditions." HP contributed the technology and the expertise, demonstrating to potential customers its prowess in creating innovative, high-impact solutions to the most difficult problems in the most trying circumstances.

Additionally, said Librie, "the systems had to be sustainable." For sustainability, HP needed to ensure that the hospital would have service contracts that met its needs, and that people would be properly trained to manage the system on an ongoing basis. "We had a great partner in PIH. This was a shared collaboration. We sat together and worked towards a shared objective."[77]

Through its work with PIH in establishing the teaching hospital in Haiti, HP is contributing to the achievement of MDGs 4, 5, and 6.[78]

HP has a clear business case for its engagement in pro bono projects such as its partnership with PIH in establishing the teaching hospital in Haiti, and working with m2m in Africa. For HP, these engagements provide an opportunity to bring technology and people together to have a positive social and environmental impact in developing markets.

"This is the theme that unifies all of our sustainability and social innovation programs in education, healthcare, and environment," Librie explained. "These experiences enable us to demonstrate HP's technology and expertise in challenging circumstances. These opportunities also open the doors to new business relationships."

BUSINESSES ARE PROFITING BY IMPROVING HEALTH WORLDWIDE

The corporate initiatives described in this chapter are designed to reduce mortality rates throughout the world, especially in developing countries where access to healthcare services and medicines is more limited than in developed countries. Access to healthcare services for all people is vital for moral, practical, and economic reasons. Companies are recognizing that they will profit by partnering with NGOs and governments in leveraging their expertise and assets—including technology, medicines, and investment capital—in advancing solutions to the healthcare challenges of the world.

CHAPTER 7

HUMAN RIGHTS

Every thought, every word, and every action that adds to the positive and
the wholesome is a contribution to peace. Each and every one of us is
capable of making such a contribution.[1]

—Aung San Suu Kyi

Thus shall we live, because we will have created a society which recognises
that all people are born equal, with each entitled in equal measure to life,
liberty, prosperity, human rights and good governance.[2]

—Nelson Mandela

A DAY DOES NOT GO BY WITHOUT NEWS OF HUMAN RIGHTS ABUSES. THESE
might be perpetrated by governments denying basic civil liberties to people or failing to guarantee a humane rule of law. In reading about violence
around the world, you might notice that national governments have shut
off people's access to the Internet: in Syria in November 2012, [3] in Iran in
February 2012,[4] and in Egypt[5] in January 2011.[6] You might have followed
stories about children forced into sex trafficking here in the United States,[7]
in Britain,[8] and worldwide.[9]

Moreover, the products and services that companies produce and that we
use daily might be tainted by human rights abuses of workers in the supply chain. As you consider the clothes that you wear, you might be concerned whether they were made in factories like the one in Bangladesh where
recently more than a thousand garment workers perished in a shabbily con-
structed multi-story building,[10] or where workers were trapped while fires
blazed around them until they died.[11] As you shop, you might wonder if
your television, computer, or cellphone is corrupted with "conflict minerals,"
minerals mined in conditions of armed conflict and human rights abuses.[12]
In fact, the materials we use daily are made with conflict minerals. These
include electronic items and cars made of conflict minerals, and even zippers,
watches, rings, and earrings.[13]

While human rights have been violated for as long as time, new media
bring vivid pictures about victims directly onto the electronic devices in our
very hands. Too often, elements of the corporate sector were responsible for
creating the human rights abuses, environmental degradation, and economic
injustices that continue to plague the world today. With knowledge comes
a growing discomfort with the pain and suffering of others. Consumers feel

they are especially complicit with respect to the products they purchase, wear, and use.[14] Employees, customers, and investors are ready to be activated.

Governments have not been particularly effective in addressing human rights abuses worldwide. In the case of freedom of expression and privacy on the Internet, for example, governments can even be central to the problem. As you will see in this chapter, however, some corporations working in partnership with NGOs are becoming potent players in addressing the complex problems of conflict minerals, supply chain issues, and human trafficking, freedom of expression and privacy on the Internet, and other human rights issues. Not only is this the right thing to do from a moral perspective, it is good business: it protects and builds brands, elevates employee morale and loyalty, and mitigates significant financial risks. This serves the bottom line.

What does a better world look like when it comes to human rights? It seems quite simple. The ethic of reciprocity, best known as "the golden rule," says it best: "Do unto others as you would have them do unto you."

The golden rule has particular resonance in today's business world. Given many contemporary social challenges, a number of business, academic, and civic leadership organizations are recognizing the importance of *empathy* for personal and professional success.[15] Ashoka,[16] a network of 3,000 leading social entrepreneurs around the globe, has an "empathy initiative." According to Dr. Angel Cabrera, president of George Mason University, "A business that doesn't reward investors adequately, that treats employees unfairly, that cheats its customers or harms its community is a failure. Empathy is an essential element of business because, without understanding the needs and desires of others, it is impossible to satisfy them."[17]

Businesses that play leading roles in advancing human rights do not always act out of purely altruistic motives. Some companies do the right thing because they have been shamed in the media for a horrific scandal, and the public humiliation has damaged sales; other companies are proactive to mitigate risk. Additionally, businesses have learned that there can be tremendous financial risks and costs associated with human rights abuses. Case studies published by the World Resources Institute (WRI), showed that resistance from communities and other stakeholders can delay permits, construction, operations, and revenues, cause conflicts with local labor markets, increase costs for financing, insurance, and security, and reduce output. According to the WRI report, "Development without Conflict: The Business Case for Community Consent," community resistance can arise at any point in a project cycle, and can have negative impacts on the company far beyond the scope of the project in dispute, "including negative impacts on stock prices, brands, and reputations, and greater difficulty in securing financing, insurance, and community cooperation on future projects."[18]

Damage to the company's reputation and potential project cancellations can add up to billions of dollars. In his book, *"Just Business,"* John Ruggie cited a Goldman Sachs study (2008) of 190 projects operated by multinational oil companies. Ruggie described an important finding of this confidential report, to which he had access: "Nontechnical risks accounted for nearly half of all risk factors faced by the oil majors, with 'stakeholder-related risk' constituting the single largest category of nontechnical risk."[19] John Ruggie also reported that one particular company "may have accrued $6.5 billion in such costs over a two-year period, amounting to a double-digit percentage of its annual profits."

Ruggie commented on the staff time devoted to managing conflicts within communities. "If these conflicts are left unattended, they may escalate, which can lead to property damage and injury, or worse, to community members and company employees."[20]

In the last chapter of this book—Chapter 8—you will learn how businesses engage community stakeholders early in the planning process, and in ongoing discussions, in order to avert such harm to communities and the companies' bottom line.

Companies that are effective in addressing human rights issues do so with a keen understanding of the value to their brand, and the credibility they will garner among customers, employees, and investors. Additionally, as you will see in this chapter, many of the most effective business initiatives to address human rights are done through coalitions and partnerships with NGOs.

In the modern era, key stakeholders have recognized that success in achieving human rights requires the full engagement of businesses. Following World War II, the United Nations put forward the Universal Declaration of Human Rights (UDHR), a formal charter for human rights.[21] The UDHR represented the international community's commitment to never allow atrocities like those of World War II to happen again. Eleanor Roosevelt was recognized as the driving force for the Declaration's adoption by the UN General Assembly on December 10, 1948. The UDHR addresses the state's duty to protect against human rights abuses by third parties, including *business enterprises*, through regulation, policymaking, investigation, and enforcement.

Launched in 2000, the United Nations Global Compact provides a framework for development and implementation of responsible and sustainable business practices. "The Global Compact asks companies to embrace universal principles and to partner with the United Nations. It has grown to become a critical platform for the UN to engage effectively with enlightened global business," states UN Secretary-General Ban Ki-moon on the Global Compact website.[22] Companies are required to endorse ten principles related to human rights, labor, environment, and anti-corruption.[23] Already, more than ten thousand business and non-business entities from 145 countries worldwide are participating in the Global Compact.[24]

In 2005, UN Secretary-General Kofi Annan appointed Professor John Ruggie as the special representative of the Secretary-General on human rights and transnational corporations and other business enterprises to further define the human rights responsibilities of business. Following six years of multi-stakeholder discussions, the United Nations Human Rights Council (UNHRC) unanimously endorsed the *United Nations Guiding Principles on Business and Human Rights: Implementing the United Nations "Protect, Respect, and Remedy" Framework*, on June 16, 2011.[25]

The Guiding Principles are intended to provide operational clarity for the principles of the Global Compact, requiring companies to ensure that they are not engaged in human rights abuses.[26]

The Guiding Principles encompass three axioms applying to all states and businesses: "the state duty to *protect* against human rights abuses by third parties, including business; the corporate responsibility to *respect* human rights; and greater access by victims to effective *remedy*, both judicial and non-judicial."[27]

While this chapter features specific approaches that some companies are taking as part of coalitions to eliminate human rights abuses, many corporate actors have created and continue to perpetuate such threats. Only with such an understanding can we move forward together to find solutions. The purpose of this book is to look ahead by providing best practices and rallying the corporate sector to continue to think creatively and collaboratively about building a better world. Businesses that manage vast human and financial capital across nations have the power to implement the golden rule throughout the world: That which is hateful to you *don't* do unto others. Companies are learning that it is not only humane to follow this doctrine, but it is also more profitable in a world where customers, employees, and investors will no longer tolerate child sex trafficking in the hotels where they sleep, deaths in factories where their dresses are sewn, child labor involved in the harvest of their cocoa products, or extreme violence contaminating their hand-held mobile phones. Corporations are recognizing the win-win of providing respect, dignity, safety, and a fair wage for employees and customers worldwide.

BUSINESSES COMBAT HUMAN TRAFFICKING TO END FORCED LABOR AND SEXUAL EXPLOITATION

At the 2012 Clinton Global Initiative Annual Meeting, nine global companies launched the Global Business Coalition Against Human Trafficking (gBCAT) to fight human trafficking. gBCAT's founding members include Carlson, Coca-Cola, Delta Air Lines, ExxonMobil, LexisNexis, ManpowerGroup, Microsoft, NXP, and Travelport.[28] gBCAT's mission is to mobilize the power, resources, and thought leadership of the business community to end human trafficking, including all forms of forced labor and sex trafficking. In a speech at CGI, President Barack Obama praised the coalition for its commitment to fight trafficking: "The good news is more and more responsible companies are holding themselves to higher standards. And today, I want to salute the new commitments that are being made. That includes the new Global Business Coalition Against Trafficking—companies that are sending a message: Human trafficking is not a business model, it is a crime, and we are going to stop it."[29]

"Our core programs are designed to assist companies in training and education for employees, vendors, and sub-contractors; awareness programs to combat sex trafficking, notably in travel and tourism; identifying and preventing forced labor in supply chains and operations; and the transfer of best practices," explained Robert Rigby-Hall, co-chair, gBCAT, and chief human resources officer at NXP Semiconductors.[30]

"Those of us who formed gBCAT are passionate about stopping all forms of human trafficking," he said. "We see ourselves as advocates in our industries to engage other companies in gBCAT."

Businesses are beginning to join the fight against global trafficking, with some companies taking the lead. To these companies—whose stories will be discussed in this chapter—combatting trafficking is a moral issue and a business imperative, raising employee morale, engendering good will with customers, and protecting the brand.

21 million people worldwide are victims of forced labor, bonded labor, child labor, and sexual servitude, according to the International Labour Organization (ILO).[31] The World Bank indicates that human trafficking is a high-profit, low-risk business.[32]

The most common form of human trafficking is sexual exploitation, according to the *Global Report on Trafficking in Persons 2012*,[33] by the United Nations Office on Drugs and Crime (UNODC). The second most common form of human trafficking is forced labor, although this may be a misrepresentation because forced labor is less frequently detected and reported than trafficking for sexual exploitation.

The victims of human trafficking are predominantly women (59 percent). Children comprise a growing percentage of trafficking victims, up from 20 percent during the period from 2003 to 2006 to 27 percent between 2007 and 2010. Between 2007 and 2010, victims of 136 different nationalities were detected in 118 countries across the world. 27 percent of victims are trafficked domestically.[34]

According to the World Bank, "not only are children often sexually exploited in the sex industry targeted for child pornography and pedophiles, but children are also trafficked to work on untangling fishing nets, sewing goods in sweatshops, picking cocoa, and begging. Traffickers may lure children and/or their parents into leaving home with the promise of a better life. On some occasions, desperate parents will sell their children to a trafficker so that they have fewer mouths to feed. Forced conscription of children into armed conflict is another form of trafficking which enslaves children in war zones and removes their freedom."[35]

A turning point for human trafficking came with the adoption of The Protocol to Prevent, Suppress and Punish Trafficking in Persons, especially Women and Children,[36] by General Assembly resolution of the United Nations in 2000.[37] The Trafficking Protocol was entered into force on December 25, 2003.[38] For the first time, it provided a legally binding instrument on trafficking with an agreed-upon definition. The Trafficking Protocol defined human trafficking to include forced labor, sexual exploitation, and the removal of human organs:

> *"Trafficking in persons" shall mean the recruitment, transportation, transfer, harbouring or receipt of persons, by means of the threat or use of force or other forms of coercion, of abduction, of fraud, of deception, of the abuse of power or of a position of vulnerability or of the giving or receiving of payments or benefits to achieve the consent of a person having control over another person, for the purpose of exploitation. Exploitation shall include, at a minimum, the exploitation of the prostitution of others or other forms of sexual exploitation, forced labour or services, slavery or practices similar to slavery, servitude or the removal of organs.*

Additionally, based on the Trafficking Protocol, trafficking includes activity that occurs across country borders and within countries; it victimizes men, as well as women and children, and is perpetrated by individuals as well as by organized crime. One of the Trafficking Protocol's purposes is to facilitate international cooperation in investigating and prosecuting trafficking. Another is to protect and assist human trafficking's victims with full respect for their rights as established in the Universal Declaration of Human Rights.[39]

In an overview of human trafficking, the World Bank discusses the factors that make people most at-risk for trafficking. Risk factors include age, gender, poverty, illness, lack of educational opportunity, marginalization or discrimination based on ethnicity, race, disability, and religion. Also most vulnerable are victims of climate change and natural disorder, conflict and war, social exclusion, drug and alcohol addiction and mental illness, lack of rule of law, and government corruption or inaction.[40]

According to the United Nations Office on Drugs and Crime, 154 countries have ratified the Trafficking Protocol. Furthermore, there is evidence that trafficking from Eastern Europe and Central Asia has been declining since 2000. Nonetheless, the number of convictions for human trafficking remains quite low. According to the UN Report, "the conviction rates for trafficking are at the same level as rare crimes such as homicides in Iceland or kidnappings in Norway."[41]

Lest one think that human trafficking only occurs in countries with poor governance, trafficking is prevalent in New York City. According to a study conducted in 2011, the number of trafficked persons in the New York metropolitan area "significantly exceeds official estimates. The report estimates that private service providers in the New York City metropolitan area have interacted with at least 11,268 survivors of trafficking since 2000 and at least 1,606 over the last year."[42] Furthermore, The Polaris Project, a global NGO fighting human trafficking and modern day slavery, shows that human trafficking occurs in all 50 of the United States—victimizing men, women, and children in cities, suburbs, and rural communities.[43]

Governments alone have not been able to combat human trafficking. Businesses have a tremendous opportunity and responsibility to address this vital challenge in partnership with NGOs and governments. Carlson, a global hospitality and travel company, was the first US-based global hospitality company to sign the travel industry's international "Code of Conduct for the Protection of Children from Sexual Exploitation in Travel and Tourism"[44] as early as 2004. The Code, aiming to prevent sexual exploitation of children at tourism destinations, was developed by ECPAT (End Child Prostitution and Trafficking), a global children's rights NGO.

By 2003, over 40 companies, tour operators, travel agencies, tourism associations, and tourism unions endorsed the Code, committing themselves to implement the measures shown below. The number of tourists impacted by the Code was estimated to reach over 30 million per year, travelling to destinations in over 16 countries worldwide.[45] The Code commits endorsers to do the following.

1. To establish a corporate ethical policy against commercial sexual exploitation of children.
2. To train the personnel in the country of origin and travel destinations.
3. To introduce clauses in contracts with suppliers, stating a common repudiation of sexual exploitation of children.
4. To provide information to travelers through catalogues, brochures, in-flight films, ticket-slips, websites, etc.
5. To provide information to local "key persons" at destinations.
6. To report annually.

As of April 2013, the Code has 1,200 international signatories in 40 countries.[46] Carlson, however, remained the only global corporation based in the United States that signed the Code of Conduct until 2011.[47] The story of how and why Carlson came to be the first US-based company to sign the Code is illuminating. In 2004, Marilyn Carlson Nelson, chairman and former chief executive officer of Carlson, was approached by Ambassador John R. Miller to sign the Code. At the time, Ambassador Miller was leading the State Department's efforts to combat sex trafficking under President Bush.

Nelson and the company already had a history of supporting children at risk for abuse and exploitation. In 1999, Her Majesty Queen Silvia of Sweden had invited Carlson to join her and a number of corporations in establishing The World Childhood Foundation, an NGO whose very mission is to "defend the rights of the child and to promote better living conditions for vulnerable and exploited children at risk all over the world."[48]

When Ambassador Miller asked Nelson to sign the Code, she was personally inclined to say yes, but she wanted to review the decision with her executive team. Discussions were complicated by concerns over potential legal exposure and public relations—the very hindrances that have kept other US companies from signing the Code. Nonetheless, the Carlson team agreed to proceed simply because they felt it was the right thing to do. Nelson reported the decision to sign the Code to Ambassador Miller.[49]

Signing the Code would involve a tremendous investment on Carlson's part. With hundreds of thousands of employees at 1,300 hotels in operation and under development, and a global footprint spanning 160 countries under many brands, the training demands and logistics were massive. Carlson encompasses Radisson, Park Plaza, Park Inn by Radisson, and Country Inns & Suites. Additionally, Carlson added a clause in their supplier contracts that they would not work with companies involved in child trafficking.

Carlson's executive team embarked on the decision of signing the Code with some trepidation. They did not anticipate the response they would receive from employees and customers. "To our surprise," said Deborah Cundy, vice president, Office of the Chairman at Carlson, "things caught on fire with this issue! Employees were thrilled. Customers were thrilled. All of our fears were washed away!"[50]

Stating the business case for signing the Code of Conduct, Cundy said, "To begin with, child trafficking is illegal criminal activity. We don't want that in our hotels. It endangers our employees and our guests. Also, there's just this sense of righteous indignation. There were lots of reasons not to do this, but none of them more compelling than the case to do it. We're really proud of it. We didn't do it to win accolades. But I can't tell you how many people get in touch with me to praise our leadership. Employees feel proud...so thrilled...such expressions of gratitude."

Elaborating on her decision to sign the Code, Nelson explained further that "it's one more indication of moral authority. In today's world, particularly the millennials want to feel comfortable that they're working in an organization that lives its credo and its mission. That means that if you talk about an inclusive and respectful environment, then it's totally consistent to want to protect and stand for human rights."

Moreover, Nelson emphasized that trafficking is illegal regardless of sovereignty. "Businesses around the world are recognizing that corruption undermines business and trade. Taking a stand against corrupt practices supports the rule of law and court system." Nelson pointed out that human trafficking is often conducted by organized crime. "I don't think that any hospitality company is eager to have this take place in its establishment." She added that the "safety and security of our employees and guests is important." Like Cundy, Nelson noted how much pride the company's position has engendered among employees, as well as good will among customers, partners and suppliers.

Nelson pointed out that "most companies are identifying a range of risk, particularly brand risk. I think that it's impossible to control all of the variables when you have a global collection of hotels, but to at least have established a policy and procedure to protect against illegal activities like this is an important element of protection from brand risk."[51]

Eventually, during the past couple of years, Hilton, Wyndham, and Delta Airlines have signed the Code. Hilton signed the Code a year or so after a highly publicized sex prostitution ring scandal at one of their franchise hotels in Beijing.[52] Wyndham was introduced to ECPAT and the Code via the Interfaith Center on Corporate Responsibility, Christian Brothers Investment Services, Mercy Investment Services, and a few additional socially responsible investment companies; this underscores the importance of investors as drivers.[53]

Wyndman signed the ECPAT Code in 2011 under pressure following a child sex trafficking scandal at a Wyndham-franchised hotel.[54] This demonstrates the power of the media and the concerns of businesses regarding investors, customers, and employees.

Hilton has 540 hotels in 78 countries on six continents.[55] Starwood Hotels and Resorts Worldwide, Inc. has 1,134 properties in nearly 100 countries and 171,000 employees at its owned and managed properties.[56] Delta Air Lines serves more than 160 million customers each year, and employs 80,000 employees worldwide, offering service to nearly 318 destinations in 59 countries on six continents.[57] The Code has far reach and impact when its six measures are implemented through all of these businesses.

According to Carol Smolenski, executive director of ECPAT-USA, additional signatories to the Code include Real Hospitality Group, a property management company, and Nix Conference and Meeting Management. "These two companies are perfect examples of the range and opportunity for businesses to be industry leaders in combatting child trafficking."[58] The companies not only did the right thing, but benefitted their businesses by protecting and building their brands, reducing risks, elevating employee morale, and attracting socially responsible investors.

HIGH TECH COMPANIES FORMED A COALITION TO ADDRESS CONFLICT MINERALS

In the early 2000's, Leonardo DiCaprio and other celebrities began raising awareness about endangered species, and then human rights, related to mining minerals in Central Africa. DiCaprio's movie *Blood Diamond* provided horrific visuals connecting mass rape and murders to the sourcing of diamonds in the same region during the Sierra Leone civil war.[59]

Similar violence surrounds the sourcing of rare minerals used particularly in the manufacture of electronics. High tech companies felt threatened by negative publicity in the media by "conflict minerals" and knew they had to act. The electronic industry decided to band together in collaboration with BSR, a global NGO whose mission is to work with business to create a just and sustainable world. Together they formed the Electronic Industry Citizenship Coalition (EICC), whose goal was to harmonize the standards and assessment methods they would all use to hold each other accountable for social and environmental issues. The EICC was formed in 2004 with seven members. Today it has more than 70 member companies.[60]

The EICC, together with the Global e-Sustainability Initiative (GeSI), commissioned a joint study on mineral extraction associated with conflict as it relates to the electronics supply chain. The two business groups then formed a joint working group to develop a three-year action plan for a multi-stakeholder, multi-industry approach to a solution.

GeSI's mission is to be a globally recognized thought leader, partner of choice, and proactive driver of the information and communications technology (ICT) sustainability agenda as measured by the development and use of its tools, broad member base, and contribution to relevant policies.[61] The Public-Private Alliance for Responsible Minerals Trade (PPA)[62] is another multi-stakeholder collaboration that addresses conflict minerals in the Democratic Republic of the Congo (DRC) and Central Africa.

How is this relevant to us? "Conflict Minerals are minerals mined in conditions of armed conflict and human rights abuses, notably in the eastern provinces of the DRC. The minerals, also known as 3TG are: Tantalum (Columbite-Tantalite), Tin (Cassiterite), Tungsten (Wolframite) and Gold."[63]

Americans use conflict minerals daily, including brushing teeth with tin (contained in toothpaste); dressing in jewelry and watches made of tin, tantalum, tungsten (the 3TG), and gold; using electronics made of the 3TG; and driving in cars made of the 3TG.

Unfortunately, many people are unaware of which products contain 3TG or where they are sourced from. As a result, it is possible to unknowingly fuel the armed conflict and human rights abuses by using 3TG.[64]

Two NGOs—the Enough Project, which fights genocide and crimes against humanity in Africa,[65] and Global Witness, which runs investigations and advocacy campaigns against natural resource-related conflict and corruption and associated environmental and human rights abuses[66]—along with the media, stirred public awareness about conflict minerals. Tech companies responded. The EICC formed in 2004 and soon produced the first version of the Electronic Industry Code of Conduct. The code includes expectations of suppliers across a broad range of labor and environmental issues but did not contemplate conflict minerals in its earliest forms. As this issue matured, however, EICC proved to be the ideal organization to manage conflict minerals.[67]

As described by Tim Mohin, who was director of Sustainable Development for Intel at the time, "the epiphany was how to manage the issue. Not company by company. But to band together." Today, Mohin is director of Corporate Responsibility, Advanced Micro Devices. He is the author of *Changing Business from the Inside Out: A Treehugger's Guide to Working in Corporations*,[68] and chair of the board of the EICC.[69] Mohin shared how high-tech companies looked at the supply chain to pinpoint the choke point, which is where the smelters refine the minerals into metals.

As Deborah Albers at Dell Inc. explains, "Most companies do not have direct relationships with mining companies. Minerals are procured from multiple sources including recycled material, metal inventories, and virgin ore, and a final product may contain a number of these metals...Minerals are often mixed with recycled metals from other geographic locations and smelted together. This makes identifying the country of origin of one combined material difficult, if not impossible...These materials are not used in their raw form because they must be refined first; therefore the smelter is the right point at which to focus a common solution."[70]

As a result, explained Mohin, "we decided to approach the smelters by using an audit approach. We would require that they get their materials from conflict-free sources. For smelters that qualified, they'd be certified as conflict-free."[71]

In August 2012, the Securities and Exchange Commission (SEC) issued a final rule mandated by Section 1502 of the Dodd-Frank Wall Street Reform and Consumer Protection Act. The rule requires companies to publicly disclose their use of conflict minerals that originated in the DRC or an adjoining country.[72]

An unfortunate consequence of the monitoring and audits was the initial avoidance of minerals derived from the DRC, which took a devastating financial toll on people in the community, particularly in 2011. While avoidance of minerals from the DRC and surrounding region is still very much an issue, there are a few multi-industry programs to source conflict-free minerals from the area, such as the Conflict Free Tin Initiative (CFTI), which launched legal mining in eastern Congo[73] and is expected to produce its first refined tin in 2013.[74]

Companies have a self-interest in a conflict-free supply of minerals in order to produce their products, limit risk with regard to compliance and interruption of business, and protect their brands. By acting on that imperative, companies advance their profits, while promoting human rights.

COMPANIES SEEK TO ADDRESS SUPPLY CHAIN VIOLATIONS OF WORKER SAFETY AND PERSONAL SECURITY

Labor conditions and the treatment of workers present the modern global corporation with a serious human rights challenge and responsibility. Recently, highly publicized, tragic, and avoidable deaths of garment workers have brought greater public scrutiny of the condition of workers producing goods for the developed world. Some companies are beginning to take steps to address the humanitarian issues for their workers and within their supply chains. Companies are becoming motivated out of a desire to protect their brands, manage risk, and satisfy investors and customers.

Historically, a major impetus for improved worker conditions and safety has come from international quasi-governmental bodies, such as the International Labour Organization (ILO). The ILO was founded in 1919 following World War I to "pursue a vision based on the premise that universal, lasting peace can be established only if it is based on social justice."[75] The ILO became the first specialized agency of the United Nations in 1946 with a mission to "promote rights at work, encourage decent employment opportunities, enhance social protection, and strengthen dialogue on work-related issues."[76]

The ILO's governing body has identified eight "fundamental" conventions, addressing basic principles and rights at work, including "freedom of association and the effective recognition of the right to collective bargaining; the elimination of all forms of forced or compulsory labor; the effective abolition of child labor; and the elimination of discrimination in respect of employment and occupation."[77]

Countries that ratify the conventions commit themselves to applying them in national law. In 1995, the ILO began a campaign to achieve universal ratification of the conventions. "There are currently over 1,200 ratifications of these conventions, representing 86 percent of the possible number of ratifications." [78] The eight conventions are given below.

1. Freedom of Association and Protection of the Right to Organise Convention
2. Right to Organise and Collective Bargaining Convention
3. Forced Labour Convention
4. Abolition of Forced Labour Convention
5. Minimum Age Convention
6. Worst Forms of Child Labour Convention
7. Equal Remuneration Convention
8. Discrimination (Employment and Occupation) Convention

The fatalities and injuries due to safety hazards in apparel factories in the developing world can be understood as human rights abuses because of the tragic personal toll on the workers and their families. On May 4, 2013, following the Rana Plaza Building collapse in Bangladesh that claimed over one thousand lives,[79] the ILO High Commission issued a statement committing its tripartite partners (governments, employers, and workers) "to increase their efforts to provide every single worker in Bangladesh with a safe work place, and to ensure workers' rights and representation, regardless of whether that work place may be a garment factory, a retail shop or a bank."[80]

In May 2013, Abercrombie & Fitch became the second major American retailer—joining Phillips-Van Heusen, owner of Calvin Klein, Tommy Hilfiger, and Izod, which had signed on a year earlier—to sign an agreement to improve factory safety in Bangladesh. As reported in the *Financial Times*, the agreement had already been signed by 35 major European retailers and brands, including including H&M, Carrefour, Mango, Primark, Marks & Spencer, and Inditex, the parent of Zara.[81]

"Under the legally enforceable plan, retailers and apparel companies have committed to having rigorous, independent factory inspections, and to helping underwrite any fire safety and building repairs needed to correct violations."[82] As of May 2013, Gap has been reluctant to sign due to concerns about legal liabilities. Walmart has also been hesitant to agree.[83]

US retail companies are facing pressure from the media, US lawmakers,[84] and citizen campaigns to sign the agreement.[85] Moreover, two investors—the

Amalgamated Bank LongView Funds, and the Interfaith Center on Corporate Responsibility—together representing a total of $2.45 trillion in assets—called on American companies like Walmart, Target, Sears, and Gap to join the accord to ensure compliance with safety standards in Bangladesh and to disclose all of the factories they use.[86]

Additional investors that have signed letters to US retailers urging them to sign include Boston Common Asset Management, Christian Brothers Investment Services, Domini Social Investments, Trillium Asset Management, and Wespath Investment Management, investing on behalf of the United Methodist Church.

Investors recognize the power of companies in addressing these vital human rights issues. At the same time, these investors are exercising their influence to pressure businesses to advance progress. As reported in *The New York Times*, these investors wrote in their letter: "Acting alone, companies can and do bring about meaningful and positive changes in human rights in the countries where they source and manufacture. But when faced with intransigence of the type we have historically seen in Bangladesh on worker safety issues, we are convinced that systemic change will only occur when companies take action together."[87]

A few companies have begun to lead the way in addressing human rights issues for workers in the developing world by engaging with NGOs and quasi-governmental partners. This is an ongoing story.

COMPANIES PURSUE PROTECTIONS OF FREEDOM OF EXPRESSION AND PRIVACY ON THE INTERNET

On March 12, 2013, Google disclosed that in prior years, it had been gathering private passwords, e-mails, and other personal information from unsuspecting individuals in the course of creating online maps in 38 US states.[88] Who else might be invading your email or listening in on your mobile calls? What data is being collected about your medical and mental health, and your personal buying habits, and how is it being bought, sold and shared?[89] What personal information do we reveal about ourselves without realizing how it might be used by data collectors? [90] In what parts of the world must you be cautious about what you say online and the ramifications?

The way in which governments have used the Internet as a tool to repress freedom of expression is a grave concern. According to Amnesty International, "the Internet itself can become a tool of repression where the monitoring of communications, the censoring and filtering of information and the amassing of immense databanks of information enhance the ability of repressive governments to restrict the freedoms and basic human rights of their citizens."

The Chinese government has done so with the cooperation of global corporations.[91] In a widely publicized case, China sentenced Shi Tao, a Chinese poet and journalist, to ten years in prison for sending an email to the United States. By Yahoo!'s own admissions, Yahoo! China provided account-holder information, in compliance with a government request, that led to Shi Tao's sentencing.[92]

Global corporations are finding that coalitions can effectively address vital global challenges. In the case of freedom of expression and privacy on the Internet, China is only part of the problem. It is much bigger. "When we first established the Global Network Initiative (GNI)," said Dunstan Allison-Hope, "everyone assumed it was about China. People referred to it as 'the China Initiative.' Then came the Arab Spring, and restrictions on Internet use in many other countries. Now people see that freedom of expression and privacy on the Internet is a global issue, even here in the United States."

Hope is managing director of Advisory Services at BSR, which co-facilitated the GNI into existence. The GNI is a multi-stakeholder group, including companies, NGOs, investors, and academics, whose mission is to protect and advance freedom of expression and privacy in information and communications technologies (ICT).

Interestingly, government is not invited to the table with the GNI, Hope said. "With the issues we deal with, governments are the ones undertaking surveillance or mandating censorship and filtering, so for many people government is part of the problem not the solution."[93] Hope is the author of *Protecting Human Rights in the Digital Age*.[94]

According to chief privacy officers at ICT companies, the ability of a company to ensure its consumers of the privacy of their data puts a company at a competitive advantage. As reported by Somini Sengupta in the *New York Times*, "established companies are trying to gain market advantage by casting themselves as more privacy-friendly than their rivals." [95] In her article, "Web Privacy Becomes a Business Imperative," Sengupta described the security measures that were discussed at a gathering of Internet and ICT companies in San Francisco in early March 2013. People from Apple, Facebook, Microsoft, Google, and Mozilla shared new approaches to help their customers protect their privacy. "They're [customers] asking for a different level of privacy on your service. You have to listen to that. It's critical to your business," said Alex Fowler, Mozilla's chief privacy officer.[96]

When asked about the motivation of businesses to promote freedom of expression and privacy on the Internet, Hope explained that this position is "consistent with the UN Guiding Principles on Business and Human Rights that it is the responsibility of business to respect human rights." Additionally, he believes that companies seek to protect the rights of their users and customers. "It is in the interests of their users—and therefore of them as companies—that strong privacy and freedom of expression protections exist globally, and the GNI is one mechanism to help try to achieve that. The ICT companies exist to promote freedom of expression, not restrict it, and to help their users communicate without interference from governments."[97]

Demonstrating the concern of corporations for freedom of expression and privacy on the Internet, the following eight companies recently decided to collaborate with the GNI's initiative to exchange best practices, learning, and tools: Alcatel-Lucent, France Telecom-Orange, Millicom, Nokia Siemens Networks, Telefonica, Telenor, TeliaSonera, and Vodafone.

"This is a positive step from some of the world's largest companies providing communications and Internet access to consumers around the world, and we hope that this effort will lead to full implementation of human rights standards through membership in GNI," said Arvind Ganesan, director of business and human rights at Human Rights Watch, a member of the GNI. "This is an opportunity for GNI to learn from telecom companies about the complex human rights challenges they face and for them to learn from GNI about how they can develop an accountable system to safeguard human rights."[98]

Another multi-stakeholder group in this arena is the Center for Democracy and Technology (CDT),[99] whose mission is to conceptualize and implement public policies that will keep the Internet open, innovative, and free. CDT deals with matters such as the Cyber Intelligence Sharing and Protection Act, or CISPA, a bill that was reintroduced into the House on February 13, 2013. CISPA "allows private Internet communications and information of American citizens to go directly to the NSA, a military intelligence agency that operates secretly with little public accountability," according to CDT president Leslie Harris. "Once that private information is in the hands of the military, it can be used for purposes completely unrelated to cybersecurity."[100] CDT also deals with privacy of personal health data,[101] and freedom of expression on the Internet.[102]

A third nonprofit that addresses freedom of expression and privacy on the Internet is the Berkman Center for Internet and Society at Harvard University. The Berkman Center's mission is to explore and understand cyberspace, to study its development, dynamics, norms, and standards, and to assess the need or lack thereof for laws and sanctions.[103]

Protecting privacy on the Internet is challenging for ICT companies, given the demands placed on them by governments to reveal personal information about their users. You might imagine that more totalitarian governments placed demands on ICT companies for personal user data. In fact, however, "the countries that made the most requests and received information from Microsoft for Skype noncontent information last year, in descending order, were Britain, the United States, Germany, France and Taiwan, which together accounted for about 80 percent of the requests," according to the *New York Times*.[104]

"Noncontent information" is defined as an account holder's name, sex, email address, IP address, country of residence, and dates and times of data traffic, whereas "content information" is described as actual content of a communication, like the subject heading of an email, the contents of an email, or a picture stored on SkyDrive, its cloud computing service.

While companies might be required to comply with law enforcement requests, they are stepping forward to disclose information to the public about such requests. In fact, the *New York Times* article reported that Microsoft was joining the ranks of Google, Twitter, and other Web businesses in disclosing the number of requests it had received from government law enforcement agencies for data on its hundreds of millions of customers around the world. Microsoft said it planned to update its transparency report every six months.

Both the Center for Democracy and Technology (CDT) and The Internet Association celebrated a victory in April 2013 when the Senate Judiciary Committee passed the Electronic Communications Privacy Amendments Act (ECPA) of 2013. The Internet Association represents the interests of America's leading Internet companies, such as Amazon, Google, Facebook, and Expedia. The Internet Association is "dedicated to advancing public policy solutions to strengthen and protect Internet freedom, foster innovation and economic growth, and empower users."[105] Passage of the ECPA is regarded as a significant step "to ensure emails and documents we store in the cloud receive the same Fourth Amendment Protections as postal mail and documents we store in desk drawers in our homes," said Greg Nojeim, senior counsel at the CTD.[106]

Companies are advancing the important human right of free expression. This protects their customers, serves the core business values, and promotes its competitive position in the marketplace.

THE UNITED NATIONS GUIDING PRINCIPLES PROVIDE A FRAMEWORK FOR COMPANIES TO DEFINE THEIR HUMAN RIGHTS RESPONSIBILITIES AND ASSESS THEIR IMPACTS

Human trafficking, freedom of expression and privacy on the internet, and conflict minerals are just a few human rights issues where corporations have opportunities and responsibilities. "How does a global company with the breadth of operations of Microsoft talk about human rights? How do we protect the rights of users? Supply chains? How do we get our arms around these issues? These are the questions we were asking," explained Dan Bross, senior director, Corporate Citizenship, Microsoft. "On June 16, 2011, the Ruggie Principles provided clarity," Bross continued, referring to the United Nations Guiding Principles. "That gave us the framework that we needed to think about our responsibilities."[107]

By early 2013, more than 10,000 business and non-business entities from 145 countries worldwide are participating in the Global Compact. The Guiding Principles further clarify a company's human rights obligations under the Global Compact.[108]

Microsoft signed onto the Global Compact in 2006. When the Guiding Principles were issued by the United Nations in 2011, Microsoft tasked Bross to form and lead a cross-company working group to develop the company's human rights statement and related work. Bross worked with the company's business segments to define the company's responsibilities within its supply chain—to respect Microsoft's users and employees.

"We looked at our mission and our responsibilities as a corporate citizen and came up with a statement which is now online," he said. The statement reads as follows: "Our commitment to respect fundamental human rights of our employees, people working for our suppliers, and our customers reflects Microsoft's company mission to help people and businesses throughout the world realize their full potential."[108] The statement continues on to commit to the Guiding Principles.[109]

The statement concludes by noting that: "To help advance the thinking and discussion in the area of ICT [information and communications technology] and human rights responsibilities and commitment, we established a Technology and Human Rights Center."[110]

Once committed to the Guiding Principles, Microsoft moved forward to assess the human rights impacts of its operations on an ongoing basis through a Human Rights Impact Assessment (HRIA) process. BSR says that an HRIA is "part of every company's responsibility to treat all human beings with respect and dignity." BSR anticipates that "HRIAs will become a key component of companies' strategies for new product development, market entry, and other key business decisions."[111] Microsoft is working with BSR to develop its human rights impact assessment approach based on the company's commitments and responsibilities.[112]

Bross cautions that some companies are afraid of exposing risks through the human rights assessment. His view, however, is that "it's already a corporate responsibility to assess risk. We're merely adding human rights. This work is a journey, not a destination. We as a company are seeking to institutionalize, systematize, synthesize, and operationalize human rights issues...to figure out the human rights checklist we need to go through when developing new products, devices, and services. This is just part of a system of doing business."

"It's the government's responsibility is to *protect* human rights, but it's the company's responsibility is to *respect* human rights," Bross pointed out. "The Guiding Principles gave us the framework to fulfill that responsibility." He also noted that adherence to the Guiding Principles is voluntary, although companies are judged in the court of public opinion based on their respect for human rights. Bross also commented on the role of NGOs and the media in holding companies accountable for meeting their social and environmental responsibilities.[113]

BSR finds that companies benefit from the results of the human rights impact assessment as well as the process itself. "We have found that the process of conducting an HRIA can help build internal capacity, strengthen stakeholder relations, and yield important insights into the effectiveness of existing company policies, processes, and tools," according to the BSR report.[114]

Additional benefits to companies that perform human rights impact assessments include maintaining a good reputation, identifying and managing risks, creating a legal and social license to operate, increasing the motivation and productivity of workers, understanding the society in which the company works, attracting investors, and advancing sustainable development.[115]

"The HRIA process serves as a key tool for Microsoft to develop a strong point of view and strategy on human rights," Bross said. "Aligning the HRIA with the company's strategy and human rights principles resulted in clear, actionable recommendations that enabled Microsoft to manage its risks and maximize its opportunities for positive impact."[116]

COMPANIES RECOGNIZE THAT THE GOLDEN RULE IS GOOD FOR BUSINESS AND A BETTER WORLD

As employers of tens of millions of people worldwide, purchasers at the tops of massive supply chains, and owners of vast global property and agribusinesses, global corporations affect the rights of many people who live on this planet. Laws and the commitment to enforcement vary from one country to another. Multinational corporations, however, are in a powerful position to respect—and even sometimes to protect—human rights throughout the world. The voices of customers, employees, and investors matter. Companies can increase their profits while improving the human condition.

CHAPTER 8

SUCCESSFUL COMPANIES ENSURE EFFECTIVE BOARD GOVERNANCE, ENGAGE STAKEHOLDERS, AND COLLABORATE WITH NGOS AND EACH OTHER

We are given our identities by other persons and other things. We are named by everything we ever knew and by everything we ever did.
　　　　　　　　　　　　　　　　　—Amos Oz and Fania Oz-Salzberger [1]

DEFEATING POVERTY, MITIGATING THE PACE OF GLOBAL WARMING AND THE destruction of natural ecosystems, and advancing education, healthcare, and human rights are ambitious goals. National governments do not have the authority and resources to offer sufficient solutions, nor has the international community achieved binding and actionable agreements to address global problems. Only multinational corporations have the might, the financial motivation, the worldwide influence, and the long-term wherewithal to accomplish these purposes. Furthermore, businesses that are leading the way are showing that innovative solutions to social, environmental, and economic challenges can be profitable.

Multinational companies at the sustainability forefront also understand that there are three keys to success: First, ensuring effective board governance of the company's sustainability strategy and achievements; second, engaging with stakeholders, including customers, employees, investors, and communities, in an iterative conversation on global problem-solving; and third, collaborating with other companies and NGOs to advance the company's sustainability agenda. This chapter will provide best practices in these areas.

EFFECTIVE BOARD GOVERNANCE

The board of directors has the legal and fiduciary responsibility to ensure the company's prosperity. As shown in this book, risks in the twenty-first century include scarcity of resources, high costs of fossil fuels, labor conflicts, community resistance resulting from human rights abuses, and the lack of a qualified workforce for high technology jobs. As also presented in this book, growth opportunities abound for companies that pursue innovative solutions to global challenges. These are boardroom issues.

Since accountability for the company's sustainability strategy rests with the board, it is essential for the board to have a sustainability committee to help facilitate oversight. The board should receive and review reports from the committee to fulfill its own duties of oversight, and also know that management incentives and practices are aligned with sustainability goals.

SUSTAINABILITY IS A MATTER FOR BOARD OVERSIGHT

Given the centrality of sustainability to the vitality and value of the company, there are a number of key considerations for the board of directors. These are some of the more significant issues for board members to understand.

1. How the sustainability agenda will drive innovation, growth, and profits.
2. Risks, including environmental (energy, and natural resources, among others) and social (labor, and community, among others).
3. The company's policies and practices related to disclosure and transparency in order to support stakeholder engagement, promote trust, and foster communications and relationships with customers, employees, investors, and other stakeholders.
4. Accountability systems and management practices to ensure that ongoing evaluation, metrics, and incentives (including compensation practices) are in place so that sustainability goals have the highest likelihood of success.
5. Plans for reporting on sustainability goals, progress, impediments, and remedies to the board of directors.

BOARD COMPOSITION

In order to ensure that a company is competitive in the global marketplace, it is important for boards to be composed of people with the diversity of experience, expertise, and perspectives to address the most vital challenges and opportunities. Boards that are entrenched with minimal turnover, homogenous composition, insufficient numbers of members who grew up in the Internet and advanced technology era, and/or few or no international members and women, run the risk of missing opportunities to advance the company by fully embracing innovation and capturing new markets.[2]

BOARD COMMITTEES

It is a best practice for the board of directors to have a committee specifically designated to oversee the company's sustainability strategy and its performance, and to discuss it with the board. Unilever's board, for example, has a "corporate responsibility committee." Its role is to "oversee Unilever's conduct as a responsible business, including monitoring the progress—and potential risk—of the Plan and ensuring this is fed back to the Board." Unilever's board committee meets quarterly and is composed of three non-executive directors.[3]

Nike also has a corporate responsibility committee of the board of directors "to review significant policies and activities and make recommendations regarding labor and environmental practices, community affairs, charitable and foundation activities, diversity and equal opportunity, and environmental and sustainability initiatives."[4] Nike's board committee meets four times a year and is composed of four non-executive directors. Nike's committee meetings are attended by the company chairman or CEO.

It is important for the committee to have a clearly defined role, to meet on a regular basis, to be composed of non-executive directors with relevant expertise, and to be joined by the CEO or chairman at meetings. The chief sustainability officer should be responsible to the committee.

COMPANIES MAXIMIZE SUSTAINABILITY RESULTS BY ENGAGING WITH STAKEHOLDERS

A company will maximize its social, environmental, and economic impacts by engaging with key stakeholders for meaningful input. Stakeholders include, among others, customers, employees, investors, and communities where the company operates.

STAKEHOLDER ENGAGEMENT

The hallmark of an effective sustainability program is its engagement with a variety of stakeholders in meaningful discussions about company decisions that will have social, environmental, and economic impacts. Examples might include the location or relocation of a major facility in an emerging market, the sourcing of natural resources from a particular geographic location, pricing a product that will affect a segment of the community that is price-sensitive, or creating a new product or service that is designed to address a social or environmental challenge. Companies involve stakeholders in a variety of formats, including large and small group discussions— sometimes scheduled for a couple of hours, or up to two full days. Sessions are often facilitated by outside professionals, who bring expertise and a fresh perspective

The wisdom of involving stakeholders lies in understanding that in today's communications environment, stakeholders will ensure that their voices are heard, whether they are invited or not, and they can make themselves heard quite publicly—very possibly throughout the world in a matter of moments. Companies are learning that it is to their benefit to welcome stakeholders to the table and incorporate their valuable input as they make critical strategic business decisions.

Businesses are also realizing that it is smart to have continuous, ongoing conversations with community stakeholders in order to avert conflicts on human rights, where human lives and billions of corporate dollars can be at stake.

Building good will with communities where employees live and work helps ensure that employees are motivated, and that local citizens, businesses, and organizations are supportive. This, in turn, helps to ensure that the company will profit through higher productivity, a good brand, and increased sales.

Global corporations are also recognizing the value of creating stakeholder advisory councils (SACs) or enhancing the role and functionality of their existing SACs. With SACs, companies can convene a small group of highly qualified experts together with the company's executives for candid discussions about corporate strategies and their implications for social, environmental, and economic impacts.

Several of the companies featured in this book have stakeholder advisory councils. They practice a range of approaches with regard to their composition, frequency and duration of meetings, and agendas. Based on observations of numerous SACs, these are good practices for corporations in establishing or strengthening SACs.

1. *Determine the company's vision* of its greater potential in terms of its social, environmental, and economic impact. Again, this must be aligned with the corporate mission and goals. And again, review this at least every other year, or with a change in company leadership.

2. *Determine the SAC's purpose*—the compelling value the sustainability advisory council (SAC) will be tasked to achieve. This must focus on the company's goals for sustainability, including being fully aligned with the corporate mission.

3. *Establish the role and responsibilities of the SAC*, based on its purpose, and articulate how council members are expected to help advance the company in achieving its greater potential with regard to sustainability. Most companies are very clear that the role of the council is strictly advisory, with no oversight.

4. *Determine the ideal composition*, based on the role of the SAC. Consider what will be required to achieve the best results including diversity of perspectives, experience, and expertise.

5. *Determine the number and duration of meetings* to accomplish the SAC's purpose.

6. *Create thoughtful and purposeful agendas* based on the role of the council and the company's key sustainability challenges and opportunities.

As one experienced SAC member noted, "Through discussions with SAC members, the company's CEO can have an unfiltered, candid, and confidential conversation about the future of the business."[5]

7. *Plan new member orientations* in order to maximize the value of council member participation. A number of companies invite new members to spend a day or two at a key manufacturing site and to meet with members of the executive team to learn about the business before participating in their first council meeting.

8. *Consider terms and term limits.* Company practices vary widely. The primary benefit of term limits is that it encourages a pace of rotation, which provides greater opportunities for fresh and diverse membership and thinking.

9. *Demonstrate the impact of the SAC's contribution.* A best practice is to include in the company's sustainability report, and other appropriate communications, a summary of the SAC's key contributions and how the SAC's work has influenced company decisions and policies.

10. *Recognize and appreciate the time and contribution of members.* This can include thoughtful acknowledgements from the CEO and the chief sustainability officer, as well as conveniences with travel and meeting arrangements.

CORPORATE SUSTAINABILITY REPORTS

Just as companies provide annual financial reports to disclose information related to their financial value, so corporations are seeing the merits of demonstrating their social, environmental, and economic impacts—sometimes referred to as "sustainability reports." The Global Reporting Initiative (GRI)—an NGO whose mission is to "make sustainability reporting standard practice for all organizations"—provides a sustainability framework that is in its fourth design iteration in fourteen years.[6]

The International Integrated Reporting Council (IIRC), also an NGO, seeks to create "the globally accepted international framework that elicits from organizations material information about their strategy, governance, performance and prospects in a clear, concise and comparable format."[7]

The Sustainability Accounting Standards Board (SASB) is a US-based nonprofit "engaged in the development and dissemination of industry-specific sustainability accounting standards."[8]

According to the Governance and Accounting Institute,[9] there is a dramatic rise in sustainability reporting among companies in the S&P 500 Index and the Fortune 500. In just one year, there was a jump from 19 percent of the S&P 500 reporting in 2011, to 53 percent of the S&P 500 reporting in

2012. Among Fortune 500 companies, there was an increase from 20 percent reporting in 2011 to 57 percent reporting in 2012.

The G & A Institute indicates that reporting benefits companies. "Increased transparency and disclosure build better relationships with stakeholders that can impact a company's reputation, valuation, and right to operate."[10] Additionally, companies that can show their commitment to sustainability can attract investment dollars. According to "the Impact of Sustainable and Responsible Investment," published by the US SIF Foundation in 2013, "testaments to the growing impact of SRI [socially responsible investment] on the investment market place can be found in the creation of SRI indices and in the development of the Principles for Responsible Investment (PRI) whose signatories—with assets over $ 30 trillion—are now estimated to represent 20 percent of the estimated total value of global capital markets."[11]

Eric Roston, sustainability editor of Bloomberg.com, noted the relevance of these reports. "GRI provided structure, rigor, and definition for companies to report on a broad range of social and environmental issues. The metrics were developed to help companies measure and disclose their performance on topics that are non-traditional in reporting. There are a number of important organizations that are developing different elements within sustainability reporting including GRI, SASB, IIRC, and CDP. Ideas and practices are maturing every year. The next phase will be more industry specific standards."[12] According to Roston, this information provided by companies can be very useful to institutional investors, journalists, governments, and NGOs.

Additional information is provided in chapter two about The Sustainability Consortium (TSC). TSC is the first organization that is developing and disseminating a standardized framework to measure and communicate sustainability-related information throughout the product value chain.[13] This information is already being used by major retail purchasers, like Walmart, to assess their supply chains.[14]

It is estimated that energy costs can comprise as much as 20 percent of a manufacturing company's production costs. Recall that in Chapter 3, Gail Klintworth of Unilever noted that only 4 percent of the company's greenhouse gas emissions are in operations, while 24 percent are around sourcing.[15] Research provided by TSC can help companies make decisions to reduce costs and mitigate risks—both fundamental to corporate sustainability and profitability. Eventually, suppliers who want to be competitive are likely to shift to more energy efficient practices, which then becomes a virtuous cycle. Once again, it is the corporate sector that is driving systemic change that can alter the pace of climate change.

SOCIAL MEDIA

Another effective form of stakeholder engagement is via social media, including blogging and tweeting. "Even the stodgiest companies have found their way onto Twitter. They have discovered...it's more like a conversation they need to join or risk losing influence over how consumers view them or their brands," says the *Wall Street Journal*.[16] In fact, as of July 2012, 82 percent of the Fortune 100 Global companies have at least one Twitter account.[17] Furthermore, companies in the Fortune 100 were mentioned online more than ten million times in a one-month period, and on most occasions that was on Twitter.

Additionally, a survey reported in *Harvard Business Review*[18] says that people are more likely to trust a company whose CEO and team engage in social media, and that people are likely or more willing to buy from a company whose mission and values are defined through their leaderships' involvement in social media. The BRANDfog 2012 CEO, Social Media and Leadership Survey demonstrated that "executive engagement in social media raises the brand profile and instills confidence in a company's leadership team."[19] Through social media, corporate leaders—including CEOs and chief sustainability officers—have an opportunity to shape their messages, engage in ongoing dialogs with influencers in the corporate and NGO sectors, and hear and address the interests of customers, employees, and investors as well as others.

Social media is an open forum that builds trust and relationships. Companies are learning that if they are not part of the conversation, it will happen without them.

COMPANIES ENHANCE THEIR CSR RESULTS THROUGH PARTNERSHIPS

Companies will maximize the success of their sustainability efforts by collaborating with NGOs and other businesses.

CORPORATE-NGO PARTNERSHIPS

Corporations bring valuable resources to bear in achieving social, environmental, and economic impacts. Companies have much to gain, however, by accessing and leveraging the expertise, community relationships, and credibility of particular NGO partners for specific initiatives/programs within a company's overall sustainability strategy. As seen in chapters two through seven, global corporations often have different, and even multiple, NGO partners for each of the company's particular sustainability projects. There are a number of ways to maximize the benefits and opportunities of NGO partnerships.

1. *Be clear in the mission and goals of your company program.* State the mission or purpose of the program, how it aligns with the company's overall sustainability mission and corporate mission, the goals for the initiative, and how the company will measure results.

2. *Determine the company's greatest assets in achieving the mission and goals.* Identify the company's strengths and gaps—with regard to expertise, credibility, and relationships with individuals and institutions whose engagement and support will be essential for the program's success.

3. *Identify the initiative's primary leadership within the company.* Identify the lead person at the company and clearly define the person's role. Also identify additional parties within the company who will be consulted, and articulate their roles in the program. Ensure that each of these people understands what is expected of them.

4. *Be strategic in identifying one or more NGO partners.* Consider the gaps that were identified in #2, above—with regard to expertise, credibility, and relationships with individuals and institutions whose engagement and support will be essential for success. Research and identify several NGOs that could potentially bring such values to a partnership relationship.

5. *Consider the benefits that the company has to offer to prospective NGO partners.* In creating a short list of potential partners, consider the possible value that the company could offer to each NGO in terms of a win-win relationship. Think in terms of the NGO missions and how the company can help the organization to achieve its purposes while the company accomplishes its own interests, and consider the resources that the company can bring to bear, such as expertise, technology, and funding.

6. *Explore potential partnership relationships with each NGO that has been identified.* Meet and explore what is possible with each potential partner.

7. *Choose the NGO partner(s).* Make the selection based on the value that each partner brings in helping to maximize the success of the initiative as well as the company's confidence and trust in the NGO's ability to deliver what it promises. Be sure that the company project and overall sustainability mission aligns with the mission of each NGO partner.

8. *Identify the NGO leadership for the initiative.* Be clear about the person who has primary responsibility for the initiative at the NGO, and clearly define the person's role. Also identify additional parties within

the NGO who will be consulted, and articulate their roles in the initiative. Ensure that each of these people understands what is expected of them.

9. *Establish clear expectations and measurable goals.* Create a clear plan that is mutually agreeable and mutually beneficial. Establish a system for regular reports and discussions—perhaps quarterly—to provide opportunities to continuously assess and potentially refine planning as needed.

10. *Consider the value of a committee.* Depending on the size and scope of the initiative, and the stakeholders who are involved, consider establishing an advisory committee or council. If a committee is established, articulate its role clearly, and create agendas thoughtfully with the group's purpose in mind.

11. *Provide reports about the program's progress.* Provide clear, accurate, and timely reports to key stakeholders about the progress of the initiative, showing measurable outcomes for each goal. Give opportunities for interested parties to offer input and respond to them accordingly.

12. *Recognize and appreciate people and organizations that contribute assistance.* Thank people and organizations for their assistance in reports and on the website where appropriate.

BUSINESS COALITIONS

As shown in a number of chapters, companies are forming coalitions with each other and with NGOs to address social, environmental, and economic challenges together. One example is the Digital Energy and Sustainability Solutions Campaign (DESSC), the coalition of information and communications technology (ICT) companies and associations, NGOs, customers and other stakeholders who recognize how ICT enables improvements to the environment and drives long-term economic growth. The DESSC seeks to advance strategies to improve energy efficiency and reduce greenhouse gas emissions, improve broadband penetration to encourage innovations through intelligent connected devices, and raise funding for clean energy.

Another example is the Global e-Sustainability Initiative (GeSI), an NGO whose members include over 30 of the world's leading service providers and vendors from the ICT sector, including AT&T, Ericsson, HP, Microsoft, Sprint, and Verizon. GeSI envisions a sustainable world through responsible ICT-enabled transformation. Their work, together with the Electronic Industry Citizenship Coalition, includes the development of an action plan to address conflict minerals. The Sustainable Apparel Coalition seeks to expand the adoption of the Higg Index for measuring the environmental and social performance of apparel products. The Global Business Coalition Against Human Trafficking, praised by President Obama at the Clinton Global Initiative Annual Meeting 2012, fights human trafficking. The Global Network Initiative, originally launched by BSR, addresses freedom of expression and privacy on the Internet. And BSR's HERproject works with multiple corporations to foster women's economic empowerment.

Aron Cramer, CEO of BSR, foresees further expansion of business coalitions. "Coalitions are an essential tool and in some ways the best tool related to sustainability," he said. "The leaders in this field are most acutely aware of what they can and cannot accomplish. That's an interesting change in perspective. Usually we see leaders thinking they can do the most. In this case, however, they know that on their own they can only get to a certain point. They realize they can make greater progress with coalitions."[20]

Another venue for further collaboration is the Clinton Global Initiative, which works year-round to foster partnerships among companies, NGOs, and governments to advance nine broad and cross-cutting tracks, each representing a topical global challenge or strategic approach. The tracks include the built environment, education and workforce development, energy, environmental stewardship, girls and women, global health, market-based approaches, response and resilience, and technology.[21] The annual meetings,[22] held each fall in New York City, are celebrated events where members convene to learn, share, and recognize partnership announcements together with President Clinton, who participates throughout the three days.

To date CGI members have made more than 2,300 commitments, which have improved the lives of over 400 million people in more than 180 countries. When fully funded and implemented, these commitments will be valued at more than $73.1 billion.[23]

LOOKING TO THE FUTURE

Global corporations have the human capital, the financial resources, the technology, the international footprint, the power of markets, and the profit motivation to build a better world. NGOs will be essential partners— essential for their expertise and their commitment to mission. Governments will be vital partners—vital as representative bodies. By engaging together through an iterative process, we will achieve "A Better World."

Companies can build profitable brands and businesses by capturing the wisdom of stakeholders from the far corners of the world, including women and girls who have been disenfranchised, young employees who are adept with new technology, social media, and solutions, consumers communicating on the Internet worldwide, grassroots NGOs in the communities where they do business, and investors who understand that companies are more valuable when they incorporate sustainability into planning.

The stories in this book show that companies are the likeliest institutions to build a better world, that they are beginning to show promise of their capacity to do so, and that you can play a part in making this so.

NOTES

1   ONLY GLOBAL CORPORATIONS HAVE THE RESOURCES, GLOBAL REACH, AND SELF-INTEREST TO BUILD A BETTER WORLD

1. Amartya Sen, *Development as Freedom* (New York, NY: Anchor Books, 1999).
2. "Engaging Tomorrow's Consumer," *World Economic Forum*, January 2013, http://www.accenture.com/SiteCollectionDocuments/PDF/Accenture -Engaging-Tomorrows-Consumer.pdf (June 29, 2013).
3. Alice Korngold and Elizabeth Voudouris, "Corporate Volunteerism: Strategic Community Involvement," in *Corporate Philanthropy at the Crossroads*, pp. 23–40 (Burlingame, Dwight F., and Dennis R. Young, eds, Bloomington: Indiana University Press, 1996). Alice Korngold, Alice, *Leveraging Good Will: Strengthening Nonprofits by Engaging Businesses*, (San Francisco: Jossey-Bass, A Wiley Imprint, 2005)..
4. Alice Korngold, "Clifford Chance's Innovative Approach to CSR," *Fast Company*, February 5, 2009, http://www.fastcompany.com/1150791/clifford -chance%E2%80%99s-innovative-approach-csr (June 11, 2013).
5. Alice Korngold, *Leveraging Good Will: Strengthening Nonprofits by Engaging Businesses* (San Francisco: Jossey-Bass, 2005), pp. 27–48.
6. Alice Korngold, "Corporate Social Responsibility: Leveraging Good Will," *Fast Company,* February 17, 2009, http://www.fastcompany.com/1172036 /corporate-social-responsibility-leveraging-good-will (June 29, 2013).
7. Alice Korngold, "How Green Is Your Boardroom?," *Fast Company*, June 13, 2011, http://www.fastcompany.com/1759311/how-green-your-boardroom (June 29, 2013).
8. Robert Hunter Wade, "The Rising Inequality of World Income Distribution," *Finance & Development*, December 2001, Vol. 38, Number 4, http://www .imf.org/external/pubs/ft/fandd/2001/12/wade.htm (June 29, 2013).
9. Susan E. Rice, "The National Security Implications of Global Poverty" in *Confronting Poverty: Weak States and U.S. National Security*, Chaper 1 (Rice, Susan E. et al., Washington, D.C.: Brookings Institution Press, 2010), http://www.brookings.edu/~/media/press/books/2010/confrontingpoverty /confrontingpoverty_chapter.pdf (June 9, 2013).

168   NOTES

10. "Global Risks 2013—Eighth Edition," *World Economic Forum*, http://www3
.weforum.org/docs/WEF_GlobalRisks_Report_2013.pdf (September 3, 2013).
11. John Ruggie, *Just Business* (London: W.W. Norton, 2013).

2   ECONOMIC DEVELOPMENT

1. Mark Engler, "Dr. Martin Luther King's Economics: Through Jobs, Freedom,"
The Nation, February 1, 2010. http://www.thenation.com/article/dr-martin
-luther-kings-economics-through-jobs-freedom.
2. "New Estimates Reveal Drop in Extreme Poverty 2005–2010," *The World
Bank*, February 29, 2012, http://econ.worldbank.org/WBSITE/EXTERNAL
/EXTDEC/0,,contentMDK:23129612~pagePK:64165401~piPK:64165026
~theSitePK:469372,00.html (June 9, 2013).
3. "Our Shared Opportunity: A Vision for Global Prosperity," *Center for
Strategic International Studies*, 2013, http://csis.org/files/publication/130304
_Nesseth_DevCouncilReport_Web.pdf, (June 9, 2013).
4. "New Estimates Reveal Drop in Extreme Poverty 2005–2010," *The World
Bank*, February 29, 2012, http://econ.worldbank.org/WBSITE/EXTERNAL
/EXTDEC/0,,contentMDK:23129612~pagePK:64165401~piPK:64165026
~theSitePK:469372,00.html (June 9, 2013).
5. "United Nations Millennium Development Goals," *United Nations*, http://
www.un.org/millenniumgoals/ (June 9, 2013).
6. "Our Shared Opportunity: A Vision for Global Prosperity," *Center for
Strategic International Studies*, http://csis.org/files/publication/130304
_Nesseth_DevCouncilReport_Web.pdf (June 9, 2013).
7. "The Business Case for Development: How Companies Can Drive Sustainable
Development and How Government Donors Can Leverage Their Impact,"
July 24, 2012, *Initiative for Global Development*, http://www.igdleaders.org
/insight/business-case-for-development/ (September 2, 2013).
8. Damian Hattingh et al., "The Rise of the African Consumer," *McKinsey
& Company*, October 2012. http://www.mckinsey.com/global_locations
/africa/south_africa/en/rise_of_the_african_consumer (June 9, 2013).
9. "New Estimates Reveal Drop in Extreme Poverty 2005–2010," *The World
Bank*, February 29, 2012, http://econ.worldbank.org/WBSITE/EXTERNAL
/EXTDEC/0,,contentMDK:23129612~pagePK:64165401~piPK:64165026
~theSitePK:469372,00.html (June 9, 2013).
10. Laurence Chandy and Homi Kharas, "The Contradictions in Global Poverty
Numbers," Brookings, March 6, 2012, http://www.brookings.edu/research
/opinions/2012/03/06-contradictions-poverty-numbers-kharas-chandy
(June 9, 2013).
11. Laurence Chandy (Fellow at Brookings), interview with the author, April 18,
2013.
12. Ibid.
13. "About BRAC USA," brac, http://www.brac.net/content/about-brac-usa#
.UiT4xD9ejN0 (September 2, 2013).

14. Alice Korngold, "BRAC Is the Largest Global Anti-Poverty Organization, and It's a Secret," May 17, 2011, http://www.fastcompany.com/1753519 /brac-largest-global-anti-poverty-organization-and-its-secret (June 9, 2013).

15. Susan Davis (founder, president, and CEO, BRAC USA), interview with the author, April 19, 2013.

16. "Climate Change and Poverty Reduction *UNDP*," *United Nations Development Programme*, http://www.undp.org/content/undp/en/home /ourwork/environmentandenergy/strategic_themes/climate_change/focus _areas/climate_change_andpovertyreduction/ (June 9, 2013).

17. Robert Hunter Wade, "The Rising Inequality of World Income Distribution," *Finance & Development*, December 2001, Vol. 38, Number 4, http://www .imf.org/external/pubs/ft/fandd/2001/12/wade.htm (June 9, 2013).

18. "A New Strategic Vision for Girls and Women: Stopping Poverty before It Starts," *UK Department for International Development*, 2011, https://www .gov.uk/government/uploads/system/uploads/attachment_data/file/67582 /strategic-vision-girls-women.pdf (June 9, 2013).

19. "Global Risks 2013—Eighth Edition," *World Economic Forum*, 2013, http:// reports.weforum.org/global-risks-2013/ (June 9, 2013).

20. "Divided We Stand: Why Inequality Keeps Rising," OECD, 2011, p. 24, http://www.oecd.org/els/soc/49499779.pdf (September 2, 2013).

21. The World Bank, Gini Index, http://data.worldbank.org/indicator/SI.POV .GINI (August 27, 2013).

22. Robert Hunter Wade, "The Rising Inequality of World Income Distribution," *Finance & Development*, December 2001, Vol. 38, Number 4, http://www .imf.org/external/pubs/ft/fandd/2001/12/wade.htm (June 9, 2013).

23. "The Great Divide: Global Income Inequality and Its Cost," http://www .globalpost.com/special-reports/global-income-inequality-great-divide -globalpost (June 9, 2013).

24. Ibid.

25. "History—Organisation for Economic Cooperation and Development," *OECD*, http://www.oecd.org/about/history/ (June 9, 2013).

26. "The Great Divide: Global Income Inequality and Its Cost," http://www .globalpost.com/special-reports/global-income-inequality-great-divide -globalpost (June 9, 2013).

27. Susan E. Rice, "The National Security Implications of Global Poverty," in *Confronting Poverty: Weak States and U.S. National Security*, Chapter 1 (Rice, Susan E. et al., Washington, D.C.: Brookings Institution Press, 2010), http://www.brookings.edu/~/media/press/books/2010/confrontingpoverty /confrontingpoverty_chapter.pdf (June 9, 2013).

28. Thomas Friedman, "Without Water, Revolution," *The New York Times*, May 18, 2013, http://www.nytimes.com/2013/05/19/opinion/sunday/friedman-without -water-revolution.html?pagewanted=1&_r=3&hpw (June 9, 2013).

29. Joshua W. Busby, "Climate Change and National Security," *Council on Foreign Relations*, November 2007, http://www.cfr.org/climate-change /climate-change-national-security/p14862 (June 9, 2013).

30. Joshua W. Busby, "Climate Change and National Security," *Council on Foreign Relations*, November 2007, http://www.cfr.org/climate-change /climate-change-national-security/p14862 (June 9, 2013).

31. Joshua W. Busby, "Climate Change and National Security," *Council on Foreign Relations*, November 2007, http://www.cfr.org/climate-change /climate-change-national-security/p14862 (June 9, 2013).

32. "About Us," *Clinton Global Initiative*, http://www.clintonglobalinitiative .org/aboutus/ (June 9, 2013).

33. "Homepage," The Dow Chemical Company, http://www.dow.com/ (June 9, 2013).

34. Jacqueline Novogratz (founder, president, and CEO, Acumen), interview with the author, September 24, 2012.

35. Bo Miller (global director, Corporate Citizenship, The Dow Chemical Company; president and executive director, The Dow Chemical Company Foundation), interview with the author, January 3, 2013.

36. "Homepage," WaterHealth, http://www.waterhealth.com/ (September 7, 2013).

37. Yazmina Zaidman (director of Communications and Strategic Partnerships, Acumen), interview with the author, March 7, 2013.

38. Siri Roland Xavier et al., "Global Entrepreneurship Monitor—2012 Global Report," *Global Entrepreneurship Monitor*, http://www.gemconsortium.org /docs/download/2645 (June 9, 2013).

39. "OECD iLibrary: Statistics / OECD Science and Technology Industry Scoreboard / 2011 Policy Environment," *OECD*, 2011, http://www.oecd-ilibrary .org/sites/stI_scoreboard-2011-en/05/08/index.html;jsessionid=2tc41oft697pq .delta?contentType=&itemId=/content/chapter/stI_scoreboard-2011–51 -en&containerItemId=/content/serial/20725345&accessItemIds=/content /book/stI_scoreboard-2011-en&mimeType=text/html (September 2, 2013).

40. George Eby Matthew, "Emerging Markets Are Still Difficult for Entrepreneurs," *Forbes*, November 11, 2011, http://www.forbes.com/sites /infosys/2011/11/11/emerging-markets/ (June 9, 2013).

41. Michael Levett and Ashley Chandler, "Maximizing Development of Local Content across Industry Sectors in Emerging Markets: How Private-Sector Self-Interest Can Help US Development Policy," *Center for Strategic and International Studies*, May 2012, http://csis.org/files/publication/120517 _Levett_LocalContentDevel_web.pdf (June 9, 2013).

42. Ibid.

43. John Harrington (public affairs manager, Africa and Asia Pacific, ExxonMobil), interview with the author, February 15, 2013.

44. Harry Pastuszek, "The Drive for Local Content," *PetroleumAfrica*, March 2013, http://www.petroleumafrica.com/magazine/ (August 27, 2013).

45. John Harrington (public affairs manager, Africa and Asia Pacific, ExxonMobil), interview with the author, February 15, 2013.

46. Suzanne McCarron (president, ExxonMobil Foundation), interview with the author, February 15, 2013.

47. Deirdre White (president and CEO, PYXERA Global), interview with the author, February 27, 2013.

48. Deirdre White, "Local Content, National Content, and the Changing Attitudes of an Industry," *borderlessblog*, October 1, 2012, http://cdcdevelopment solutions.org/blog/2012/10/local-content-national-content-and-the -changing-attitudes-of-an-industry (June 9, 2013).
49. Ibid.
50. Deirdre White, "Regional Content as an Alternative to Local Content: Is It Feasible?," *borderlessblog*, http://www.cdcdevelopmentsolutions.org/blog /2012/10/regional-content-as-an-alternative-to-local-content-is-it-feasible (June 9, 2013).
51. Brooke Avory (CiYuan program manager, BSR), interview with the author, January 9, 2013.
52. "Homepage" *BSR*, http://www.bsr.org/ (June 9, 2013).
53. Brooke Avory (CiYuan program manager, BSR), interview with the author, January 9, 2013.
54. Luella Chavez D'Angelo (chief communications officer, Western Union), interview with the author, September 22, 2012.
55. Samantha Walker (Global Marketing manager, Western Union), email to the author, April 19, 2013.
56. Alice Korngold, "Clinton Global Initiative: Western Union Announces NGO Global Pay," *Fast Company*, September 23, 2012, http://www .fastcompany.com/3001516/clinton-global-initiative-western-union -announces-ngo-global-pay (June 9, 2013).
57. Hikmet Ersek (president and CEO, Western Union), interview with the author, September 22, 2013.
58. Elaine Weidman-Grunewald (vice president, Sustainability and Corporate Responsibility, Ericsson Group worldwide), interview with the author, November 21, 2012.
59. Ibid.
60. Elaine Weidman-Grunewald, email to author, April 19, 2013.
61. "The Potential Economic Impact of Mobile Communications in Myanmar," *Ericsson*, November 13, 2012, http://www.ericsson.com/res/docs/2012 /myanmar-report-2012–13nov.pdf (September 2, 2013).
62. "New Study Quantifies the Impact of Broadband Speed on GDP," Ericsson, September 27, 2011, http://www.ericsson.com/news/1550083 (June 9, 2013).
63. Elaine Weidman-Grunewald, interview with the author, November 21, 2012.
64. Ibid.
65. "Homepage," *Refugees United*, http://info.refunite.org/ (June 9, 2013).
66. Alice Korngold, "Refugees United, The Social Network That's More Important than Facebook, Goes Mobile," *Fast Company*, September 23, 2010, http://www.fastcompany.com/1690690/refugees-united-social-network -thats-more-important-facebook-goes-mobile (June, 9 2013).
67. Elaine Weidman-Grunewald, email to the author, April 19, 2013.
68. "Homepage," Vodafone, http://www.vodafone.com/content/index.html (June 9, 2013).
69. "Homepage" *Safaricom: M-PESA*, http://www.safaricom.co.ke/business /solutions-by-business-size/large-corporate/m-pesa (June 9, 2013).

70. Ignacio Mas and Dan Radcliffe, "Mobile Payments go Viral: M-PESA in Kenya," *The World Bank*, March 2010, http://papers.ssrn.com/sol3/papers .cfm?abstract_id=1593388 (September 7, 2013).

71. Tavneet Suri, and Billy Jack, "Reaching the Poor: Mobile Banking and Financial Inclusion," *Slate*, February 27, 2012, http://www.slate.com/blogs/future _tense/2012/02/27/m_pesa_ict4d_and_mobile_banking_for_the_poor _.html (June 9, 2013).

72. Michael Joseph (managing director, Mobile Money, Vodafone), interview with the author, May 21, 2013.

73. "Homepage," *UK Department for International Development*, https://www .gov.uk/government/organisations/department-for-international-development (September 2, 2013).

74. Michael Joseph (managing director, Mobile Money, Vodafone), interview with the author, May 21, 2013.

75. Ibid.

76. Ibid.

77. Ibid.

78. "Vodacom Tanzania Reports Five Million M-PESA Subs; Transactions Top USD823m," *TeleGeography*, May 2, 2013, http://www.telegeography.com /products/commsupdate/articles/2013/05/02/vodacom-tanzania-reports -five-million-m-pesa-subs-transactions-top-usd823m/ (June 9, 2013).

79. "M-PESA Launched in South Africa," *How We Made It in Africa*, September 1, 2010, http://www.howwemadeitinafrica.com/m-pesa-launched-in-south -africa/3611/ (June 9, 2013).

80. Jon Russell, "Vodafone Launches M-Pesa Mobile Banking in India, Targeting 700m 'Unbanked' People," *The Next Web*, April 17, 2013, http://thenextweb .com/in/2013/04/17/vodafone-launches-m-pesa-mobile-banking-service-in -india-targets-700m-unbanked-people/ (June 9, 2013).

81. Michael Joseph (managing director, Mobile Money, Vodafone), interview with the author, May 21, 2013.

82. "World Development Report 2012, Gender Equality and Development," *The World Bank*, http://siteresources.worldbank.org/INTWDR2012/Resource s/7778105–1299699968583/7786210–1315936222006/Complete-Report .pdf#page=458&zoom=121,40,441 (June 9, 2013).

83. Ibid.

84. "Homepage," *BSR*, http://www.bsr.org/ (June 9, 2013).

85. "HERproject," *BSR*, http://herproject.org/ (June 9, 2013).

86. "Effects of a Workplace Health Program on Absenteeism, Turnover, and Worker Attitudes in a Bangladesh Garment Factory," U.S. Agency for International Development Bureau for Global Health, April 2007, http://herproject.org /downloads/BSR_HERproject_Bangladesh_ROI_Study.pdf (June 9, 2013).

87. Racheal Meiers (director, HERproject, BSR), interview with the author, December 13, 2013.

88. Racheal Yaeger, "HERproject: Health Enables Returns," *BSR*, August 2011, http:// www.bsr.org/reports/HERproject_Health_Enables_Returns_The_Business _Returns_from_Womens_Health_Programs_081511.pdf (June 9, 2013).

89. Racheal Meiers (director, HERproject, BSR), interview with author, December 13, 2013.

90. "FAQs – HERproject," *BSR*, http://herproject.org/about/faq (June 9, 2013).

91. "Exploring the Links between International Business and Poverty Reduction," *Oxfam America, The Coca-Cola Company, and SABMiller*, December 2011, http://www.oxfamamerica.org/files/coca-cola-sab-miller-poverty-footprint -dec-2011.pdf (June 9, 2013).

92. Ibid.

3   CLIMATE CHANGE AND ENERGY

1. From Theodore Roosevelt's Seventh Annual Message to Congress, December 3, 1907, http://www.pbs.org/weta/thewest/resources/archives/eight/trconserv .htm.

2. "Global Climate Change: Effects," *National Aeronautics and Space Administration*, http://climate.nasa.gov/effects (June 12, 2012).

3. "Global Climate Change: Consensus," *National Aeronautics and Space Administration*, http://climate.nasa.gov/scientific-consensus (June 12, 2012).

4. Eric S. Blake et al., "Tropical Cyclone Report Hurricane Sandy," *National Hurricane Center*, October 29, 2013, http://www.nhc.noaa.gov/data/tcr /AL182012_Sandy.pdf (June 12, 2013).

5. Fiona Harvey, "Climate Change Will Increase Threat of War, Chris Huhne to Warn," *The Guardian,* July 6, 2011, http://www.guardian.co.uk /environment/2011/jul/06/climate-change-war-chris-huhne (June 12, 2013); Joshua W. Busby, "Climate Change and National Security," *The Council on Foreign Relations,* November 2007, http://www.cfr.org/climate-change /climate-change-national-security/p14862 (June 12, 2013); John Vidal, "Climate Change: How a Warming World Is a Threat to Our Food Supplies," April 13, 2013, *The Guardian*, http://www.guardian.co.uk/environment /2013/apr/13/climate-change-threat-food-supplies (June 12, 2013).

6. "Climate Change: Basic Information," *United States Environmental Protection Agency*, http://www.epa.gov/climatechange/basics/ (June 11, 2013).

7. "Warming of the Climate System Is Unequivocal," *UN Chronicle*, January 6, 2007, http://www.un.org/wcm/content/site/chronicle/home/archive/issues2007 /greenourworld/pid/21621 (August 27, 2013).

8. S. Solomon, D. Quinn, M. Channing, Z. Chen, M. Marquis, K. B. Averyt, M. Tignor, and H. L. Miller (eds.) "Summary for Policymakers," *Intergovernmental Panel on Climate Change* (Cambridge, UK, and New York: Cambridge University Press, 2007), http://www.ipcc.ch/pdf/assessment -report/ar4/wg1/ar4-wg1-spm.pdf (June 12, 2013).

9. "Framework Convention on Climate Change," *United Nations*, 2013, http:// unfccc.int/essential_background/basic_facts_figures/items/6246.php (June 12, 2013).

10. "World Population Prospects, the 2010 Revision," *United Nations Department of Economic and Social Affairs*, http://esa.un.org/unpd/wpp /Other-Information/faq.htm#q1 (June 12, 2013).

11. Richard Dobbs et al., "Resource Revolution: Meeting the World's Energy, Materials, Food, and Water Needs," *McKinsey &Company*, November 2011, http://www.mckinsey.com/insights/energy_resources_materials/resource_revolution (June, 12, 2013).

12. Geoffrey Gertz and Hommi Kharas, "The New Global Middle Class: A Cross-Over from West to East," *Brookings*, March 2010, http://www.brookings.edu/research/papers/2010/03/china-middle-class-kharas (September 2, 2013).

13. World Wildlife Fund, http://wwf.panda.org/about_our_earth/all_publications/living_planet_report/demands_on_our_planet/overshoot/ (August 27, 2013).

14. "What Is the G20 / G20," *The Group of Twenty*, http://g20.org/docs/about/about_G20.html (June 12, 2013).

15. "Counting the Cost of Carbon: Low Carbon Economy Index 2011," *PwC*, November 2011, http://www.pwc.com/en_GX/gx/sustainability/publications/low-carbon-economy-index/assets/low-carbon-economy-Index-2011.pdf (June 30, 2013).

16. "Business Resilience in an Uncertain and Resource-Constrained World," *The Carbon Disclosure Project*, 2012, https://www.cdproject.net/CDPResults/CDP-Global-500-Climate-Change-Report-2012.pdf (June 12, 2013).

17. "Summit 2013—Bloomberg New Energy Finance," *Bloomberg New Energy Finance*, 2013 http://about.bnef.com/summit/ (June 12, 2013).

18. Ban Ki-moon, "Secretary-General's Remarks at Bloomberg New Energy Finance Summit [as prepared for delivery]," *United Nations*, April 24, 2013, http://www.un.org/sg/statements/index.asp?nid=6765 (June 12, 2013).

19. Suzanne Fallender (director, CSR Strategy and Communications, Intel), email to the author, May 21, 2013.

20. "National Top 50," *United States Environmental Protection Agency*, March 18, 2013, http://www.epa.gov/greenpower/toplists/top50.htm (June 12, 2013).

21. "Greenhouse Gas Equivalencies Calculator," *United States Environmental Protection Agency*, 2013, http://www.epa.gov/cleanenergy/energy-resources/calculator.html#res (June 12, 2013).

22. Suzanne Fallender (director, CSR Strategy and Communications, Intel), interview with the author, April 29, 2013.

23. Ibid.

24. Ibid.

25. "World Urbanization Prospects, The 2011 Revision," *United Nations*, March 2012, http://esa.un.org/unpd/wup/pdf/WUP2011_Highlights.pdf (June 12, 2013).

26. "Cities and Climate Change: Global Report on Human Settlements 2011," *UN Habitat*, March 29, 2011, http://www.unhabitat.org/downloads/docs/GRHS2011/P1HotCities.pdf (June 12, 2013).

27. Ibid.

28. "U.N.: World Population Increasingly Urban," *CBS News*, February 11, 2009, http://www.cbsnews.com/2100-202_162-3880698.html (September 2, 2013).

29. "World Urbanization Prospects The 2011 Revision," *United Nations*, March 2012, http://esa.un.org/unpd/wup/pdf/WUP2011_Highlights.pdf (June 12, 2013).

30. Suzanne Fallender, interview with the author, April 29, 2013.
31. "Intel Collaborative Research Institute for Sustainable Cities," *Intel Corporation*, https://www.intel-university-collaboration.net/intel-collaborative|-research -institute-for-sustainable-connected-computing (June 12, 2013).
32. "Mission & Guiding Principles," *Pecan Street Research Institute*, http://www .pecanstreet.org/about/mission-guiding-principles/ (June 17, 2013).
33. "Visualizing Sustainable Energy: Big Data," *Intel Corporation*, http://www .intel.com/content/www/us/en/big-data/big-data-pecan-street-video.html (June 17, 2013).
34. Suzanne Fallender, interview with the author, April 29, 2013.
35. "Homepage," *Digital Energy and Sustainability Solutions Campaign*, http:// www.digitalenergysolutions.org/ (June 17, 2013).
36. "Homepage, *Information Technology Industry Council*, http://www.itic.org/ (June 17, 2013).
37. "Policy Priorities," *Digital Energy & Sustainability Solutions Campaign*, http://www.digitalenergysolutions.org/policy-priorities/ (June 17, 2013).
38. "About DESSC," *Digital Energy & Sustainability Solutions Campaign*, http:// www.digitalenergysolutions.org/about/index.dot (June 17, 2013).
39. "U.N.: World Population Increasingly Urban," *CBS News*, February 11, 2009, http://www.cbsnews.com/2100–202_162–3880698.html (June 17, 2013).
40. "Triple Bottom Line Benefits for City Businesses: Networked Society City Index Part III," *Ericsson*, http://www.ericsson.com/res/docs/2012/networked -society-city-index-report-part-3.pdf (June 17, 2013).
41. "The Company," *Ericsson*, http://www.ericsson.com/thecompany (June 17, 2013); Elaine Weidman-Grunewald (vice president, Sustainability and Corporate Responsibility, Ericsson), email to the author, August 28, 2013.
42. "Triple Bottom Line Benefits for City Businesses: Networked Society City Index Part III," *Ericsson* http://www.ericsson.com/res/docs/2012/networked -society-city-index-report-part-3.pdf (June 17, 2013).
43. Ibid.
44. "Networked Society City Index Part III: Triple Bottom Line Benefits for City Businesses," http://www.ericsson.com/res/docs/2012/networked-society -city-index-report-part-3.pdf (June 17, 2013).
45. Elaine Weidman-Grunewald (vice president, Sustainability and Corporate Responsibility, Ericsson), interview with the author, January 16, 2013.
46. Elaine Weidman-Grunewald, interview with the author, April 25, 2013.
47. "Our Products," *Ericsson*, http://www.ericsson.com/ourportfolio/products (June 17, 2013).
48. "GeSI Governance: ICT Sustainability Governance," *Global e-Sustainability Initiative*, http://gesi.org/ICT_sustainability_governance (June 17, 2013).
49. "SMARTer2020," *Global e-Sustainability Initiative*, 2013, http://gesi.org /SMARTer2020 (June 17, 2013).
50. Ibid.
51. Elaine Weidman-Grunewald, interview with the author, April 25, 2013.
52. Global e-Sustainability Initiative, "Smarter2020," http://gesi.org/SMART er2020 (June 11, 2013).

53. "Buildings and Climate Change: Summary for Decision-Makers," *United Nations Environment Programme*, 2009, http://www.unep.org/sbci/pdfs /SBCI-BCCSummary.pdf (June 17, 2013).

54. David Gann, *Building Innovation: Complex Constructs in a Changing World* (London: Thomas Telford, 2000).

55. Clay Nesler (vice president, Global Energy and Sustainability for the Building Efficiency Business, Johnson Controls), email to the author, August 28, 2013.

56. Ibid.

57. "About Us," *Institute for Building Efficiency an Initiative of Johnson Controls*, 2013, http://www.institutebe.com/About.aspx (June 17, 2013).

58. "2012 Energy Efficiency Indicator: Global Results," *Institute for Building Efficiency, an Initiative of Johnson Controls*, 2012, http://www.institutebe .com/InstituteBE/media/Library/Resources/Energy%20Efficiency %20Indicator/2012-EEI-Global-Results-Executive-Summary.pdf (June 17, 2013).

59. "Homepage," *Urban Land Institute*, 2013, http://www.uli.org/ (June 17, 2013).

60. "Homepage," *International Facility Management Association*, 2013, http:// www.ifma.org/ (June 17, 2013).

61. "2012 Energy Efficiency Indicator: Global Results," *Institute for Building Efficiency, an Initiative of Johnson Controls*, 2012, http://www.institutebe .com/InstituteBE/media/Library/Resources/Energy%20Efficiency %20Indicator/2012-EEI-Global-Results-Executive-Summary.pdf (June 17, 2013).

62. Ibid.

63. Kelly Vaughn, "Empire State Building Retrofit Surpasses Energy Savings Expectations," *Rocky Mountain Institute*, May 31, 2012, http://blog.rmi.org /blog_empire_state_retrofit_surpasses_energy_savings_expectations (June 17, 2013).

64. "Website," Empire State Building, http://www.esbtour.com/en-us/m/3/3 /Default.aspx (June 17, 2013).

65. Adrian Bishop, "Empire State Building Saves $2.4million in Energy Bills," *The Earth Times*, 2013, http://www.earthtimes.org/energy/empire-state -building-saves-energy-bills/2026/ (June 17, 2013).

66. "About," *Clinton Climate Initiative*, http://www.clintonfoundation.org/main /our-work/by-initiative/clinton-climate-initiative/about.html (June 17, 2013).

67. "Clinton Foundation History," *Clinton Foundation*, http://www.clinton foundation.org/main/about/clinton-foundation-history.html (June 17, 2013).

68. Clay Nesler (vice president, Global Energy and Sustainability for the Building Efficiency Business, Johnson Controls), interview with the author, April 24, 2013.

69. "First Clinton Climate Initiative Project Signed with Johnson Controls," *The Corporate Social Responsibility Newswire*, http://www.csrwire.com /press_releases/25433-First-Clinton-Climate-Initiative-Project-Signed -With-Johnson-Controls (February 18, 2008).

70. Clay Nesler, interview with the author, April 24, 2013.

71. Homepage," *Unilever*, http://www.unilever.com/ (June 17, 2013).

72. "Unilever Sustainable Living Plain Helping to Drive Growth," *Unilever*, April 22, 2013, http://www.unilever.com/mediacentre/pressreleases/2013 /UnileverSustainableLivingPlanhelpingtodrivegrowth.aspx (June 17, 2013).

73. "Our Compass Strategy and Business Model," *Unilever*, http://www.unilever .com/investorrelations/annual_reports/AnnualReportandAccounts2012 /our-compass-strategy-and-business-model.aspx (June 17, 2013).

74. "Introduction to Unilever," *Unilever*, 2013, http://www.unilever.com/aboutus /introductiontounilever/ (June 17, 2013).

75. "Our Compass Strategy and Business Model," *Unilever*, http://www.unilever .com/investorrelations/annual_reports/AnnualReportandAccounts2012 /our-compass-strategy-and-business-model.aspx (June 17, 2013).

76. Gail Klintworth (chief sustainability officer, Unilever), interview with the author, January 22, 2013.

77. Thomas Lingard (director, Global Advocacy, Unilever), interview with the author, January 29, 2013.

78. "Unilever Publishes Its Marketing Behaviour Change Principles 'Five Levers for Change' to Inspire Sustainable Living," *Unilever*, November 23, 2011, http://www.unilever.com/mediacentre/pressreleases/2011/five-levers -change-111123.aspx (June 17, 2013).

79. Gail Klintworth, interview with the author, January 22, 2013.

80. "Global Handwashing Day's Fifth Birthday," *Unilever*, 2012, http://www .unilever.com/brands-in-action/detail/Global-Handwashing-Day-s-fifth -birthday/308767/?WT.contenttype=brands%20in%20action (June 17, 2013).

81. Ibid.

82. "About Us," *Rainforest Alliance*, http://www.rainforest-alliance.org/about (June 17, 2013).

83. "Lipton's Sustainable Tea in Turkey," *Unilever*, http://www.unilever.com /brands-in-action/detail/Lipton-s-sustainable-tea-in-Turkey/292029/?WT .contenttype=brands%20in%20action (June 17, 2013).

84. Gail Klintworth (chief sustainability officer, Unilever), interview with the author, January 22, 2013; Gail Klintworh, email to the author, August 28, 2013.

85. "Unilever Debates Global Development at Davos," *Unilever*, January 25, 2013, http://www.unilever.com/mediacentre/newsandfeatures/paul-polman -speaks-at-davos.aspx (June 17, 2013).

86. "Our Mission and Guiding Principles," *The Consumer Goods Forum*, http:// www.theconsumergoodsforum.com/mission.aspx (June 17, 2013).

87. "Working with Our Customers," *Unilever*, 2013, http://www.unilever.com /sustainable-living/customers-suppliers/customers/ (June 17, 2013).

88. Hannah Jones, "Nike Seeks to Eliminate Hazardous Chemicals from Products," *theguardian*, September 6, 2011, http://www.guardian.co.uk /sustainable-business/blog/nike-to-eliminate-hazardous-chemicals-corporate -responsibility (June 17, 2013).

89. Tyler Falk, "Nike Increases Use of Sustainable Textiles," *smartplanet*, March 20, 2013, http://www.smartplanet.com/blog/bulletin/nike-increases-use-of -sustainable-textiles/15390 (June 17, 2013).

90. "The Higg Index," *Sustainable Apparel Coalition*, http://www.apparelcoalition .org/higgindex (June 18, 2013).

91. "Nike, NASA, State Department and USAID Aim to Revolutionize Sustainable Materials," *Nike, Inc.*, April 24, 2013, http://nikeinc.com/news /nike-nasa-u-s-state-department-and-usaid-seek-innovations-to-revolutionize -sustainable-materials (June 18, 2013).

92. Ibid.

93. Hannah Jones, interview with the author, January 18, 2013.

94. "Overview," *Sustainable Apparel Coalition*, 2012, http://www.apparelcoalition .org/overview/ (June 18, 2013).

95. Jason Kibbey, interview with the author, February 28, 2013.

96. "2013 Winter Meeting," *Clinton Global Initiative*, February 20, 2013, http:// www.clintonglobalinitiative.org/ourmeetings/2013/wintermeeting/ (June 18, 2013).

97. Catherine von Altheer (communications manager, Carbon Disclosure Project), interview with the author, April 18, 2013.

98. "Homepage," *Carbon Disclosure Project*, https://www.cdproject.net/en-US /Pages/HomePage.aspx (June 18, 2013).

99. Catherine von Altheer, email to the author, May 21, 2013.

100. "Become a CDP Investor Signatory," *Carbon Disclosure Project*, https://www .cdproject.net/en-US/Programmes/Pages/becoming-a-signatory.aspx (June 18, 2013).

101. Catherine von Altheer, interview with the author, April 18, 2013.

102. Catherine von Altheer, interview with the author, May 18, 2013, and a follow-up email from von Altheer on May 21, 2013.

103. "Business Resilience in an Uncertain, Resource-Constrained World," CDP Global 500 Climate Change Report 2012, *Carbon Disclosure Project*, https:// www.cdproject.net/CDPResults/CDP-Global-500-Climate-Change-Report -2012.pdf (June 23, 2013).

104. Catherine von Altheer (communications manager, the Carbon Disclosure Project), interview with the author, April 18, 2013.

105. "Carbon Disclosure Project 2010 Global 500 Report," *Carbon Disclosure Project*, 2010, https://www.cdproject.net/CDPResults/CDP-2010-G500.pdf (June 23, 2013).

106. Catherine von Altheer, interview with the author, May 21, 2013.

107. "Business Resilience in an Uncertain, Resource-Constrained World," CDP Global 500 Climate Change Report 2012, *Carbon Disclosure Project*, https://www.cdproject.net/CDPResults/CDP-Global-500-Climate-Change -Report-2012.pdf (June 23, 2013).

108. Paul Dickinson (executive chairman and founder, CDP), interview with the author, May 3, 2013.

109. Gail Klintworth, interview with the author, January 22, 2013.

110. Stephan Mohr et al., "Manufacturing Resourse Productivity," *McKinsey & Company*, June 2012, http://www.mckinsey.com/insights/sustainability /manufacturing_resource_productivity (June 18, 2013).

111. "Sustainability Measurement and Reporting Standards," *The Sustainability Consortium*, http://www.sustainabilityconsortium.org/smrs/ (September 2, 2013).

112. Kara Hurst (CEO, The Sustainability Consortium), interview with the author, May 28, 2013.

113. "Why Join?" *The Sustainability Consortium*, http://www.sustainability consortium.org/join-tsc/ (June 18, 2013).

114. Kara Hurst, interview with the author, May 28, 2013.

115. Marc Gunther, "Walmart's Index: This Is Big. Really Big.," April 15, 2013, http:// www.marcgunther.com/walmarts-index-this-is-big-really-big/ (June 18, 2013).

116. Andrea Thomas (senior vice president, Sustainability, Walmart), email to the author, May 30, 2013.

117. Joe Romm, "Tackling Climate Change Is One of America's Greatest Economic Opportunities of the 21st Century," *Climate Progress*, April 11, 2013, http:// thinkprogress.org/climate/2013/04/11/1851271/nike-starbucks-intel-we -cannot-risk-our-kids-futures-on-the-false-hope-the-vast-majority-of-scien tists-are-wrong/ (June 18, 2013).

118. Ibid.; "Home," *Business for Innovative Climate and Energy Policy*, a program of Ceres, 2013, http://www.ceres.org/bicep (June 18, 2013).

119. "Summit 2013," *Bloomberg New Energy Finance*, 2013, http://about.bnef .com/summit/ (June 18, 2013).

120. "Climate Change," *United Nations*, 2012, http://www.un.org/en/globalissues /climatechange/ (June 18, 2013).

121. Ibid.

122. "Welcome," *Climate Strategy & Partners*, 2013, http://climatestrategy.es/ (June 18, 2013).

123. "Peter Sweatman bio," *Climate Change Capital*, http://www.climatechangecapi tal.com/about-us/people/peter-sweatman.aspx (June 18, 2013).

124. Peter Sweatman (chief executive and founder, Climate Strategy and Partners), interview with the author, April 24, 2013.

125. Joshua W. Busby, "Climate Change and National Security," *Council on Foreign Relations*, November 2007, http://www.cfr.org/climate-change/climate -change-national-security/p14862 (June 18, 2013).

126. Ibid.

127. Ibid.

128. "The Arab Spring and Climate Change," *Center for American Progress*, February 2013, http://www.americanprogress.org/wp-content/uploads /2013/02/ClimateChangeArabSpring.pdf (June 18, 2013).

129. "Homepage," *Center for American Progress*, http://www.americanprogress .org/ (June 18, 2013).

130. "Programs," *The Stimson Center*, 2013, http://www.stimson.org/ (June 18, 2013).

131. About, *The Center for Climate and Security*, 2013, http://climateandsecurity. org/about/ (June 18, 2013).

132. "The Arab Spring and Climate Change," *Center for American Progress*, February 2013, http://www.americanprogress.org/wp-content/uploads /2013/02/ClimateChangeArabSpring.pdf (June 18, 2013).

133. Stephan Faris, "The Real Roots of Darfur," *The Atlantic*, April 1, 2007, http://m.theatlantic.com/magazine/archive/2007/04/the-real-roots-of -darfur/305701/ (June 11, 2013).

134. Ben Schiller, "Mapping the 31 Million People Displaced by Natural Disasters So Far," *Fast Company*, May 30, 2013, http://www.fastcoexist.com/1682141 /mapping-the-31-million-people-displaced-by-natural-disasters-so-far (September 2, 2013).

4 ECOSYSTEMS

1. "Discover John Muir," John Muir Trust, www.discoverjohnmuir.com

2. "New Kimberly-Clark Policy Is a Victory for Ancient Forests," *Greenpeace USA*, August 5, 2009, http://www.greenpeace.org/usa/en/news-and-blogs /news/new-kimberly-clark-policy-080509/ (June 18, 2013).

3. Ibid.

4. "Homepage," *Water.org*, 2013, http://water.org/ (June 18, 2013).

5. "World Population Prospects: the 2012 Revision," *United Nations Department of Economic and Social Affairs*, http://esa.un.org/unpd/wpp/Other-Information /faq.htm#q1 (June 18, 2013).

6. Richard Dobbs et al., "Unlocking the Potential of Emerging-Market Cities," *McKinsey & Company*, September 2012, https://www.mckinseyquarterly.com /Strategy/Globalization/Unlocking_the_potential_of_emerging-market _cities_3015 (June 18, 2013).

7. "Engaging Tomorrow's Consumer," *World Economic Forum*, January 2013, http://www.accenture.com/SiteCollectionDocuments/PDF/Accenture -Engaging-Tomorrows-Consumer.pdf (June 18, 2013).

8. "Conservation by Design: A Strategic Framework for Success: Tenth Anniversary Edition," *The Nature Conservancy*, 2006, http://www.nature .org/ourscience/conservationbydesign/cbd.pdf (June 18, 2013).

9. About Us—Vision & Mission, *The Nature Conservancy*, http://www.nature .org/about-us/vision-mission/index.htm (June 18, 2013).

10. "Current State & Trends Assessment," *Millennium Ecosystem Assessment*, 2005, http://www.unep.org/maweb/en/Condition.aspx (June 18, 2013).

11. Thomas L. Friedman, "Without Water, Revolution," *The New York Times*, May 18, 2013, http://www.nytimes.com/2013/05/19/opinion/sunday/friedman -without-water-revolution.html?pagewanted=1&_r=3&hpw (June 18, 2013).

12. Joshua W. Busby, "Climate Change and National Security," *Council on Foreign Relations*, November 2007, http://www.cfr.org/climate-change/cli- mate-change-national-security/p14862 (June 18, 2013).

13. Ibid.

14. "About Rio+20," *United Nations Conference on Sustainable Development*, http://www.uncsd2012.org/about.html (June 18, 2013).

15. "The Future We Want," *United Nations Conference on Sustainable Development*, http://www.uncsd2012.org/content/documents/727The %20Future%20We%20Want%2019%20June%201230pm.pdf (June 18, 2013).

16. "United Nations Millennium Development Goals," *United Nations*, http://www.un.org/millenniumgoals/ (June 18, 2013).

17. Thomas E. Lovejoy, "The Climate Change Endgame," January 21, 2013, http://www.nytimes.com/2013/01/22/opinion/global/the-climate-change-endgame.html?smid=tw-share&_r=0 (September 7, 2013).

18. Bryan Walsh, "What the Failure of Rio+20 Means for the Climate," *Time*, June 26, 2012, http://www.time.com/time/health/article/0,8599,2118058,00.html (June 19, 2013).

19. Robert Sanders, "Scientists Uncover Evidence of Impending Tipping Point for Earth," *UC Berkeley News Center*, June 6, 2012, http://newscenter.berkeley.edu/2012/06/06/scientists-uncover-evidence-of-impending-tipping-point-for-earth/ (June 19, 2013).

20. Stephanie Kirchgaessner, "Budget Cuts Put U.S. Science to the Test," *Financial Times*, January 25, 2013, http://www.ft.com/intl/cms/s/0/ad923166–66d8–11e2-a805–00144feab49a.html#axzz2dKKXCCZL (August 29, 2013).

21. "Unilever Debates Global Development at Davos," *Unilever*, January 25, 2013, http://www.unilever.com/mediacentre/newsandfeatures/paul-polman-speaks-at-davos.aspx (June 18, 2013).

22. Investors, *Ecolab*, http://investor.ecolab.com/ (June 19, 2013).

23. "Sustainability Report 2011," *Ecolab USA, Inc.*, http://www.ecolab.com/media-center/publications/~/media/Ecolab/Ecolab%20Site/Page%20Content/Documents/Our%20Company/Publications/Sustainability%20Report/2011SustainabilityReport.ashx (June 20, 2013).

24. Ibid.

25. Ibid.

26. Ibid.

27. Emilio Tenuto (vice president, Corporate Sustainability, Ecolab), interview with the author, January 24, 2013.

28. Alliance for Water Stewardship, http://www.allianceforwaterstewardship.org/ (August 27, 2013).

29. "Homepage," *Alliance for Water Stewardship*, http://www.allianceforwaterstewardship.org/ (June 19, 2013).

30. Ed Stych, "Bill Gates' Stake in Ecolab Could Get Bigger," *Minneapolis St. Paul Business Journal*, May 7, 2012, http://www.bizjournals.com/twincities/news/2012/05/07/microsoft-gates-can-invest-in-ecolab.html (June 20, 2013).

31. Emilio Tenuto, interview with the author, January 24, 2013.

32. "Homepage," *Greenpeace*, http://www.greenpeace.org/usa/en/about/ (June 20, 2013).

33. "Kimberly-Clark and Greenpeace Agree to Historic Measures to Protect Forests," *Kleercut. Net*, August 5, 2009, http://www.kleercut.net/en/ (June 20, 2013).

34. Suhas Apte (Kimberly-Clark), email to the author, May 17, 2013.

35. "Full Circle: 2011 Sustainability Report," *Kimberly-Clark*, http://www.sustainabilityreport2011.kimberly-clark.com/files/2011_Sustainability_Report.pdf (June 20, 2013).

36. Richard Brooks (Greenpeace), interview with the author, February 20, 2013.

37. Scott Paul (Greenpeace), interview with the author, January 23, 2013.

38. Ibid.

39. Scott Paul, email to the author, May 7, 2013.

40. Scott Paul, interview with the the author, January 23, 2013.

41. Suhas Apte, interview with the author, January 2, 2013.

42. Richard Brooks, interview with the author, February 20, 2013.

43. Alice Korngold, "How Green Is Your Boardroom?," *Fast Company*, June 13, 2011, http://www.fastcompany.com/1759311/how-green-your-boardroom (June 20, 2013).

44. "Full Circle: 2011 Sustainability Report," *Kimberly-Clark*, http://www.sustainabilityreport2011.kimberly-clark.com/files/2011_Sustainability_Report.pdf (June 20, 2013).

45. Suhas Apte, interview with the author, January 2, 2013.

46. "We Learned How to Listen Better," Tom Falk (Kimberly-Clark), interviewed by David Kiron, *Massachusetts Institute of Technology Management Review*, January 15, 2013, http://sloanreview.mit.edu/feature/we-learned-how-to-listen-better/ (June 20, 2013).

47. "We Learned How to Listen Better," Tom Falk (Kimberly-Clark), interviewed by David Kiron, *Massachusetts Institute of Technology Management Review*, January 15, 2013, http://sloanreview.mit.edu/feature/we-learned-how-to-listen-better/ (June 20, 2013).

48. Robert G. Eccles, George Serafeim, and Shelley Xin Li, "Dow Chemical: Innovating for Sustainability," *Harvard Business School*, Case Study 112–064, January 2012, revised June 2013.

49. Mark Tercek (president and CEO, The Nature Conservancy), interview with the author, November 30, 2012.

50. "The Nature Conservancy—Dow Collaboration: 2012 Progress Report," *The Nature Conservancy*, http://www.nature.org/media/companies/the-nature-conservancy-dow-collaboration-progress-report-2012.pdf (June 20, 2013).

51. Mark Tercek (president and CEO, The Nature Conservancy), interview with the author, November 30, 2012.

52. "Biodiversity and Ecosystem Services Trends and Conditions Assessment Tool," *BESTCAT*, http://bestcat.org.s3.amazonaws.com/index.html (June 20, 2013).

53. Amy O'Meara, "24 Companies Representing $500 Billion Announce Commitments Underscoring Business Value of Nature," *The EcoInnovator*, June 18, 2012, http://corporateecoforum.com/ecoinnovator/?p=7184 (June 20, 2013).

54. Mark R. Tercek and Jonathan S. Adams, *Nature's Fortune: How Business and Society Thrive by Investing in Nature* (New York: Basic Books, 2013), p. 187.

55. "The New Business Imperative: Valuing Natural Capital," *The Nature Conservancy* and *Corporate EcoForum*, 2012, http://corporateecoforum.com/valuingnaturalcapital/ (June 20, 2013).

56. "About," *Corporate EcoForum*," http://corporateecoforum.com/contact/index.php (September 7, 2013).

57. "The New Business Imperative: Valuing Natural Capital," *The Nature Conservancy* and *Corporate EcoForum*, 2012, http://corporateecoforum.com /valuingnaturalcapital/ (June 20, 2013).

58. Ibid.

59. Neil Hawkins (vice president, Global Environment, Health & Safety (EHS), and Sustainability, Dow), interview with the author, January 10, 2013.

60. "Sustainable Living," *Unilever*, http://www.unilever.com/sustainable-living/ (June 20, 2013).

61. Gail Klintworth (chief sustainability officer, Unilever), interview with the author, January 22, 2013.

62. Thomas Lingard (global advocacy director, Unilever), interview with the author, January 29, 2013.

63. "Inspiring Sustainable Living: Unilever's Five Levers for Change," *Unilever*, http://www.unilever.com/images/slp_5-Levers-for-Change_tcm13–276832 .pdf (September 7, 2013).

64. "Unilever Sustainable Living Plan," *Unilever*, http://www.unilever.com /sustainable-living/uslp/index.aspx#PillarGroup1 (June 30, 2012).

65. Gail Klintworth, interview with the author, January 22, 2013.

66. "Our Strategy and Footprint," Unilever website, http://www.unilever.com /sustainable-living/sustainablesourcing/why/index.aspx (August 27, 2013).

67. "What We Do: Earth's Most Special Places," *WWF Global*, http://wwf.panda .org/what_we_do/where_we_work/ (June 20, 2013).

68. "Indonesia," *Greenpeace*, http://www.greenpeace.org/international/en/campaigns /forests/asia-pacific/ (June 20, 2013).

69. "Global Public Sector Trends in Ecosystem Services, 2009–2012," *BSR*, February 2013, http://www.bsr.org/reports/BSR_Ecosystem_Services _Policy_Synthesis.pdf (June 20, 2013).

70. "Ecosystems and Human Well-Being: Synthesis," *Millennium Ecosystem Assessment*, 2005, http://www.millenniumassessment.org/documents/document .356.aspx.pdf (September 7, 2013).

71. Sissel Waage, "5 Public sector Trends in Ecosystem Services," *Greenbiz.com*, February 8, 2013, http://www.greenbiz.com/blog/2013/02/08/5-public-sector -trends-ecosystem-services?mkt_tok=3RkMMJWWfF9wsRonv6nLZKXo njHpfsX56%2B4sXqS%2FlMI%2F0ER3fOvrPUfGjI4ASMFqI%2BSLDw EYGJlv6SgFSLHEMa5qw7gMXRQ%3D (June 20, 2013).

72. "What's Happening to Biodiversity?," *Visual.ly*, http://visual.ly/what %E2%80%99s-happening-biodiversity (June 20, 2013).

73. Thomas E. Lovejoy, "The Climate Change Endgame," *The New York Times*, January 21, 2013, http://www.nytimes.com/2013/01/22/opinion/global/the -climate-change-endgame.html?smid=tw-share&_r=1&) (June 20, 2013).

74. Richard Brooks (Greenpeace), interview with the author, February 20, 2013.

75. Liz Enochs, "McDonald's, Unilever, Pepsi, Adidas Make News at Davos," *Greenbiz.com*, January 24, 2013, http://www.greenbiz.com/news/2013/01/24 /mcdonalds-unilever-pepsi-adidas-all-make-news-davos?page=0%2C1&utm _source=twitterfeed&utm_medium=twitter&utm_campaign=greenbuzz (June 20, 2013).

76. "Consumers Still Purchasing, But May not Be 'Buying' Companies' Environmental Claims," *Cone Communications/Trend Tracker*, March 27, 2012, http://www.conecomm.com/stuff/contentmgr/files/0/1b7667e63cd5d d2858bd5a559a3a778a/files/2012_cone_green_gap_trend_tracker_release _and_fact_sheet.pdf (June 20, 2013).

77. "About Us," *BAV Consulting*, http://bavconsulting.com/about/ (June 20, 2013).

78. John Gerzema, "The Rise of Mindful Consumption," *McKinsey & Company*, http://voices.mckinseyonsociety.com/the-rise-of-mindful-consumption/ (June 20, 2013).

79. "Sustainable Finance," *WWF Global*, http://wwf.panda.org/what_we_do /how_we_work/businesses/transforming_markets/solutions/methodology /commodity_financing/sustainable_finance/ (June 20, 2013).

80. "Sustainable Capitalism," *Generation Investment Management LLP*, February 15, 2012, http://www.generationim.com/media/pdf-generation-sustainable -capitalism-v1.pdf (June 20, 2013).

81. David A. Gabel, "Study Shows Workers at 'Green' Companies Are More Productive," *Environmental News Network*, September 11, 2012, http://www .enn.com/business/article/44932 (June 20, 2013).

82. John Gerzema, "The Rise of Mindful Consumption," *McKinsey & Company*, http://voices.mckinseyonsociety.com/the-rise-of-mindful-consumption/ (June 20, 2013).

83. The Nature Conservancy, http://www.nature.org/ourinitiatives/regions/north america/unitedstates/westvirginia/explore/wv-bear-rocks-brochure .pdf (August 27, 2013).

5   EDUCATION

1. Paulo Freire, *Pedagogy of the Oppressed: 30th Anniversary Edition* (London: Bloomsbury Academic, 2000).

2. "Vital Signs—Michigan," *Change the Equation,* http://vitalsigns.changethe equation.org/tcpdf/vitalsigns/newsletter.php?statename=Michigan (June 20, 2013).

3. "Vital Signs: All Over the Map—Comparing States' Expectations for Student Performance in Science," *Change the Equation,*, http://changetheequation.org /sites/default/files/State_Science_Assessments_12_11.pdf (June 20, 2013).

4. "Our Mission and Goals," *Change the Equation*, http://changetheequation. org/our-mission-and-goals (June 20, 2013).

5. "Vital Signs—STEM Help Wanted—Demand for Science, Technology, Engineering and Mathematics Weathers the Storm," *Change the Equation*, http://changetheequation.org/sites/default/files/CTEq_VitalSigns _Supply%20%282%29.pdf (June 20, 2013).

6. "Vital Signs—STEM Help Wanted," *Change the Equation*, http://change theequation.org/sites/default/files/CTEq_VitalSigns_Supply%0%282%29 .pdf (June 20, 2013).

7. "STEM Vital Signs," *Change the Equation*, http://vitalsigns.changethe equation.org/ (June 20, 2013).

8. "The Global Race for STEM Skills," *The Observatory on Borderless Higher Education*, January 2013, http://www.obhe.ac.uk/newsletters/borderless_report_january_2013/global_race_for_stem_skills (June 20, 2013).

9. Linda Rosen (CEO, Change the Equation), interview with the author, January 4, 2013.

10. "The Economics of Higher Education," *United Stated Department of the Treasury with the Department of Education,* December 2012, http://www.treasury.gov/connect/blog/Documents/20121212_Economics%20of%20Higher%20Ed_vFINAL.pdf (June 20, 2013).

11. "The Economics of Higher Education," *United Stated Department of the Treasury with the Department of Education*, December 2012, http://www.treasury.gov/connect/blog/Documents/20121212_Economics%20of%20Higher%20Ed_vFINAL.pdf (June 20, 2013).

12. Lorraine Woellert, "Companies Say 3 Million Unfilled Positions in Skill Crisis: Jobs," *Bloomberg*, July 25, 2012, http://www.bloomberg.com/news/2012–07–25/companies-say-3-million-unfilled-positions-in-skill-crisis-jobs.html (September 7, 2013).

13. "STEMtistics: Facts & Figures," *Change the Equation*, http://changetheequation.org/stemtistics-facts-figures (June 20, 2013).

14. "STEMtistic: Bringing up the Rear," *Change the Equation*, http://changetheequation.org/stemtistic-bringing-rear-0 (June 20, 2013).

15. James Truslow Adams, *The Epic of America* (Simon Publications, 2001).

16. "The Economics of Higher Education," *United Stated Department of the Treasury with the Department of Education,* December 2012, http://www.treasury.gov/connect/blog/Documents/20121212_Economics%20of%20Higher%20Ed_vFINAL.pdf (June 20, 2013).

17. Ron Haskins, Julia B. Isaacs, and Isabel V. Sawhill, "Getting Ahead or Losing Ground: Economic Mobility in America," *Brookings*, February 2008, http://www.brookings.edu/research/reports/2008/02/economic-mobility-sawhill (June 20, 2013).

18. "The Economics of Higher Education," *United Stated Department of the Treasury with the Department of Education*, December 2012, http://www.treasury.gov/connect/blog/Documents/20121212_Economics%20of%20Higher%20Ed_vFINAL.pdf (June 20, 2013).

19. "U.S. Education Reform and National Security," *Council on Foreign Relations*, March 2012, http://www.cfr.org/united-states/us-education-reform-national-security/p27618 (June 20, 2013).

20. Ibid.

21. Ibid.

22. Mona Mourshed, Diana Farrell, and Dominic Barton, "Education to Employment: Designing a System that Works," *McKinsey & Company*, 2012 http://mckinseyonsociety.com/downloads/reports/Education/Education-to-Employment_FINAL.pdf (June 20, 2013).

23. Jenny Marlar, "Global Unemployment at 8% in 2011," *Gallup World*, April 17, 2012, http://www.gallup.com/poll/153884/global-unemployment-2011.aspx (June 20, 2013).

24. "Education at a Glance 2012: OECD Indicators *OECD*, September 20, 2012, http://www.oecd.org/edu/EAG%202012_e-book_EN_200912.pdf (June 20, 2013).

25. Ibid.

26. Ibid.

27. "High Unemployment and Growing Inequality Fuel Social Unrest around the World," *International Labour Organization*, April 27, 2012, http://www.ilo.org/global/about-the-ilo/newsroom/news/WCMS_179430/lang--en/index.htm (June 20, 2013).

28. "United Nations Millennium Goals," *United Nations*, http://www.un.org/millenniumgoals/education.shtml (June 20, 2013).

29. Mona Mourshed, Diana Farrell, and Dominic Barton, "Education to Employment: Designing a System that Works," *McKinsey & Company*, 2012, http://mckinseyonsociety.com/downloads/reports/Education/Education-to-Employment_FINAL.pdf (June 20, 2013).

30. "Education at a Glance 2012: OECD Indicators," *OECD*, September 20, 2012, http://www.oecd.org/edu/EAG%202012_e-book_EN_200912.pdf (June 20, 2013).

31. "About HP," http://www8.hp.com/us/en/hp-information/index.html (June 20, 2013).

32. "Catalyst Initiative," HP, http://www8.hp.com/us/en/hp-information/social-innovation/catalyst.html (June 20, 2013).

33. Alice Korngold, "Hewlett Packard's Corporate Global Vision," *Fast Company*, January 18, 2012, http://www.fastcompany.com/1809130/hewlett-packards-corporate-global-vision (June 20, 2013).

34. Ibid.

35. Ibid.

36. Ibid.

37. Ibid.

38. Jim Vanides (global program manager, HP Catalyst), interview with the author, December 10, 2012.

39. Ibid.

40. "Homepage," *ISTE*, https://www.iste.org/ (June 20, 2013).

41. "Homepage," *The New Media Consortium*, 2013, http://www.nmc.org/ (June 20, 2013).

42. "Catalyst Initiative," *HP*, http://www8.hp.com/us/en/hp-information/social-innovation/catalyst.html (June 20, 2013).

43. Jeannette Weisschuh (director, Education Initiatives, Sustainability and Social Innovation, Catalyst, HP), interview with the author, December 14, 2012.

44. Ibid.

45. Ibid.

46. Gabi Zedlmayer (VP, Sustainability and Social Innovation (SSI), HP), interview with the author, January 14, 2013.

47. Gavin Dykes (program director, Education World Forum), interview with the author, January 4, 2013.

48. Mona Mourshed, Diana Farrell, and Dominic Barton, "Education to Employment: Designing a System that Works," *McKinsey & Company*, 2012, http://mckinseyonsociety.com/downloads/reports/Education/Education-to-Employment_FINAL.pdf (June 20, 2013).

49. Alice Korngold, "Hewlett Packard's Corporate Global Vision," *Fast Company*, January 18, 2012, http://www.fastcompany.com/1809130/hewlett-packards-corporate-global-vision (June 20, 2013).

50. Gabi Zedlmayer (VP, Sustainability and Social Innovation (SSI), HP), interview with the author, January 14, 2013.

51. "Catalyst Initiative," *HP*, http://www8.hp.com/us/en/hp-information/social-innovation/catalyst.html (June 20, 2013).

52. "United Nations Millennium Goals," *United Nations*, http://www.un.org/millenniumgoals/education.shtml (June 20, 2013).

53. "The State of Broadband 2012: Achieving Digital Inclusion for All," *The Broadband Commission*, September 2012, http://www.broadbandcommission.org/Documents/bb-annualreport2012.pdf (June 20, 2013).

54. Ibid., "The State of Broadband 2012: Achieving Digital Inclusion for All," *The Broadband Commission*, September 2012, http://www.broadbandcommission.org/Documents/bb-annualreport2012.pdf (June 20, 2013).

55. "The Company," *Ericsson*, http://www.ericsson.com/thecompany (June 20, 2013); updated by Elaine Weidman-Grunewald (vice president, Sustainability and Corporate Responsibility, Ericsson), email to the author, August 28, 2013.

56. "Misson: Solutions for Sustainable Development," *The Earth Institute*, Columbia University, http://www.earth.columbia.edu/articles/view/1791 (June 20, 2013).

57. "About Us," *Millennium Promise*, http://www.millenniumvillages.org/millenniumpromise (June 20, 2013).

58. Elaine Weidman-Grunewald (vice president, Sustainability and Corporate Responsibility, Ericsson), interview with the author, November 21, 2012; Elaine Weidman-Grunewald, email to the author, August 28, 2013.

59. "Homepage," *GirlUp*, http://www.girlup.org/learn/education.html (June 20, 2013).

60. Ibid.

61. Elaine Weidman-Grunewald, interview with the author, November 21, 2012.

62. Suzanne Fallender (director, CSR Strategy and Communications, Intel), email to author, May 21, 2013.

63. "Pioneering Program Expands Education Opportunities across Argentina," *Intel*, 2011, http://download.intel.com/education/transformation/Ed_Transformation_CS_Argentina_LoRes.pdf (June 20, 2013).

64. Ibid.

65. "Our Board of Directors," *Achieve*, http://www.achieve.org/our-board-directors (June 20, 2013).

66. "Achieving the Common Core," *Achieve,* http://www.achieve.org/achieving-common-core (June 20, 2013).

67. "Benchmarking for Success: Ensuring U.S. Students Receive a World
-Class Education," *National Governors Association, Council of Chief State
School Officers*, and *Achieve, Inc.,* 2008, http://www.corestandards.org
/assets/0812BENCHMARKING.pdf (June 20, 2013).

68. "The Standards," *Common Core: State Standards Initiative*, 2010, http://
www.corestandards.org/the-standards (June 20, 2013).

69. "Intel 2012 Corporate Responsibility Report," *Intel*, http://www.intel.com
/content/www/us/en/corporate-responsibility/corporate-responsibility
-report-overview.html (June 20, 203).

6 HEALTHCARE

1. Tom Farle and Deborah A. Cohen, *Prescription for a Healthy Nation* (Boston:
Beacon Press, 2006).

2. "The Top 10 Causes of Death," *World Health Organization*, 2011, http://
www.who.int/mediacentre/factsheets/fs310/en/index1.html (June 20, 2013).

3. "Child Mortality in Developing Countries Has Declined by 25 percent since
1990," *The World Bank*, September 8, 2010, http://data.worldbank.org/news
/developing-countries-child-mortality-declines (June 20, 2013).

4. "The Top 10 Causes of Death," *World Health Organization*, 2011, http://
www.who.int/mediacentre/factsheets/fs310/en/index4.html (June 20, 2013).

5. "Health Systems Financing—The Path to Universal Coverage," *World Health
Organization*, 2010, http://www.who.int/whr/2010/10_summary_en.pdf
(June 20, 2013).

6. "Declaration of Alma-Ata," *International Conference on Primary Health
Care*, September 1978, http://www.who.int/publications/almaata_declaration
_en.pdf (June 20, 2013).

7. "United Nations Millennium Goals," *United Nations*, http://www.un.org
/millenniumgoals/bkgd.shtml (June 20, 2013).

8. Ibid"United Nations Millennium Goals," *United Nations*, http://www
.un.org/millenniumgoals/childhealth.shtml (June 20, 2013).

9. "United Nations Millennium Goals," *United Nations*, http://www.un.org
/millenniumgoals/maternal.shtml (June 20, 2013).

10. Ibid.

11. "Who We Are," *The NCD Alliance*, http://www.ncdalliance.org/who-we-are
(June 20, 2013).

12. "Child Mortality," *The Partnership for Maternal, Newborn & Child Health,*,
September 2011, http://www.who.int/pmnch/media/press_materials/fs/fs
_mdg4_childmortality/en/index.html (June 20, 2013).

13. "Briefing for the High-Level Dialogue on Health in Post-2015 Non-
Communicable Disease (NCDs), Global Health and Development," *The
NCD Alliance*, February 27, 2013, http://ncdalliance.org/sites/default
/files/rfiles/NCD%20Alliance%20-%20Botswana%20Briefing%20-%20
March%202013.pdf (June 20, 2013).

14. Maureen Lewis, "Governance and Corruption in Public Health Care
Systems," Center for Global Development, January 2006, http://www.cgdev

.org/publication/governance-and-corruption-public-health-care-systems-working-paper-78 (September 7, 2013).

15. "Deaths from NCDs," *World Health Organization*, 2008, http://www.who.int/gho/ncd/mortality_morbidity/ncd_total/en/ (June 20, 2013).

16. "Global Status Report on Noncommunicable Diseases 2010," *World Health Organization*, http://whqlibdoc.who.int/publications/2011/9789240686458_eng.pdf (June 20, 2013).

17. Ibid.

18. "Non-Communicable Diseases and Adolescents: An Opportunity for Action," *The AstraZeneca Young Health Programme*, http://www.jhsph.edu/research/centers-and-institutes/center-for-adolescent-health/az/noncommunicable.pdf (June 20, 2013).

19. "Homepage," *Plan*, 2013, http://plan-international.org/ (June 20, 2013).

20. Robert Wm. Blum, MD, MPH, PhD, interview with the author, March 18, 2013.

21. Sarah Shilito, email to the author, May 13, 2013.

22. Tanya Barron, interview with the author, March 6, 2013.

23. Ibid.

24. Maria Luisa Contursi (co-founder of mindyourmind), interview with the author, February 22, 2013.

25. "Who We Are," *mindyourmind*, http://mindyourmind.ca/about-mym/who-we-are (June 20, 2013).

26. Maria Luisa Contursi (co-founder of mindyourmind), interview with the author, February 22, 2013.

27. Caroline Hempstead, interview with the author, April 9, 2013.

28. Ibid.

29. "International Corporate Volunteerism 2013 Benchmarking Study," PYXERA Global, http://www.slideshare.net/CDCDevelopmentSolutions/international-corporate-volunteerism-2013-benchmarking-study (June 20, 2013).

30. Ibid.

31. Ibid.

32. Ibid.

33. Ibid.

34. Ibid.

35. Ibid.

36. Ibid.

37. "Homepage," *mothers2mothers*, http://www.m2m.org/ (June 20, 2013).

38. Robin Smalley (international co-founder and director, m2m), interview with the author, May 3, 2013.

39. "Homepage," *mothers2mothers*, http://www.m2m.org/ (June 20, 2013).

40. Robin Smalley, interview with the author, May 3, 2013.

41. Ibid.

42. "About Pfizer," *Pfizer,*, http://www.pfizer.com/about (June 20, 2013).

43. "Global Health," *Pfizer*, http://www.pfizer.com/responsibility/global_health/global_health_fellows.jsp (June 20, 2013).

44. "Homepage," PYXERA Global, http://www.cdcdevelopmentsolutions.org/ (June 20, 2013).

45. "International Corporate Volunteerism 2013 Benchmarking Study," PYXERA Global, http://www.slideshare.net/CDCDevelopmentSolutions /international-corporate-volunteerism-2013-benchmarking-study (June 20, 2013).

46. Caroline Roan (vice president, Corporate Responsibility, Pfizer Inc., and president of the Pfizer Foundation), interview with the author, March 26, 2013.

47. Ibid.

48. Deirdre Peterson (Pfizer), email to the author, April 1, 2013.

49. Ibid.

50. "Homepage," *GlaxoSmithKline*, http://www.gsk.com/ (June 20, 2013).

51. Ibid.

52. Ahsiya Mencin (director, PULSE Volunteer Partnership, GSK), interview with the author, March 25, 2013.

53. Alice Korngold, "International Corporate Volunteering: Experiential Learning Advances Diversity and Communications," *Fast Company*, http:// www.fastcompany.com/1834193/international-corporate-volunteering -experiential-learning-advances-diversity-and-communicat (June 20, 2013).

54. Ahsiya Mencin, interview with the author, March 25, 2013.

55. "About CHAI," *The Clinton Health Access Initiative*, http://www.clinton foundation.org/main/our-work/by-initiative/clinton-health-access-initiative /about.html (June 20, 2013).

56. Malika Idouaddi (supply chain optimisation project specialist, GSK, UK), interview with the author, May 6, 2013.

57. Sir Andrew Witty (chairman and CEO, GSK), interview with the author, May 20, 2013.

58. "United Nations Millennium Goals," *United Nations*, http://www.un.org /millenniumgoals/ (June 20, 2013).

59. "Immunization Facts and Figures April 2013," *UNICEF*, http://www .unicef.org/immunization/files/UNICEF_Key_facts_and_figures_on _Immunization_April_2013%281%29.pdf (June 20, 2013).

60. Dr. Allan Pamba, interview with the author, May 17, 2013.

61. "Dr. Allan Pamba, director of Public Engagement & Access Initiatives, DCMA," *GSK*, http://www.developingcountriesunit.gsk.com/The-Team /Team-Biographies/Dr-Allan-Pamba-Director-Public-Engagement-and -Access-Initiatives-DCMA (June 20, 2013).

62. Ibid.

63. Dr. Allan Pamba, interview with the author, May 17, 2013.

64. "GSK Forms Partnership with Vodafone to Help Increase Childhood Vaccination in Mozambique," *GSK*, December 10, 2012, http://www.gsk .com/media/press-releases/2012/GSK-forms-partnership-with-Vodafone-to -help-increase-childhood-vaccination-in-Mozambique.html (June 20, 2013).

65. "About the Alliance: GAVI's mission," *GAVI Alliance*, 2013, http://www .gavialliance.org/about/mission/ (June 20, 2013).

NOTES   191

66. Dr. Allan Pamba, interview with the author, May 14, 2013.
67. Dr. Allan Pamba, email to the author, May 23, 2013.
68. Dr. Allan Pamba, interview with the author, May 14, 2013.
69. Chris Librie (director, Environmental and Health Initiatives for HP Sustainability and Social Innovation), interview with the author, May 6, 2013.
70. Mark Heffernan (CFO, m2m), interview with the author, May 10, 2013; "Mark Heffernan," *mothers2mothers*, http://www.m2m.org/about-us/our -team/mark-heffernan.html (June 20, 2013).
71. Mark Heffernan, interview with the author, May 10, 2013.
72. Ibid.
73. Chris Librie, interview with the author, May 6, 2013.
74. Ibid.
75. "Hôpital Universitaire de Mirebalais," *HP*, http://www8.hp.com/us/en/hp -information/social-innovation/hopital-universitaire-de-mirebalais.html#. UYSRpcqRutY (June 20, 2013).
76. Chris Librie, interview with the author, May 6, 2013.
77. Ibid.
78. "United Nations Millennium Goals," *United Nations*, http://www.un.org /millenniumgoals/ (June 20, 2013).

7   HUMAN RIGHTS

1. Aung San Suu Kyi, Nobel Peace Prize lecture delivered in June 2012, for the prize awarded in 1991, http://www.nobelprize.org/nobel_prizes/peace /laureates/1991/kyi-lecture_en.html.
2. Nelson Mandela, upon receiving the Nobel Peace Prize in 1993, http://www .nobelprize.org/nobel_prizes/peace/laureates/1993/mandela-lecture_en.html.
3. Martin Chulov, "Syria Shuts off Internet Access across the Country," *The Guardian*, November 29, 2012, http://www.guardian.co.uk/world/2012 /nov/29/syria-blocks-internet (June 20, 2013).
4. Charles Cooper, "Iran Cuts off Internet Access," *CNET*, February 10, 2012, http://news.cnet.com/8301–13510_3–57374594–21/iran-cuts-off-internet -access/ (September 7, 2013).
5. Charles Arthur, "Egypt Cuts off Internet Access," *The Guardian*, January 28, 2011, http://www.guardian.co.uk/technology/2011/jan/28/egypt-cuts-off -internet-access (June 21, 2013).
6. "Egypt Cut off Internet Access Following Street Protests," *Bloomberg TV*, January 31, 2011, http://www.bloomberg.com/video/66308814-egypt-cut -off-internet-access-following-street-protests.html (June 21, 2013).
7. Kathleen Miles, "LA Teen Prostitutes Come from Foster Homes a Majority of the Time, County Says," *The Huffington Post*, November 28, 2012, http:// www.huffingtonpost.com/2012/11/28/la-teen-prostitutes-foster-homes -county-video_n_2207778.html (June 21, 2013).
8. Mark Townsend, "Joy Vanished into Britain's Child-Sex Trade—Why Aren't We Looking for Her?" *The Guardian*, October 15, 2011, http://www.guardian .co.uk/law/2011/oct/16/britains-child-sex-trade (June 21, 2013).

9. Nicholas D. Kristof, "The Face of Modern Slavery," *The New York Times*, November 16, 2011, http://www.nytimes.com/2011/11/17/opinion/kristof-the-face-of-modern-slavery.html (June 21, 2013).

10. Calamur, Krishnadev, "Bangladesh Factory Collapse Death Toll Crosses 1,000," *National Public Radio*, May 9, 2013, http://www.npr.org/blogs/thetwo-way/2013/05/09/182737557/bangladesh-factory-collapse-death-toll-crosses-1–000 (September 7, 2013).

11. Julfikar Ali Manik and Jim Yardley, "Bangladesh Finds Gross Negligence in Factory Fire," *The New York Times*, December 17, 2012, http://www.nytimes.com/2012/12/18/world/asia/bangladesh-factory-fire-caused-by-gross-negligence.html (June 30, 2013); Serajul Quadir, and Ruma Paul, "Bangladesh Factory Fire Kills 8; Collapse Toll Tops 900," *Reuters*, May 9, 2013, http://www.reuters.com/article/2013/05/09/us-bangladesh-fire-id USBRE94801T20130509 (June 30, 2013).

12. Frank Piasecki Poulsen, "Children of the Congo Who Risk Their Lives to Supply Our Mobile Phones," *The Guardian*, December 7, 2012, http://www.guardian.co.uk/sustainable-business/blog/congo-child-labour-mobile-minerals (June 21, 2013).

13. "Daily Use of Conflict Minerals in America," *TriplePundit*, February 25, 2013, http://www.triplepundit.com/podium/daily-use-of-conflict-minerals-america/?goback=.gde_4578112_member_218279484 (June 21, 2013).

14. Marc Gunther, "What's the Cost of Cheap Clothing?," *GreenBiz.com*, January 29, 2013, http://www.greenbiz.com/blog/2013/01/29/bangladesh-price-cheap-clothing?page=0%2C1 (June 22, 2013).

15. Sarah Halzack, "Can Empathy Play an Important Role in a Successful Career?" *The Washington Post*, March 15, 2013, http://articles.washingtonpost.com/2013–03–15/business/37738425_1_fiorina-products-empathy (June 22, 2013).

16. "About Ashoka's Empathy Initiative," *Ashoka*, http://empathy.ashoka.org/about-ashokas-empathy-initiative (June 22, 2013).

17. Angel Cabrera, "Empathy, the Glue That Holds a Business Together," *George Mason University*, March 16, 2013, http://president.gmu.edu/2013/03/empathy-the-glue-that-holds-a-business-together (June 30, 2013).

18. Steven Herz, Antonio La Vina, and Jonathan Sohn, "Development without Conflict: The Business Case for Community Consent," *World Resources Institute*, May 2007, http://pdf.wri.org/development_without_conflict_fpic.pdf (June 22, 2013).

19. Goldman Sachs Global Investment Research, "Top 190 Projects to Change the World," April 25, 2008, cited by John Gerard Ruggie, *Just Business* (London: W.W. Norton & Company Inc., 2013), p. 138.

20. John Gerard Ruggie, *Just Business* (London: W.W. Norton & Company, Inc., 2013), p. 138.

21. "The Universal Declaration of Human Rights," *United Nations*, http://www.un.org/en/documents/udhr/index.shtml (June 22, 2013).

22. "About Us," *United Nations Global Compact*, http://www.unglobalcompact.org/ (June 22, 2013).

23. "About Us—The Ten Principles," *United Nations Global Compact*, http://www.unglobalcompact.org/AboutTheGC/TheTenPrinciples/index.html (June 22, 2013).

24. "How to Participate," *United Nations Global Compact*, http://www.unglobal compact.org/HowToParticipate/index.html (June 22, 2013).

25. "Guiding Principles on Business and Human Rights," *United Nations Human Rights*, http://www.ohchr.org/Documents/Publications/Guiding PrinciplesBusinessHR_EN.pdf (June 22, 2013).

26. "The UN Protect, Respect and Remedy Framework for Business and Human Rights: Relationship to UN Global Compact Commitments," *United Nations Global Compact*, May 2010, http://www.unglobalcompact.org/docs/issues_doc /human_rights/Resources/UNGC_SRSGBHR_Note.pdf (June 22, 2013).

27. "The UN Protect, Respect, and Remedy Framework for Business and Human Rights: Relationship to UN Global Compact Commitments," *United Nations Global Compact*, May 2010, http://www.unglobalcompact. org/docs/issues_doc/human_rights/Resources/UNGC_SRSGBHR_Note .pdf (June 22, 2013).

28. "About," *Global Business Coalition Against Human Trafficking*, http://www .gbcat.org/ (June 22, 2013).

29. "Companies Join Forces to Combat Human Trafficking," *United Nations Global Initiative to Fight Human Trafficking*, http://www.ungift.org /knowledgehub/en/stories/September2012/companies-join-forces-to-combat -human-trafficking.html (June 23, 2013).

30. Robert Rigby-Hall (co-chair, gBCAT, and chief human resources officer at NXP Semiconductors), interview with the author, April 18, 2013.

31. "21 Million People Are Now Victims of Forced Labour, ILO Says," *International Labour Organization*, June 1, 2012, http://www.ilo.org /global/about-the-ilo/newsroom/news/WCMS_181961/lang--en/index.htm (September 7, 2013).

32. "Human Trafficking: A Brief Overview," *The World Bank*, December 2009, http://siteresources.worldbank.org/EXTSOCIALDEVELOPMENT /Resources/244362–1239390842422/6012763–1239905793229/Human _Trafficking.pdf (June 23, 2013).

33. "Global Report on Trafficking in Persons, 2012" *United Nations Office on Drugs and Crime*, http://www.unodc.org/documents/data-and-analysis/glotip /Trafficking_in_Persons_2012_web.pdf (June 23, 2013).

34. "Global Report on Trafficking in Persons, 2012" *United Nations Office on Drugs and Crime*, http://www.unodc.org/documents/data-and-analysis/glotip /Trafficking_in_Persons_2012_web.pdf (June 23, 2013).

35. "Human Trafficking: A Brief Overview," *The World Bank*, December 2009, http://siteresources.worldbank.org/EXTSOCIALDEVELOPMENT /Resources/244362–1239390842422/6012763–1239905793229/Human _Trafficking.pdf (June 23, 2013).

36. "Global Report on Trafficking in Persons, 2012" *United Nations Office on Drugs and Crime*, http://www.unodc.org/documents/data-and-analysis/glotip /Trafficking_in_Persons_2012_web.pdf (June 23, 2013).

37. "Human Trafficking," *United Nations Office on Drugs and Crime*, http://www.unodc.org/unodc/en/human-trafficking/what-is-human-trafficking.html (June 23, 2013).

38. "United Nations Convention Against Transnational Organized Crime and the Protocols Thereto," *United Nations Office on Drugs and Crime*, http://www.unodc.org/unodc/treaties/CTOC/ (June 23, 2013).

39. "The Universal Declaration of Human Rights," *United Nations*, http://www.un.org/en/documents/udhr/index.shtml (June 22, 2013).

40. "Human Trafficking: A Brief Overview," *The World Bank*, December 2009, http://siteresources.worldbank.org/EXTSOCIALDEVELOPMENT/Resources/244362–1239390842422/6012763–1239905793229/Human_Trafficking.pdf (June 23, 2013).

41. "Global Report on Trafficking in Persons, 2012" *United Nations Office on Drugs and Crime*, http://www.unodc.org/documents/data-and-analysis/glotip/Trafficking_in_Persons_2012_web.pdf (June 23, 2013).

42. "Study Documents Scope of Human Trafficking in New York City," *Forensic Magazine*, November 14, 2011, http://www.forensicmag.com/news/study-documents-scope-human-trafficking-new-york-city (June 23, 2013).

43. "The Victims," *Polaris Project*, http://www.polarisproject.org/human-trafficking/overview/the-victims (June 23, 2013).

44. Deborah Cundy (vice president, Office of the Chairman at Carlson), interview with the author, March 25, 2013.

45. "About The Code," *TheCode.org*, http://www.thecode.org/about/ and http://www.osce.org/what/trafficking/58770 (June 23, 2013).

46. Andreas Anstrup (general manager, The Code), email to the author, April 3, 2013.

47. Carol Smolenski (executive director, ECPAT-USA), interview with the author, March 29, 2013.

48. "Homepage," *World Childhood Foundation*, http://www.childhood.org/ (June 22, 2013).

49. Deborah Cundy (vice president, Office of the Chairman at Carlson), interview with the author, March 25, 2013.

50. Ibid.

51. Marilyn Carlson Nelson (chairman and former chief executive officer of Carlson), interview with the author, May 3, 2013.

52. "Chinese Police Investigate Hilton Hotel Prostitution Ring," *AFP*, June 21, 2010, http://www.google.com/hostednews/afp/article/ALeqM5jU2_gWNuWo-z5nBG8SsaZ3GRPHXw (June 23, 2013).

53. Carol Smolenski, email to the author, May 19, 2013.

54. "Petition to Stop Wyndham Hotel Staff From Supporting Child Sex Trafficking in Wyndham Hotels," *change.org*, July 2011, http://www.change.org/petitions/stop-wyndham-hotel-staff-from-supporting-child-sex-trafficking-in-wyndham-hotels (June 30, 2013).

55. "About Hilton," *Hilton Hotel & Resorts*, http://www3.hilton.com/en/about/index.html (June 23, 2013).

56. *Starwood Hotels & Resorts Worldwide*, http://www.starwoodhotels.com/cor porate/about/index.html (June 24, 2013).

57. "Press Kit," *Delta Airlines*, http://news.delta.com/index.php?s=18&cat=47 (June 23, 2013).

58. Carol Smolenski, interview with the author, March 29, 2013.

59. A. Maurits van der Veen, "Conflict Minerals—Naming and Shaming,", December 14, 2010, http://blog.maurits.net/2010/12/conflict-minerals-naming -and-shaming.html (June 24, 2013).

60. Tim Mohin, *Changing Business from the Inside Out: A Tree-Hugger's Guide to Working in Corporations* (San Francisco: Berrett-Koehler Publishers, 2012).

61. "Mission/vision—ICT and Sustainability," *Global e-Sustainability Initiative*, http://gesi.org/ICT_sustainability_mission_and_vision (June 24, 2013).

62. "Homepage," *Public-Private Alliance for Responsible Minerals Trade*, http:// www.resolv.org/site-ppa/ (June 24, 2013).

63. "Daily Use of Conflict Minerals in America," *TriplePundit*, February 2013 http://www.triplepundit.com/podium/daily-use-of-conflict-minerals-america/ (June 24, 2013).

64. Ibid.

65. "Homepage," *Enough*, http://www.enoughproject.org/ (June 24, 2013).

66. "Homepage," *Global Witness*, http://www.globalwitness.org/ (June 29, 2013).

67. Tim Mohin (director, Corporate Responsibility, Advanced Micro Devices), interview with the author, January 13, 2013; Tim Mohin, email to the author, May 6, 2013.

68. Tim Mohin, *Changing Business from the Inside Out: A Tree-Hugger's Guide to Working in Corporations* (San Francisco: Berrett-Koehler Publishers, 2012).

69. "Board of Directors," *Electronic Industry Citizenship Coalition*, May 15, 2013, http://www.eicc.info/about_us_board.shtml (June 29, 2013).

70. Deborah Albers, "Conflict Minerals," *Dell Inc.*, January 2013, http://i.dell.com /sites/doccontent/corporate/corp-comm/en/Documents/conflict-mineral -white-paper.pdf (June 29, 2013).

71. Tim Mohin, interview with the author, January 13, 2013.

72. "SEC Adopts Rule for Disclosing Use of Conflict Minerals," *U.S. Securities and Exchange Commission*, August 22, 2012, http://www.sec.gov/News /PressRelease/Detail/PressRelease/1365171484002#.Uium2rHD9jo (June 29, 2013).

73. Raluca Besliu, "Relaunching Legal Mining in Congo with Conflict-Free Tags?" *Digital Journal*, February 27, 2013, http://www.digitaljournal.com /article/344451 (June 29, 2013).

74. "Traders to Smelters," *Conflict-Free Tin Initiative*, March 2013, http:// solutions-network.org/site-cfti/event/to-smelter/ (June 29, 2013); and email from Tim Mohin May 6, 2013.

75. "About the ILO," *International Labour Organization*, http://www.ilo.org /global/about-the-ilo/lang--en/index.htm (June 29, 2013).

76. "About the ILO," *International Labour Organization*, http://www.ilo.org /global/about-the-ilo/lang--en/index.htm (June 29, 2013).

77. "Conventions and Recommendations," *International Labour Organization*, http://www.ilo.org/global/standards/introduction-to-international-labour-stan dards/conventions-and-recommendations/lang--en/index.htm (June 29, 2013).
78. Ibid.
79. Charlie Campbell, "Bangladesh: Eight Killed in Factory Fire; Collapse Toll Hits 1,000," *Time*, May 9, 2013, http://world.time.com/2013/05/09/latest -bangladesh-garment-factory-disaster-spotlights-continuing-safety-con cerns/ (June 29, 2013).
80. "Conventions and Recommendations," *International Labour Organization*, http://www.ilo.org/global/standards/introduction-to-international-labour -standards/conventions-and-recommendations/lang--en/index.htm (June 29, 2013).
81. Steven Greenhouse, "Abercrombie & Fitch Signs Bangladesh Safety Plan," *The New York Times,* May 15, 2013, http://www.nytimes.com/2013/05/16 /business/global/abercrombie-fitch-agrees-to-bangladesh-factory-safety-plan.html (June 29, 2013); Barney Jopson and James Politi, "US Retail Under Pressure on Bangladesh Deal," *Financial Times,* May 16, 2013 http://www.ft.com/intl/cms/s/0/33e2f2ce-be44–11e2-bb35–00144feab7de .html#axzz2dKKXCCZL (August 28, 2013).
82. Steven Greenhouse, "Abercrombie & Fitch Signs Bangladesh Safety Plan," *The New York Times*, May 15, 2013, http://www.nytimes.com/2013/05/16 /business/global/abercrombie-fitch-agrees-to-bangladesh-factory-safety -plan.html (June 29, 2013).
83. Steven Greenhouse, "Abercrombie & Fitch Signs Bangladesh Safety Plan," *The New York Times*, May 15, 2013, http://www.nytimes.com/2013/05/16 /business/global/abercrombie-fitch-agrees-to-bangladesh-factory-safety -plan.html (June 29, 2013).
84. Barney Jopson, and James Politi, "US Retail Under Pressure on Bangladesh Deal," *Financial Times,* May 16, 2013 http://www.ft.com/intl/cms /s/0/33e2f2ce-be44–11e2-bb35–00144feab7de.html#axzz2TgO4oZMx (June 30, 2013).
85. "Petition to Walmart & Gap: Join Fire Safety Program, Fix Death Trap Factories," *Change.org*, http://www.change.org/petitions/walmart-gap-join -fire-safety-program-fix-death-trap-factories (June 29, 2013).
86. Steven Greenhouse, "Groups Press Big Retailers on Safety Overseas," *The New York Times*, May 16, 2013, http://www.nytimes.com/2013/05/17 /business/global/investors-and-religious-groups-press-retailers-on-safety .html?hpw (June 29, 2013).
87. Steven Greenhouse, "Groups Press Big Retailers on Safety Overseas," *The New York Times*, May 16, 2013, http://www.nytimes.com/2013/05/17/ business/global/investors-and-religious-groups-press-retailers-on-safety .html?hpw (June 29, 2013).
88. David Streitfeld, "Google Concedes that Drive-By Prying Violated Privacy," *The New York Times*, March 12, 2013, http://www.nytimes.com/2013/03/13 /technology/google-pays-fine-over-street-view-privacy-breach.html?_r=0 (June 29, 2013).

89. Lois Beckett, "Everything We Know about What Data Brokers Know about You," *ProPublica*, March 7, 2013, http://www.propublica.org/article/every thing-we-know-about-what-data-brokers-know-about-you (June 29, 2013).

90. Somini Sengupta, "Letting Down Our Guard with Web Privacy," *The New York Times*, March 30, 2013, http://www.nytimes.com/2013/03/31 /technology/web-privacy-and-how-consumers-let-down-their-guard.html? pagewanted=all&_r=1& (June 29, 2013).

91. "Undermining Freedom of Expression in China—The Role of Yahoo!, Microsoft, and Google," *Amnesty International*, July 2006, http://www .ethicsworld.org/corporatesocialresponsibility/PDF%20links/Amnesty.pdf (June 29, 2013).

92. "Yahoo! in China—Background," *Amnesty International*, http://www .amnestyusa.org/our-work/countries/asia-and-the-pacific/china/yahoo-in -china-background (June 29, 2013).

93. Dunstan Allison-Hope (managing director, Advisory Services, BSR), interview with the author, January 7, 2013.

94. Dunstan Allison-Hope, "Protecting Human Rights in the Digital Age," *BSR*, February 2011, http://globalnetworkinitiative.org/sites/default/files /files/BSR_ICT_Human_Rights_Report.pdf (June 29, 2013).

95. Somini Sengupta, "Web Privacy Becomes a Business Imperative," *The New York Times,* March 3, 2013, http://www.nytimes.com/2013/03/04/technol-ogy/amid-do-not-track-effort-web-companies-race-to-look-privacy-friendly .html?pagewanted=all (June 29, 2013).

96. Ibid.

97. Dunstan Allison-Hope, interview with the author, March 19, 2013.

98. "Key Telecommunications Players Collaborate with the Global Network Initiative on Freedom of Expression and Privacy Rights," *Global Network Initiative*, March 12, 2013, http://globalnetworkinitiative.org/news/key -telecommunications-players-collaborate-global-network-initiative-freedom -expression-and (June 29, 2013).

99. "About," *Center for Democracy & Technology*, https://www.cdt.org/about (June 29, 2013).

100. "Cybersecurity Legislation Still Fundamentally Flawed: CDT Opposes CISPA," *Center for Democracy & Technology*, February 13, 2013, https:// www.cdt.org/pr_statement/cybersecurity-legislation-still-fundamentally -flawed-cdt-opposes-cispa (June 29, 2013).

101. Deven McGraw, "For Health Data, Big Isn't Better," *Center for Democracy & Technology,* February 27, 2013, https://www.cdt.org/commentary/health -data-big-isnt-better (June 29, 2013).

102. Emily Barabas, "Internet Defamation Double Whammy in The UK: New Court Decision Plus New Legislation Threaten Online Free Expression," *Center for Democracy & Technology*, February 27, 2013, https://www.cdt.org /blogs/emily-barabas/2702internet-defamation-double-whammy-uk-new -court-decision-plus-new-legislation (June 29, 2013).

103. "About," Berkman Center for Internet and Society at Harvard University, http://cyber.law.harvard.edu/ (August 28, 2013).

104. Kevin J. O'Brien, "Microsoft Releases Report on Law Enforcement Requests," *The New York Times*, March 21, 2013, http://www.nytimes.com /2013/03/22/technology/microsoft-releases-report-on-law-enforcement -requests.html?smid=tw-share (June 29, 2013).

105. "Homepage," *The Internet Association*, http://internetassociation.org/ (June 29, 2013).

106. Alex Fitzpatrick, "Email Warrant Measure Gets Senate Judiciary Nod," *Mashable*, April 25, 2013, http://mashable.com/2013/04/25/email-warrant -measure-passes-comittee/ (June 29, 2013).

107. Dan Bross, interview with the author, Janaury 7, 2013.

108. "Guiding Principles for the Implementation of the UN 'Protect, Respect and Remedy' Framework," *United Nations Global Compact*, April 24, 2013, http://www.unglobalcompact.org/Issues/human_rights/The_UN_SRSG _and_the_UN_Global_Compact.html (June 29, 2013).

109. "Human Rights," Corporate Citizenship, Microsoft, https://www.microsoft .com/about/corporatecitizenship/en-us/working-responsibly/principled -business-practices/human-rights/ (August 28, 2013)

110. Ibid.

111. "Conducting an Effective Human Rights Impact Assessment," *BSR*, March 2013, http://www.bsr.org/reports/BSR_Human_Rights_Impact_Assessments .pdf (June 29, 2013)

112. Dan Bross, "How Microsoft Did It: Implementing the Guiding Principles on Business and Human Rights," *BSR*, December 4, 2012, http://www.bsr.org /en/our-insights/bsr-insight-article/how-microsoft-did-it-implementing-the -guiding-principles-on-business-and-hu (June 29, 2013).

113. Dan Bross, interview with the author, Janaury 7, 2013.

114. "Conducting an Effective Human Rights Impact Assessment," *BSR*, March 2013, http://www.bsr.org/reports/BSR_Human_Rights_Impact _Assessments.pdf (June 29, 2013).

115. Olga Lenzen, and Marina d'Engelbronner, "Guide to Corporate Human Rights Impact Assessment Tools," *Aim for Human Rights*, January 2009, http://www.humanrightsimpact.org/fileadmin/hria_resources/Business _centre/HRB_Booklet_2009.pdf (June 29, 2013).

116. "Conducting an Effective Human Rights Impact Assessment," *BSR*, March 2013, http://www.bsr.org/reports/BSR_Human_Rights_Impact _Assessments.pdf (June 29, 2013).

8   SUCCESSFUL COMPANIES ENSURE EFFECTIVE BOARD GOVERNANCE, ENGAGE STAKEHOLDERS, AND COLLABORATE WITH NGOS AND EACH OTHER

1. Amos Oz and Fania Oz-Salzberger, *Jews and Words* (New Haven: Yale University Press, 2012).

2. Alice Korngold, "Are S&P 500 Boards Equipped for the New Challenges of the Global Marketplace?" *The Huffington Post*, July 14, 2013 http://

www.huffingtonpost.com/alice-korngold/are-sp-500-boards-equippe
_b_3593214.html (July 24, 2013).

3. "Our Governance," *Unilever*, http://www.unilever.com/sustainable-living
/ourapproach/Governance/ (June 29, 2013).

4. "About," *Nike, Inc.*, http://www.nikebiz.com/crreport/content/about/1–4–2
-board-of-directors.php?cat=governance-accountability (June 29, 2013).

5. Aron Cramer (president and CEO, BSR), interview with the author, May 9,
2013.

6. "Homepage," *Global Reporting Initiative*, https://www.globalreporting.org
/Pages/default.aspx (June 29, 2013).

7. "The IIRC," *The International Integrated Reporting Council*, http://www
.theiirc.org/the-iirc/ (June 29, 2013).

8. "Homepage," *Sustainability Accounting Standards Board*, 2013, http://www
.sasb.org/ (June 29, 2013).

9. "Homepage," *Governance & Accountability Institute, Inc.*, http://www.ga
-institute.com/ (June 29, 2013).

10. "2012 Corporate ESG/Sustainability/Responsibility Reporting—*Does It
Matter?*" *Governance & Accountability Institute, Inc.*, http://www.ga-institute
.com/fileadmin/user_upload/Reports/SP500_-_Final_12–15–12.pdf (June 29,
2013), p. 36.

11. "The Impact of Sustainable Development and Responsible Investment," *US
SIF* http://www.ussif.org/files/Publications/USSIF_ImpactofSRI_916F.pdf
(October 21, 2013), p. 3.

12. Eric Roston (sustainability editor, Bloomberg.com), interview with the
author, April 3, 2013.

13. "Sustainability Measurement and Reporting Standards," *The Sustainability
Consortium*, April 9, 2010, http://www.sustainabilityconsortium.org/smrs/
(June 29, 2013).

14. Marc Gunther, "Walmart's Index: This Is Big. Really Big." April 15, 2013,
http://www.marcgunther.com/walmarts-index-this-is-big-really-big/ (June 29,
2013).

15. Gail Klintworth (chief sustainability officer, Unilever), interview with the
author, January 22, 2013.

16. Elizabeth Holmes, "Tweeting Without Fear—How Three Companies Have
Built Their Twitter Strategies," *The Wall Street Journal*, December 9, 2011,
http://online.wsj.com/article/SB10001424052970204319004577086140865
075800.html (June 29, 2013).

17. Shea Bennett, "Twitter Is the Number One Social Network amongst Global
Companies [STUDY]," *All Twitter*, July 18, 2012, http://www.mediabistro.
com/alltwitter/global-social-media-check-up_b25552 (June 29, 2013).

18. David K. Williams and Mary Michelle Scott, "New Research on Why CEOs
Should Use Social Media," *HBR Blog Network*, July 27, 2012, http://blogs.hbr
.org/cs/2012/07/new_research_on_why_ceos_shoul.html (June 29, 2013).

19. Ann Charles and Aman Singh, "2012 CEO, Social Media, and Leadership
Suvey," BRANDfog, http://www.brandfog.com/CEOSocialMediaSurvey
/BRANDfog_2012_CEO_Survey.pdf.

20. Aron Cramer, interview with the author, May 9, 2013.
21. "About Us: Tracks," *Clinton Global Initiative*, http://www.clintonglobal initiative.org/aboutus/tracks.asp (June 29, 2013).
22. "Meetings," *Clinton Global Initiative*, http://www.clintonglobalinitiative .org/ourmeetings/ (June 29, 2013).
23. "About Us," *Clinton Global Initiative*, http://www.clintonglobalinitiative .org/aboutus/ (June 29, 2013).

ABOUT THE AUTHOR

ALICE KORNGOLD HAS BEEN A SOCIAL ENTREPRENEUR, CONSULTANT, AND author for more than 30 years. At the forefront of corporate social responsibility (CSR) since the early 1990s, Korngold is president of her own international consulting firm, Korngold Consulting, LLC, which is based in New York City. She and her team consult for global corporations on corporate social responsibility and sustainability, facilitate strategic partnerships with NGOs and nonprofits, and train and place business executives on NGO and nonprofit boards of directors for leadership development. Korngold also consults to the boards of directors of global, national, and regional NGOs and nonprofits—advancing them to achieve their greater ambitions and long-term sustainability.

In the early 1990s, Korngold pioneered the nation's most highly acclaimed "board-matching program," through which over a thousand corporate executives were trained and placed on nonprofit boards. With national foundation funds, she assisted 20 US cities in establishing nonprofit board-matching and leadership development programs for corporate executives. Korngold has advocated that by integrating nonprofit board service with corporate philanthropy and business volunteerism companies could leverage their community engagement strategies for the greater benefit of the company, its employees, and communities.

Korngold is the author of *Leveraging Good Will: Strengthening Nonprofits by Engaging Businesses* (Jossey-Bass, a Wiley Imprint, 2005). She is the co-author of "Corporate Volunteerism: Strategic Community Involvement," a chapter in *Corporate Philanthropy at the Crossroads* (Indiana University Press, 1996). She blogs for *Fast Company, Guardian Sustainable Business*, and *The Huffington Post*.

Korngold has guest lectured at the graduate business schools of Harvard University, Dartmouth College, New York University, and Columbia University.

Korngold co-chairs the New York Leadership Council of GlobalGiving. She received a BA and an MS Ed. in Psychological Services from the University of Pennsylvania.

Index